ReFocus: The Films of Annemarie Jacir

ReFocus: The International Directors Series

Series Editors: Robert Singer, Gary D. Rhodes and Stefanie Van de Peer

Board of advisors:
Lizelle Bisschoff (Glasgow University)
Stephanie Hemelryck Donald (University of Lincoln)
Anna Misiak (Falmouth University)
Des O'Rawe (Queen's University Belfast)

ReFocus is a series of contemporary methodological and theoretical approaches to the interdisciplinary analyses and interpretations of international film directors, from the celebrated to the ignored, in direct relationship to their respective culture – its myths, values, and historical precepts – and the broader parameters of international film history and theory.

Titles in the series include:

ReFocus: The Films of Susanne Bier Edited by Missy Molloy, Mimi Nielsen and Meryl Shriver-Rice

ReFocus: The Films of Francis Veber Keith Corson

ReFocus: The Films of Xavier Dolan Edited by Andrée Lafontaine

ReFocus: The Films of Pedro Costa: Producing and Consuming Contemporary Art Cinema Nuno Barradas Jorge

ReFocus: The Films of Sohrab Shahid Saless: Exile, Displacement and the Stateless Moving Image Edited by Azadeh Fatehrad

ReFocus: The Films of Pablo Larraín Edited by Laura Hatry

ReFocus: The Films of Michel Gondry Edited by Marcelline Block and Jennifer Kirby

ReFocus: The Films of Rachid Bouchareb Edited by Michael Gott and Leslie Kealhofer-Kemp

ReFocus: The Films of Andrei Tarkovsky Edited by Sergey Toymentsev

ReFocus: The Films of Paul Leni Edited by Erica Tortolani and Martin F. Norden

ReFocus: The Films of Rakhshan Banietemad Edited by Maryam Ghorbankarimi

ReFocus: The Films of Jocelyn Saab: Films, Artworks and Cultural Events for the Arab World Edited by Mathilde Rouxel and Stefanie Van de Peer

ReFocus: The Films of François Ozon Edited by Loïc Bourdeau

ReFocus: The Films of Teuvo Tulio Henry Bacon, Kimmo Laine and Jaakko Seppälä

ReFocus: The Films of João Pedro Rodrigues and João Rui Guerra da Mata Edited by José Duarte and Filipa Rosário

ReFocus: The Films of Lucrecia Martel Edited by Natalia Christofoletti Barrenha, Julia Kratje and Paul Merchant

ReFocus: The Films of Shyam Benegal Edited by Sneha Kar Chaudhuri and Ramit Samaddar

ReFocus: The Films of Denis Villeneuve Edited by Jeri English and Marie Pascal

ReFocus: The Films of Antoinetta Angelidi Edited by Penny Bouska and Sotiris Petridis

ReFocus: The Films of Ken Russell Edited by Matthew Melia

ReFocus: The Films of Kim Ki-young Edited by Chung-kang Kim

ReFocus: The Films of Jane Campion Edited by Alexia L. Bowler and Adele Jones

ReFocus: The Films of Alejandro Jodorowsky Edited by Michael Newell Witte

ReFocus: The Films of Nuri Bilge Ceylan Edited by Gönül Dönmez-Colin

ReFocus: The Films of Claire Denis Edited by Peter Sloane

ReFocus: The Films of Yim Soon-rye Edited by Molly Kim

ReFocus: The Films of Annemarie Jacir Iqra Shagufta Cheema with Stefanie Van de Peer

edinburghuniversitypress.com/series/refocint

ReFocus:
The Films of Annemarie Jacir

Iqra Shagufta Cheema with Stefanie Van de Peer

EDINBURGH
University Press

Edinburgh University Press is one of the leading university presses in the UK. We publish academic books and journals in our selected subject areas across the humanities and social sciences, combining cutting-edge scholarship with high editorial and production values to produce academic works of lasting importance. For more information visit our website: edinburghuniversitypress.com

© Iqra Shagufta Cheema and Stefanie Van de Peer, 2024, 2025

Grateful acknowledgement is made to the sources listed in the List of Illustrations for permission to reproduce material previously published elsewhere. Every effort has been made to trace the copyright holders, but if any have been inadvertently overlooked, the publisher will be pleased to make the necessary arrangements at the first opportunity.

Edinburgh University Press Ltd
13 Infirmary Street
Edinburgh, EH1 1LT

First published in hardback by Edinburgh University Press 2024

Typeset in 11/13 Ehrhardt MT by
IDSUK (DataConnection) Ltd

A CIP record for this book is available from the British Library

ISBN 978 1 4744 8091 8 (hardback)
ISBN 978 1 4744 8092 5 (paperback)
ISBN 978 1 4744 8093 2 (webready PDF)
ISBN 978 1 4744 8094 9 (epub)

The right of Iqra Shagufta Cheema and Stefanie Van de Peer to be identified as the authors of this work has been asserted in accordance with the Copyright, Designs and Patents Act 1988, and the Copyright and Related Rights Regulations 2003 (SI No. 2498).

Contents

List of Figures	vi
Acknowledgements	vii
Introduction: Annemarie Jacir's Transnational Oeuvre *Iqra Shagufta Cheema*	1
1 Experimenting with Realities in Jacir's Short Films *Stefanie Van de Peer*	23
2 Heterotopias and Thirdspaces: Construction of Space in Jacir's Films *Iqra Shagufta Cheema*	39
3 Locations of Memory: Home and Homeland *Iqra Shagufta Cheema*	62
4 Transvergent Transnationalism: Borders, Homes and Humans *Iqra Shagufta Cheema*	86
5 Characters at the Margins *Iqra Shagufta Cheema*	111
6 Curatorial Politics and Practices *Stefanie Van de Peer*	123
Conclusion: An Interview with Annemarie Jacir	140
Index	145

Figures

2.1 *When I Saw You*: Ghayda and Tarek in the refugee camp after a tense moment when Ghayda is unhappy about Tarek's performance in school and Tarek is upset about his father's absence. Credit: Philistine Films — 43

2.2 *Wajib*: Shadi and Abu Shadi driving by the Star of David in Nazareth. Credit: Philistine Films — 50

2.3 *Salt of this Sea*: Soraya and Emad sitting on top of a hill while Soraya shares her grandfather's memories. Credit: Philistine Films — 53

3.1 *Salt of this Sea*: Soraya and Irit, the Israeli artist, in the middle of their heated exchange in Soraya's ancestral home. Credit: Philistine Films — 69

3.2 *When I Saw You*: Tarek in the fedayeen base playing with the fedayeen just before Ghayda stumbles in looking for him. Credit: Philistine Films — 74

3.3 *Wajib*: Shadi and Abu Shadi after delivering a wedding invitation to the house of one of their friends. Credit: Philistine Films — 80

4.1 *Salt of this Sea*: Soraya, Emad and Marwan looking at the Al Aqsa in the distance after illegally crossing into Jerusalem. Credit: Philistine Films — 90

4.2 *Wajib*: Shadi and Abu Shadi accompany Amal to try on wedding dresses and to inform her that her mother won't be attending her wedding. Credit: Philistine Films — 97

4.3 *When I Saw You*: The fedayeen commander, Abu Akram, trains fedayeen while Tarek assists him in keeping count of their sets of crunches. Credit: Philistine Films — 106

Acknowledgements

I would like to thank Stefanie without whom this project would not have been possible. When I reached out to the editors at Edinburgh University Press as a doctoral student, I learned that only people with doctoral degrees could publish books with academic presses. Stefanie generously offered to become my co-author to enable me to sign an advanced book contract – she has, since then, been an invaluable mentor for me; she not only contributed two chapters to this book but also provided feedback on my work. Academia is a better place because of people like her.

I would also like to thank my friend, Ayesha Ali, who introduced me to the world of film and TV and helped me access them when I had neither permission from my family to watch films, nor the resources to access them. I owe thanks also to my friend, Andrew Smith, who remained indefatigable through many hours of binge-watching films with me and inadvertently enabled me to become a better viewer.

Iqra Shagufta Cheema

I would like to thank Manal Shqair for reading my chapters in draft form and commenting with such creativity that it challenged me to dig deeper into an understanding of and solidarity with the Palestinians, who are subject to everyday terror and oppression.

Stefanie Van de Peer

This book is dedicated to all artists and people who create and sustain hope amid prohibitive tyranny and violence.

INTRODUCTION

Annemarie Jacir's Transnational Oeuvre

Iqra Shagufta Cheema

'I found cinema was a perfect metaphor for what is happening in Palestine today and has been happening for the last 57 years', comments Annemarie Jacir (Armes 2015: 276). Filmmaking in Palestine is fractured by war, disaster, oppression and insurgency – and remains largely unrecorded officially, shrouded in taboos and sensationalism. It is defined by exile and by the requirement for permits to enter the Palestinian territories, thus portraying the Palestinian stories in fragmentary ways. Hamid Naficy describes Palestinian cinema as 'one of the rare cinemas in the world that is structurally exilic, as it is made either in the condition of internal exile in occupied Palestine or under the erasure and tensions of displacement and external exile in other countries' (2006: 91). To make films under such limiting conditions requires dissent and creativity – and 'Palestinians are creative – and must be – in order to survive' (Ghazoul et al. 2011: 5). One filmmaker whose work imaginatively captures these problematics of Palestinian filmmaking is Annemarie Jacir.

While Palestinian cinema is expected to portray issues of occupation and representation, Jacir, like many other artists and filmmakers, dreams of being recognised and acknowledged not only as a Palestinian woman but also as an artist – for the mastery of her craft, for her art. Jacir shares that creating art to 'humanize' or 'explain' Arabs or Palestinians is 'limiting' and 'insulting' and it 'kills the potential of what [she] considers art' (Ghazoul et al. 2011: 6). Palestinian cinema is not solely about a place, since 'Palestine is not in Ramallah. It's in the people, in the camps and those who have insisted to keep up a struggle and a dream' (Ghazoul et al. 2011: 5). In 2004, *Filmmaker Magazine* named Jacir as one of the '25 new faces of independent cinema' (Sinclair 2017). She is frequently hailed as the first Palestinian woman filmmaker (a title she disapproves). She has been called 'the most influential, best-loved and well-respected cinematic representative of her displaced people' (Rothe 2018) and her storytelling voice is considered 'one of the loudest and most important in the world of international cinema' (Sinclair 2017).

In this introduction, we summarise the fragments of the lived experiences of Annemarie Jacir as a Palestinian-American filmmaker. After a brief discussion of her education and early life that led to her career as a filmmaker, we focus on her family – particularly her sister Emily Jacir who is an artist of growing global reputation – and her familial connections to Palestine as her homeland. We outline her career development from a poet and film student to an international prize-winning auteur and an influential filmmaker from Palestine and from the Arab world. Furthermore, in addition to her creative work, we discuss the funding structures of her films and her mentorship for her contemporaries and younger filmmakers through workshops.

BIOGRAPHICAL NOTES

Annemarie Jacir was born in one of the oldest Christian families in Bethlehem, Palestine, on 17 January 1974. Her ancestral home, the Jacir Palace, was the grandest of the city's mansions. However, her family lost their fortune in the financial crash of the 1930s and the house was sold; since then it has been a prison and a school and now forms part of a five-star hotel. Her father worked for the United Nations Relief and Works Agency for Palestine Refugees (UNRWA), then moved to Saudi Arabia, where the family lived as outsiders. Jacir lived between Riyadh, Saudi Arabia, and Bethlehem until the age of sixteen. She received her early education at an international school in Saudi Arabia. When she was sixteen, she moved to the United States to study politics and literature at a private girls' school in Dallas. She was involved in theatre in her high school where she directed plays. She also got the opportunity to spend time in a video-editing room, playing with images and editing.

She was interested in film but was unclear about the eventual trajectory of her interest in the form. After graduating, she moved to Los Angeles where she worked as an assistant on various film sets, before finding a role as a script reader in the literary department of a talent agency. This proved critical to her training in the 'craft and formatting of screenwriting' (Lodderhose 2021). However, Jacir did not feel that Los Angeles was right for her; she says, 'I didn't feel like I had a place there . . . It wasn't the kind of cinema that really interested me and there was something about the whole place that didn't feel so creative to me' (Lodderhose 2021).

Jacir's creative discomfiture in Los Angeles and Hollywood's discomfiture with Jacir's Palestinian identity were not mutually exclusive. On several occasions, she was advised to hide her Palestinian identity and her roots while in Hollywood. 'I've never hidden the fact that I'm Palestinian . . . I have a lot of identities, female and Palestinian being two of them. But I was told more than once in LA that if I wanted to break into the industry: "Don't say that you're a Palestinian in this city, don't talk about it"' (Lodderhose 2021). The fact that her one identity transgressed all her other identities was striking. This solidified for her that Hollywood was not the right place for her at that time. She decided to apply for graduate school and was accepted into Columbia University in New York. She moved from the west coast to the east, leaving Hollywood behind to pursue her own ambitions. She lived in New York for about six years.

During the graduate programme, she proposed her thesis film, which was about 'a Palestinian film crew navigating their way through Israeli checkpoints in occupied territory as they attempt to reach Jerusalem'. However, she was told that 'the best place for her script was in the garbage' (Lodderhose 2021). Unwilling to give up, Jacir proceeded to crowdfund her short film *Like Twenty Impossibles*, which became her best-known short and was selected for the Cannes Film Festival and was also nominated for an Oscar. After New York, Jacir returned to Palestine where she met her now husband, Ossama Bawardi, on the set of her first feature film, *Salt of this Sea*. They live in Jordan, following a period in 2008 when the Israeli authorities denied her re-entry to the West Bank. She shot *Salt of this Sea* in a few places where it was illegal to film, indicating her 'mini-rebellions all along the way' ('Bristol Palestine Film Festival' 2022).

Often recognised as the first Palestinian woman filmmaker by the Western media, Jacir contests this identity. She believes that 'it doesn't matter who is first at anything. What matters is there is no last and that there are more and more . . . and more importantly, there are lots and lots of female filmmakers in Palestine, some of them working since before [she] was born' (Rothe 2022). She maintains that she does 'not believe in women's cinema' ('In Berlin' 2020). Despite the feminist portrayal of her characters and the feminist cinematic ecology of her films, she does not like to be labelled as the 'woman' filmmaker and does not engage with the feminist politics of her films.

She has written, directed and produced over sixteen films, which have premiered at several film festivals such as Cannes, Berlinale, Venice, Locarno and Telluride, and have won multiple awards. Her short films include *The Satellite Shooters* (writer, producer and director, 2001), *The Post Oslo History* (director, 2001), *Like Twenty Impossibles* (writer and director, 2003), *Until When* (producer, 2004), *A Few Crumbs for the Birds* (co-director and writer, 2005), *An Explanation (and then burn the ashes)* (director, producer and writer, 2006), *Palestine: Summer 2006* (director, producer and writer, 2006), *For Cultural Purposes Only* (contributing writer, 2009), *Haneen* (producer, 2010), *Horizon* (creative producer, 2013), *In Overtime* (producer, 2014), *Nafas* (writer, 2019), *Give Up the Ghost* (creative producer, 2019), *From Palestine with Love (Postcard from the Future)* (director, 2022), and *The Oblivion Theory* (forthcoming). Her feature films include *Salt of this Sea* (2008), *When I Saw You* (2012) and *Wajib* (2017) – all three were selected as Palestinian entries for the Oscar for Best Foreign Language Film. She also directed an episode of the third season of the critically acclaimed American TV series *Ramy* (Ramy Youssef, 2022). In 2021, she won Eurimages Co-production Development Award for 'an adaptation and relocation' of José Eduardo Agualusa's novel *A General Theory of Oblivion* to 'Gaza at the time of the First Palestinian Intifada', which is co-produced by Incognito Films, France, and One Two Films, Germany (Abbatescianni 2021). She also served on the competition jury of the 70th Berlin International Film Festival. Along with her filmmaking and mentorship, she has taught at Columbia University, Bethlehem University and Birzeit University, as well as in refugee camps in Palestine, Lebanon and Jordan. She has also served as a juror at the Cannes Film Festival. In 2018, she was invited to join the Academy of Motion Picture Arts and Sciences.

Jacir regularly collaborates with other filmmakers as an editor, writer, director and producer. She also mentors other artists and curates their work to promote independent cinema. In the spirit of this collaboration and mentorship, she founded Philistine Films, an independent production company that has 'an interest in challenging, thought-provoking and original movies from filmmakers with distinctive visions' (Philistine Films website). Various directors and artists have collaborated under the banner of Philistine Films, including Ossama Bawardi, Dahna Abourahme, Kamran Rastegar, Suzy Salamy, Rami Yasin, Zain Duraie, Mai Masri and Catherine Rios. With the goal of fostering and promoting a 'self-sufficient' and professional film industry, Philistine Films organises technical and educational film training workshops; these include screenwriting workshops, directing workshops and technical crew training workshops. It also hosts artists and film festivals, for example it invited Ken Loach to Ramallah in 2011, and organises and hosts the travelling film festival and database, Dreams of a Nation. Jacir also co-founded the Dar Yusuf Nasri Jacir for Art and Research, an artist-run space in her home town, Bethlehem, with her elder sister Emily Jacir.

EMILY JACIR

Emily Jacir has been an important inspiration, collaborator and co-creator of Annemarie's work and art. She is an artist of international reputation and a central figure in Palestine's artistic circles. She has actively supported, fostered and established the local art community since 1999, both individually and collaboratively. She has held solo exhibitions at the Guggenheim Museum, New York (2009), Beirut Art Center (2010), Darat al Funun, Amman (2014–15), Whitechapel Gallery, London (2015), the Irish Museum of Modern Art, Dublin (2016–17) and Alexander and Bonin, New York (2018). Her work has also been a part of major international group exhibitions, at the Museum of Modern Art, New York; San Francisco Museum of Modern Art; Fondazione Sandretto Re Rebaudengo, Turin; the 8th Istanbul Biennial (2003); Whitney Biennial (2004); Sharjah Biennial 7 (2005); 15th Biennale of Sydney (2006); 29th Bienal de São Paulo, Brazil (2010); Sharjah Biennial (2011); *documenta 13* (2012);[1] and five consecutive Venice Biennales. Along with her photography and installations, she has curated multiple film programmes. She curated a selection of short films called 'Palestinian Revolution Cinema (1968–1982)', which went on tour in 2007. She has also curated many Arab film programmes in New York City, including the first Palestinian Film Festival in 2002.[2] She has taught at the International Academy of Art, Palestine, since its opening year, 2006. From 2011 to 2012, she led the Ashkal Alwan Home Workspace Program in Beirut and created the curriculum and programming during its founding year, 2010–11. She was also among the founders of the International Academy of Art Palestine in Ramallah, which lasted from 2007 to 2017.

Like Annemarie, Emily's art explores themes of exile, surveillance, settlements and freedom. *Memorial to 418 Palestinian Villages Destroyed, Depopulated and Occupied by Israel in 1948* (2001) – an abandoned refugee tent, hand-stitched by exiled Palestinians, Israelis and others – is a desperate witness to enduring memory. *Where We Come From* (2001–03) documents the requests made by people who are denied access to their homeland – some of these requests include 'to play soccer with a boy in Haifa', 'to water a tree in my village', 'to put flowers on my mother's grave'. It also includes snapshots of Jacir whose American passport and 'freedom of movement' stamp enable her to carry out these requests.[3] *Crossing Surda* (2003) records the two kilometres distance Palestinians have to walk between military checkpoints on the last permitted road between Ramallah and thirty Palestinian villages.[4] *Accumulations* (2005) displays political and apolitical emails, including news about bombings, newsletters from an anti-discrimination committee, solicitations for a romantic rendezvous, and Happy New Year wishes.[5] *Retracing bus no. 23 on the historic Jerusalem–Hebron Road* (2006) recalls the journey on the Jerusalem-Hebron road in the 1960s and shows the intrusion, isolation, restriction, enclosure and devastation of the community.[6]

FINANCING AND MAKING PALESTINIAN FILMS

With 75 percent of Palestinians living as refugees, the migrant experience is inherent to Palestinian life. In Annemarie Jacir's films and other work, Palestine is a complex living and breathing place with human stories at its heart. Her works inclusively bring it all together, highlighting how Palestine and its people are inextricably interconnected. Interviews with Jacir consistently point towards her innovative, speculative and creative self, which thrives on challenges. We include an interview with the filmmaker in this book to get her own perspective on her creative process and products. Overall, Jacir's life and career incorporate the social, political and historical circumstances that define her transnational life, and in turn her transnational sociopolitical experiences also shape her works. In her films, she highlights the tragedies that Palestinians experience but also the joys they create for themselves.

Cinema, for Jacir, serves as a medium to present Palestinian stories internationally as well as portraying them in their full humanity – especially since the settler violence against Palestinians has only increased recently. Jacir shares: 'There are so many stories, so many things. We have been reduced to invisibility all our lives . . . Then there is this silence imposed on us, which has lasted and still lasts. Cinema is just a different way for us to express ourselves.'[7]

While Jacir finds the expectation that she will humanise and normalise Palestinians as an artist, her films strike a balance between the political and the personal to create a viewing experience that is both artistically and politically wonderful. It is difficult to make independent films with limited funding and distribution opportunities, but it is also a 'privilege' because 'you are working with people, you are telling a story, have an audience, so for [Jacir], you have a duty to be part of the world around you'. She maintains that she doesn't feel as though she 'represents Palestine or the Palestinians, but at the same time, these stories come from real places, people, real experiences in life' (Barat 2013). Her films are popular and critically successful internationally, but it is not easy to get recognition as a Palestinian or Arab artist. In 2014, after watching Jacir's film *When I Saw You*, Hugh Grant tweeted that he had 'discovered Arab Cinema', Jacir indirectly affirmed the sentiments implicit in Hugh's 'discovery' of Arab cinema when she shared that 'Palestinian cinema had a brief moment where it was very "fashionable" about six years ago' (Gilbert 2012). Despite the popularity of Arab cinema, Palestinian Cinema remains mired in certain political and cultural expectations. Palestinian cinema has, in some ways, become a festival cinema, a 'fashionable' topic to be seen to engage with in international film festival programmes, as was shown by Nick Denes (2014). Since many reputable film festivals are held in North America or Europe, it is difficult to distribute films without considering Western trends and tastes.

When Saudi Arabia reopened its cinemas on 18 April 2018, Western companies started 'flocking to booths of Saudi filmmakers at festivals', which left filmmakers from other countries off the radar of foreign producers' (Saadi 2018). Unsurprisingly then, the number of Arab films released each year remains 'modest' – Palestine has never released 'more than three features in one year' ('In Berlin' 2020). However, since the most recent Israeli–Palestinian conflict which started in May 2021, interest in Palestinian narratives has relatively increased, but so have Israeli attempts to block Palestinian representation. As we draft this introduction, *Farha* (2021), a coming-of-age film about the Nakba by Palestinian-Jordanian director Darin J. Sallam, faces an organised Israeli campaign to stop its further distribution (Elassar 2022). *Farha* premiered at the Toronto Film Festival in September 2021 and was subsequently screened in Busan, Rome, Gothenburg, Lyon, Jeddah and Palestine, and was then streamed on Netflix. Jacir had pointed out that 'with digital cinema, with new technologies, more and more Palestinians can make films and have access to resources' (Gilbert 2012), something that the international distribution and exhibition of Palestinian films now certainly confirms. During an interview, Jacir shared that there would be 12–13 films from Palestine in 2021 ('In Berlin' 2020).

Besides the geopolitical difficulties of shooting and distributing Palestinian cinema, financing these films also remains a challenge. Jacir financed most of her films through co-productions between European and Arab producers and investors. But even European funding has dwindled over the years due to economic crises, which has increased the challenges for Palestinian (and other) filmmakers (Saadi 2018). When seeking European funding, Palestinian filmmakers are also frequently asked why they don't have an Israeli partner. Having a partner with Israeli citizenship makes the investment less risky for the financiers. Jacir comments that European producers or financiers seek 'an Israeli partner or coproducer so that they feel safe'. This is one of the reasons why many 'Palestinians with Israeli citizenship' such as Elia Suleiman, Hany Abu Assad and Tawfiq Abu Wael have 'been doing well'. Jacir further maintains that 'it's similar to the Palestinian writers inside Israel in the sixties, who managed to create amazing works, like Mahmoud Darwish, Emile Habibi, and Tawfiq Zayyad. Except for Rashid Masharawi, I don't know of a single West Banker or Gazan who has been able to get out there and make a feature film' (Saadi 2018). In 2020, the Bristol Palestine Film Festival commissioned a mural by Bethlehem-based Palestinian artist Taqi Spateen, in close collaboration with Benoit Bennett and community volunteers. This mural features four significant figures in Palestinian cinema: Annemarie Jacir, Muayad Alayan, Najwa Najjar and Mohammad Bakri. The founder of the festival, David Owen, commented on Jacir:

> I think the first time I came across her was at the Dreams of the Nation project. I read an article that she'd written, and it just took the right angle. Her politics is perfect, real human rights. She's open-minded, a staunch activist and she's been a bit of a mover and shaker within Palestinian film. She has to make different decisions, like I'm not accepting funding from that organisation like the Israeli Film Council. Other Palestinian filmmakers have, and I don't have a judgement on that, but her choice not to has made her journey tougher . . . ('Bristol Palestine Film Festival' 2020)

Funding for films usually comes with restrictions that seek to 'dictat[e] the vision of a movie', according to Jacir, which could be 'the biggest challenge facing Arab cinema today' since 'it competes with other international films trying to tap into the same limited pool of money' (Saadi 2018). This challenge can sometimes lead to filmmakers 'los[ing] sight of what they want to say; of the story they want to tell' (Saadi 2018). But simultaneously Jacir maintains that due to 'constantly being blocked, [they] have to think about what [they] are doing and why [they] are doing it . . . that is why Palestinian cinema, and many cinemas in the world, are good' ('Ceasefire Interview' 2022). Impressively enough, Jacir's films not only maintain their politics but also critically reflect and engage with the challenges of shooting and making films in Palestine and about Palestine.

A SHORT OVERVIEW OF JACIR'S FILMS

Like Twenty Impossibles

Like Twenty Impossibles/Ka'inana Ashrun Mustachio was Jacir's first short to receive international acclaim. This 17-minute film was shot during the Second Intifada in 2001 across a year and a half in Occupied Palestine. The film narrativises the impossibility of everyday mobility in a country that is trapped in an expansive web of checkpoints and monitored areas. A young filmmaker, Anne-Marie (Reem Abu-Sbaih), returns to the West Bank after spending years in the United States. The film captures the challenges faced by the filmmaker and the Palestinian film crew as they travel to Jerusalem for a film shoot.

Jacir recalls shooting during 'one of the region's most violent times in modern history' as a young writer, director and editor: 'It was crazy . . . it was such a violent time and I remember being caught in the middle of some really terrifying moments where I really feared for my life' (Lodderhose 2021). In 2003, the film premiered as an official selection at the Cannes Film Festival; it was the first short Arab film to enter the festival. Jacir was the first Palestinian female director to walk the red carpet at Cannes. It was subsequently shown at multiple film festivals and won about nineteen awards internationally. It was named best short film at numerous international film festivals.[8] The film's cast included Tarek Abu Assab, Ashraf Abu Moch, Reem Abu Sbaih, Ismael Dabbag, Raja'i Khateeb, Rami Mussalem and Shadi Zumorrod.

A semi-autobiographical metacommentary on the politics and challenges of filmmaking in Palestine, *Like Twenty Impossibles* explores both emotional and political borders to investigate artistic responsibilities as well as the fragmentation and uncertainty camouflaging the lives of Palestinian residents and artists. This is a challenge that Jacir later partially explores and also surmounts in her first feature film, *Salt of this Sea*.

Salt of this Sea

Salt of this Sea is the story of Soraya (Suheir Hammad), a Palestinian-American born in Brooklyn to a working-class Palestinian refugee family. She learns that her grandfather's savings were frozen in his bank account in Jaffa when he was exiled in 1948. Determined to undo the loss of her ancestral money – but really the loss of her ancestral home and homeland – she returns to Palestine. In some ways, the film can be read as the coming-of-age story of a Palestinian-American woman in the way Soraya changes when she encounters various Palestinian realities. She meets Emad (Saleh Bakri), a young Palestinian whose ambition, contrary to Soraya's, is to leave his homeland forever. Due to her American upbringing, Soraya's decisions stem from her dominanlty individualistic perception of her own self and the world around her, which eventually results in Emad's arrest and her deportation. Emad is taken to jail while she is sent back to the US. Along with highlighting post-1948 generational trauma, the film also presents the contrast between the contrasting ways these realities impact Soraya as an American and her friends as Palestinians. This film takes the audience through various Palestinian locations, simultaneously capturing the threats of traversing these borders and boundaries. It was shot in Ramallah, Dawayma, Jaffa and Haifa.[9] Though the film received some criticism for being too 'sermonizing' and lecture-like, it effectively captures the material, geographical, familial and political trajectories of Palestinian experiences.

Salt of this Sea was Palestine's official Oscar entry for Best Foreign Language Film (2008) and the first feature film to be directed by a Palestinian woman. Along with international acclaim, the film also received about twelve international awards.[10] It was the Palestinian submission for the 81st Academy Award for Best Foreign Language Film. The film's cast includes the Palestinian-American poet Suheir Hammad and the then-emerging Palestinian actor Saleh Bakri. Other cast members are Riyad Ideis, Dana Drigov, Um Hussein Al Malhi and Yahya Barakat, among others. This was Saleh Bakri's first role in an Arab film. He has subsequently starred in all of Jacir's feature films. We watched this film on the streaming platform, Kanopy, via institutional access.

The challenges of financing and producing a Palestinian film are clear in the credits of *Salt of this Sea*. Jacir was unable to procure any support from the Arab world because 'there was not any' (Saadi 2018). The million euros required to produce the film were gathered by various production companies and one television network – Rotana Film Production, JBA Production, Philistine Films, Thelma Film AG, Louverture Films, Clarity World Films, Augustus Films, TSR and Mediapro – from eight different countries including France, the United States, the Netherlands, Spain, Belgium and Switzerland (Armes 2015: 19). In the credits, Jacir also acknowledges the support of at least four organisations for 'funding or tutoring scriptwriting', including the Paul Robeson Foundation, Sundance

Screenwriters Lab, Paris Cinema Project and Berlinale Co-Production & Talent Project Market (Armes 2015: 20). This film was eventually produced with mostly European funding and was premiered at Cannes.

Besides funding, shooting the film was also a challenge. When Jacir started the film, she was told that 'it would be impossible to make. Shooting in the West Bank was easy, but [she] wanted to shoot in Israel without an Israeli producer or Israeli support' (Ghazoul et al. 2011). Jacir also did not have Israeli citizenship. Though usually resistant to being called the first person to do something,[11] Jacir accepts that 'it's the first time a Palestinian production and crew, without any Israeli support or participation, [had] shot in Israel'. She further comments:

> Of course, the army blocked us: My crew was denied permissions, our locations were rejected, and I was also prevented from being in several locations. So we did it guerrilla style – otherwise there would have been no film. Israel as a shooting location was a very aggressive environment for us, but I can't tell you how satisfying it was to be a Palestinian film crew shooting in a place like Jaffa, especially when so many members of the crew were refugees from Jaffa. It was very special. (Ghazoul et al. 2011)

To make this film, Jacir watched 'every bank-robbery movie ever made', including *Dog Day Afternoon*, *They Drive by Night*, *Gun Crazy* and *Bonnie and Clyde*, and listened to music by Saul Williams, Asmahan, M.I.A. and Billie Holiday (Ghazoul et al. 2011). Additionally, she admits the influence of John Cassavetes' *Shadows*. To prepare the actors to play their characters, she 'rented a house in the Amari refugee camp and asked Saleh Bakri to live there'. She did not allow Bakri to meet Suheir Hammad 'until only ten days before shooting'. She maintains that she 'wanted to work on their characters and build who they are – to work on that life they come from before they ever meet in the story' (Murphy 2013). The film opens with documentary clips of the Nakba which Jacir 'dug . . . up from the Israeli archives' and which were 'difficult to obtain'. These clips portray rare images of 'the actual destruction of homes. Real documentary images of houses in Jaffa being destroyed' (Ghazoul et al. 2011). Jacir observes:

> The archival spirit and unceasing need to document that which was destroyed is homage to the indefatigable work of Walid Khalidi. And the lyricism and declamatory style of the film, in its script and its vision, hint at the poetry of Mahmoud Darwish. (Ghazoul et al. 2011)

Jacir declares *Salt of this Sea* her 'love letter to Palestine' (Ghazoul et al. 2011).

When I Saw You

When I Saw You/Lamma Shoftak was Jacir's second feature film, which premiered in 2012. While *Salt of this Sea* portrays the trauma of al-Nakba, *When I Saw You* is about the trauma of the Naksa, the 1967 occupation and expulsion of Palestinians, after which Israel took control of the West Bank and Gaza Strip and left '300,000 Palestinians displaced' (Sinclair 2017). Sharing her motivation for the film, Jacir notes:

> I had what I call the privilege of Palestine. All my life I was going back and forth. My grandparents, aunts and uncles lived in Bethlehem, so we were able to come in and out and we spent three or four months of the year in Palestine ever since I was a baby. So I have known Palestine all my life and it's the one place that has always been constant . . . Later, I was denied entry and found myself in Jordan five years ago. I suddenly found myself in the position of most Palestinians [in 2008]. I was looking at Palestine from across the border and could no longer reach there . . . Suddenly everything was just taken from me – like that. That's when the idea of *When I Saw You* came about. I found myself stuck in Jordan and very depressed, trying to figure out what I could do with this depression. I found the story of Tarek, a boy with hope, that's what I needed to focus on. (Barat 2013)

The film is set in the Harir refugee camp in Jordan and captures the 'feeling of hope' in the wake of the Naksa, the second mass expulsion of Palestinians, 'when the Palestinian armed liberation movement was on the ascendance' (Murphy 2013). Jordan is changing with the arrival of Palestinian refugees. Tarek (Mahmoud Asfa), an 11-year-old boy whose father is missing, is placed in the refugee camp along with his mother, Ghayda (Ruba Blal). He detests his life in the camp, the tents, the prefab houses, the ration queues and the bathrooms. His hope of return is ruined by the revelation that there are generations of refugees who have been living in the camp since 1948. Impatient and determined, he leaves the refugee camp to return to his home in Palestine. He loses the way to his Palestinian house but finds a group of fedayeen who become home for him.[12] In the fedayee base, he finds love, joy, determination, intellect, chatter and, most importantly, a new hope. The film was received well by Arab audiences but met with criticism for romanticising the fedayeen's struggles for liberation.

The film was the Palestinian entry for the Best Foreign Language Film at the 85th Academy Awards. It was funded by the Dubai Film Festival, along with some funding from Greece. Jacir made the film after she had settled in Amman, Jordan. Like her first feature film, *When I Saw You* also received multiple accolades.[13] The lead child actor, Mahmoud Asfa, was nominated for the

Young Artist Award for leading performance in foreign film and was the winner of the Best Actor Award at the Olympia International Film Festival. The film's cast includes Saleh Bakri, Ruba Blal, Mahmoud Asfa, Anas Algaralleh, Ali Elayan, Ruba Shamshoum, Ahmad Srour and Firas W. Taybeh, among others. We watched this film on Vudu.

This is arguably the most criticised among Jacir's films because it zooms in on a child's perspective and his perspective of the Palestine–Israel conflict and naive insistence on return to the homeland. Tarek never lets go of his conviction and desire of return. He asks a 'very logical question: "If you walked [away], why can't you walk back"' (Barat 2013). Jacir portrays different generations comparatively to highlight their complicity, their resignation and their differential hopes of return. Jacir comments that Tarek is 'the only person who remains on track with what he wants. It's [her] question to [her] leadership: why didn't you stay focused like Tarek?' to pursue the dream of return (Blincoe 2014). Overall, 'embodying a widely shared Palestinian fantasy of escape and freedom, the film brings magic to the bleak reality of displacement and stagnant refugee camps, as lived by millions of Palestinians over the past century' (Sinclair 2017).

Like her first feature film, *Salt of this Sea*, *When I Saw You* also came with financing, casting and shooting challenges. Raising finance for the film took two years, but Jacir was able to raise it all from 'the Arab community', while 'all the producers of the film [were also] Palestinian, so that was a huge achievement'. At the same time, they 'only had half the budget [they] needed so a lot of compromises had to be made' (Gilbert 2012). Shooting in Jordan required 'location permission from the Jordanian army', which turned out to be a difficult to obtain for 'a politically "sensitive" film' (Gilbert 2012; Mobarak 2012; Murphy 2013). While most people easily get shooting permits, the permit was denied to Jacir:

> Everyone is shooting in Jordan these days because it's like the film set for Iraq and for a lot of stuff. They never say no to anything. They said no to us. Yeah, they said no to us. We had the film commission, we were like, 'What's up?' And they're like, 'It's the subject. You're hitting on our raw nerve – the Palestinian/Jordanian tension and what happened in those years . . .' We got the film commission involved, we had to show the script and have a lot of discussions, and they let it go. But we also had one location where we couldn't get some of our crew members through. It's also because the location we were shooting for the refugee camp is way in the north of Jordan. It's like the Jordanian/Syrian/Israeli border. So it's full of military and they're like, 'We don't want cameras around.' Nobody wants cameras. (Mobarak 2012)

The film contains numerous references to 'specific (Palestinian revolutionary) films and photographs' of the period of hope and determination after the

Naksa; even the freeze frame at the end is 'a homage to the period' (Romani 2014). Ruba Shamshoum sings in the film but she 'never read the script'. The song she sings is 'about this rebirth of Palestinian nationalism'. The film contains many scenes that 'begin with either red, black or green [the colours of the Palestinian flag]. Like the mother sewing [in the beginning], it's with a white thread, Tarek brushing his mother's black hair – it's a repetition in the film.' Ruba's song is also about colours – 'the red of the poppies, the green of cactus, the black of the night' (Murphy 2013).

The fedayeen's location in the forest is 'the real location that the Palestinian fighters were hiding in and were constantly moving those tents from one part of the forest to another part of the forest'. When they were 'scouting' the location for shooting, they found 'all kinds of stuff' including bullets. The film captures an Israeli attack on the fedayeen base which prompts them to take refuge in a tunnel. Jacir comments that these tunnels were 'huge' and interconnected. They found a tunnel which was 'like a hospital. Like you go inside and then suddenly it opens up and there were six rooms. Huge rooms. [They] found medical supplies like IV bags, all kinds of stuff because after [fedayeen] got out of there it was just abandoned. No one goes there much anymore. So, it was really interesting to be in the actual location of where this was happening' (Mobarak 2012).

Casting and choosing locations itself required time. It took a long time for Jacir to find Mahmoud Asfa, who plays Tarek. She along with her team visited 'community centers, schools, refugee camps, and theaters' and saw 'about 200 boys' until they found him in Irbid refugee camp in the north of Jordan. Jacir cast the 'guys who played the fighters' because 'they looked good, they had long hair, they looked the part. And later [she] found out that a lot of them were children of the fighters' (Murphy 2013). She comments that she 'did a lot of research, a lot of visual research like photographs and film archives for both the refugee camp look and then also the fighters'. Jacir's research for this film highlights not only multiple political international movements but also the transnationalism of her films.

From her research, she learned that the fedayeen were 'documented a lot' because they became 'sexy in the international press at some point'. So, there were 'actually a lot of photographs of those guys and how they were living in tents and what they were wearing' (Mobarak 2012). The film contains multiple scenes where fedayeen talk about international revolutionary movements at the time. 1967 was a 'tremendously important year' for Palestinians but it was also 'a time of great hope' in terms of political movements and uprisings. People in the world 'were going through a kind of rebirth; an infectious sense of hope that they could change their own lives. Student movements, anti-colonial movements, civil rights' (Gilbert 2012). Jacir comments: 'I wanted to tell a story about this important time, not to be nostalgic but rather because it is so relevant. I started writing the script at a time [when] I was in need of hope in my own life, and in what I saw going on around me and in my own generation' (Gilbert 2012). While it seems idealistic and romanticised, this was the charm and nature of many of these political or anti-war or anti-colonialist movements for the young people who joined them. Fedayeen were aware of these simultaneous revolutionary events around the world. They 'knew about student movements in France, they knew about anti-war movements in the US' and followed 'Leftist ideology' (Mobarak 2012).

These movements were not only aware of each other, but they also actively supported each other via any means possible. When Jacir's team was in the location, they 'found stuff donated and they actually had the names of the countries that were donating.' East Germany and Russia were both sending donations. Cuba and China were also donating and training the fedayeen. In *When I Saw You*, the fedayeen receive donations of weapons and boots. They had a 'whole process of smuggling in stuff', with the help of 'Jordanian peasants' who lived in the area (Mobarak 2012). In a way, Jacir's next film explores the aftermath of the end of this kind of transnational political support and the resulting disillusionment.

Wajib

Wajib was Jacir's third feature film. It was screened in the Contemporary World Cinema section of the 2017 Toronto International Film Festival. It was also selected as the Palestinian entry for the Best Foreign Language Film at the 90th Academy Awards. The film won thirty-six international awards.[14] The cast includes Mohammad Bakri (who is himself a well-known documentary maker as well as an actor), Saleh Bakri (Mohammad Bakri's son), Ossama Bawardi, Lama Tatour, Maria Zreik, Rebecca Esmeralda Telhami and Tarik Kopty.

In this lyrical road movie, a Muslim father and his son drive through Nazareth in the wake of Christmas to hand-deliver wedding invitations to often eclectic and eccentric houses, as per local custom. The son, Shadi (Saleh Bakri), is an architect and lives in Italy but is visiting Nazareth for his sister's wedding. The father, Abu Shadi (Mohammad Bakri), is divorced and feels bitter because of his wife and his son leaving him to move to other countries and choosing people he dislikes: his wife remarried, and his son is dating the daughter of a Palestinian Liberation Organization (PLO) leader. The film explores a different geography and demographic as it takes the audience through the narrow streets and wider roads. It captures a family that is broken by choice rather than because of political turmoil. It shows people of various religious faiths and inclinations in Nazareth. Simultaneously, it comments on the artistic and architectural history, arts and politics of Nazareth and Europe.

Jacir was inspired to work on this film when she witnessed her own husband delivering wedding invitations, doing his duty. The tradition of hand-delivering wedding invitations is 'a Palestinian tradition' that is also practised by other Mediterranean countries. While it is obsolete in most places, people in Nazareth still practise it (Elphick 2017). Nazareth is in northern Israel, with a 70 per cent Muslim and 30 per cent Christian population. It is home to the largest community of Arabs, who are predominantly Christians and who identify as Palestinians but live as Israeli citizens (Sinclair 2017). Called 'Jacir's funniest film yet' (Sinclair 2017), *Wajib* also 'highlight[s] the persisting tensions felt between Palestinians living inside Israel and Palestine, and in the diaspora – of being caught between preserving traditions as a form of resistance to the brutal occupation and being a forward-thinking and productive population' (Sinclair 2017).

For *Wajib*, Jacir gleaned funding from a number of diverse sources, including France and Colombia. This funding, however, came with 'technical strings attached over a period of five years' (Saadi 2018). Often, filmmakers receive funding that influences their vision of the film, and Jacir considers herself lucky that the funding did not come with ideological or artistic demands attached (Saadi 2018). To secure Colombian funding, she had to hire a Colombian actor, so she requested her casting director to 'find a Palestinian with a Colombian passport to star in the movie'. She found a woman in Ramallah, who she cast in the role of the widow (Saadi 2018).

Jacir was also 'reticent' about casting a real father and son together in the roles of Shadi and Abu Shadi. She talked to Mohammad Bakri about this possiblity and her reticence, but then she had a dream about it. She comments, 'whenever I dream about an actor, I cast them. It's happened a couple of times and I've never been wrong with that. I had my dream, then I woke up. I said, "It's him. He's the one"' (Elphick 2017). The film's strength lies in the portrayal of the affective and ideological diversity of lives in Nazareth. Like Jacir's previous two films, this film is also attentive to the landscape and cinematises it lyrically, poetically and nostalgically. We watched this film on Amazon Prime, where it was temporarily available.

Latest and Upcoming Work

Under the title *Postcards from the Future*, eleven renowned world cinema personalities produced short films that were screened every evening on the giant screen of Locarno's Piazza Grande to 8,000 spectators, during the 75th Locarno Film Festival (3–13 August 2022). These filmmakers included Annemarie Jacir, along with Ukrainian screenwriter Natalya Vorozhbit, Swiss director Fredi M. Murer, Russian filmmaker Alexander Sokurov, French director Bertrand Mandico, US filmmaker Kevin B. Lee, English director Claire Simon, Israeli writer and director Nadav Lapid, and Swiss Rwandan filmmaker Kantarama Gahigiri, each of whom directed a 3–4 minute short that describes their vision of the future (Rothe 2022). Jacir comments that Locarno gave her a 'small budget', which she used to 'hire some guys from Jenin, got them permits and brought them to Haifa'. She worked with her regular team, including Ossama Bawardi, Nael Kanj, Athar Sbeit and Ashraf Dowani. For the project, they 'constructed this giant wall which is the exact same dimensions as the apartheid wall in Palestine'. A young sound designer, Hussein Alaroury, made a soundtrack that was 'quite haunting and accompanie[d] the stillness of the images'. The most significant thing about this clip is that it was screened in the Piazza Grande, one of the largest screens in Europe. For this screening, Jacir wanted something that 'would really show the weight and ugliness of the apartheid wall, for audiences to experience' (Rothe 2022).

In 2022, Jacir directed the third episode, called 'Egyptian Cigarettes', of the groundbreaking American TV series, *Ramy*. While the series has received acclaim for its non-traditional and non-stereotypical portrayal of Arab-Americans, Jacir's episode received particular attention because it includes what has been described as 'the most uncomfortable scene ever' and because it approaches sensitive subjects such as the Holocaust, checkpoints between the West Bank and Jerusalem, privilege, class, age and sexuality, all in the span of one episode. In the episode, Ramy (Ramy Youssef) – who, like Jacir's own characters, simultaneously incites sympathy, anger and frustration – flies in the first-class with his lapsed Jewish friend/Israeli-American business partner and his closeted gay uncle (Laith Nakli) to Israel to negotiate a deal for his diamond business. His uncle, excited to be able finally to see his homeland, is taken directly to an interrogation room and then deported back to the US. Ramy, meanwhile, enters Israel and even crosses into the Occupied Palestine to pursue his sexual interests only to reveal the multilayered complexities of the politics and complicitiy of diasporic Palestinians.

Jacir has just finished the script for her next project. She hopes that it will qualify under the British-Palestinian co-production agreement. But she has also been 'reaching out to international partners' who want to be part of her new film, which she calls 'the project of her life' (Aftab 2020). Jacir is also developing a TV series based on Susan Abulhawa's bestselling novel *Mornings in Jenin*, which is a 'multigenerational story of a Palestinian family forced out of their village into the Jenin refugee camp' (Vivarelli 2020). The book 'follows the Abulheja family – Yehya and Basima and their two sons – who are forced to leave their homestead in Palestine by the newly formed state of Israel in 1948, and it follows them through half a century of trials and tribulations in five countries' (Vivarelli 2020). Originally published in 2010, this novel has been translated into 30 languages. As shown by her previous and current projects, it is the locational, psychological, cognitive and experiential range of Jacir's subject matter, along with her funding and distribution, that makes her oeuvre transnational.

CHAPTER OVERVIEW

The chapters in this book explore the themes of exile, memory, trauma, time, displacement, determination, transnationalism and diaspora in the Palestinian experience. The first chapter, 'Experimenting with Realities in Jacir's Short Films', takes a closer look at Jacir's short and experimental films. The films announce some of the central themes in her work, such as the place of memory, politics of space, transvergence of transnationalism, and the role of aesthetic experiences, which will return in our analyses of the feature films in the following chapters. This chapter also comments on Jacir's intellectual and self-reflexive politics as a writer and filmmaker, and her reflection on her responsibilities as an artist. The second chapter, 'Heterotopias and Thirdspaces: Construction of Space in Jacir's Films', explores the role and centrality of various spaces and spatial politics in Jacir's feature films. It reflects on the deployment of space as the site of personal, communal and political crises as well as the potential site of resolution of these crises. The third chapter, 'Locations of Memory: Home and Homeland', explores the impact of memories of home and homeland on characters' affective, social and political lives. It highlights and analyses the ways in which characters' personal, familial and geographical memories of the past shadow their present lives and inform their future decisions. The fourth chapter, 'Transvergent Transnationalism: Borders, Homes and Humans', studies Jacir's cinema as transvergent transnationalism because of the overwhelmingly exilic, diasporic and refugee experiences of her characters. The fifth chapter, 'Characters at the Margins', redirects its attention from the major characters and protagonists to the minor characters to discuss the diversity and nuance that these characters render to the plots of these films. The sixth chapter, 'Curatorial Politics and Practices', provides a detailed summary and commentary on the works and festivals that Jacir has curated. It also comments on her inspiration for these curations and creations. The concluding section, 'An Interview with Annemarie Jacir', is a conversation with the filmmaker where she responds to questions about her creative inspiration, cinematography, her role as a Palestinian woman director, and her future plans.

While we were working on this book, the new waves of Israeli settler violence in the Palestinian territories erupted in May 2021 and then 2023. Writing a book about one of the most influential Palestinian filmmakers comes with a strong sense of responsibility not only to the films and the filmmaker but also to the characters. Neither of us is from Palestine, but we are both deeply invested in the Palestinian cause and Palestinians' right to their land and homes, and a right to freedom from oppression and violence. As a Muslim woman from Pakistan, Iqra is sensitive to the politics of Muslim representation in Western media, so she approaches this work with the sensitivity and awareness of the problematics of making and distributing Palestinian films but also the criticality of talking about Palestinian cinema and films. With an interest in women's cinema from the Arab world, Stefanie is likewise dedicated to critically engaging with representational issues, both in front of and behind the camera. Jacir is a particularly interesting filmmaker, as the diversity of themes and narratives in her work reflects a pluralistic approach to the power of film to change people's perspectives. As a privileged white European academic working in a UK context, as a curator of international film festival programmes, and as an editor for the series this book appears in, Stefanie is acutely aware of the position of power she takes up, and is dedicated to assisting in the widening of visibility and accessibility of work that broadens the story of film history.

During the writing of this book, we developed a mentorship and friendship based in a shared understanding of the significance of Jacir's work and her politics as a Palestinian working transnationally. Our admiration for the films and the filmmaker fed our discussions and our writing, and we hope that this book becomes a useful source for those interested in Palestinian cinema or Arab women's cinema. We hope this book archives Jacir's cinema and her growth as a filmmaker as well as our appreciation for her work.

REFERENCES

Abbatescianni, Davide (2021), 'Annemarie Jacir: Director of *The Oblivion Theory*', *Cineuropa*, https://cineuropa.org/en/interview/398673/ (accessed 19 April 2023).

Aftab, Kaleem (2020), 'Annemarie Jacir Period Film in Development with Producer Ossama Bawardi', *Variety*, 31 October, https://variety.com/2020/film/global/ossama-bawardi-annemarie-jacir-1234820513/ (accessed 19 April 2023).

Armes, Roy (2015), *New Voices in Arab Cinema*, Bloomington: Indiana University Press.

Barat, Frank (2013), 'Why can't we walk back? A Conversation with Palestinian Filmmaker Annemarie Jacir', *+972 Magazine*, 13 December, https://www.972mag.com/why-cant-we-walk-back-a-conversation-with-palestinian-filmmaker-annemarie-jacir/ (accessed 19 April 2023).

Berger, Laura (2020), 'Annemarie Jacir is Bringing "Mornings in Jenin" to Television', Women and Hollywood, 23 December, https://womenandhollywood.com/annemarie-jacir-is-bringing-mornings-in-jenin-to-television/ (accessed 19 April 2023).

Blincoe, Nicholas (2014), 'Annemarie Jacir: An Auteur in Exile', *The Guardian*, 5 June, https://www.theguardian.com/film/2014/jun/05/annemarie-jacir-auteur-in-exile-palestinian-director-when-i-saw-you (accessed 19 April 2023).

'Bristol Palestine Film Festival: Interview' (2020), *That's What She Said Magazine*, 28 November, https://twssmagazine.com/2020/11/28/bristol-palestine-film-festival-interview/ (accessed 19 April 2023).

'Ceasefire Interview Palestinian Director, Annemarie Jacir' (2022), *Alchetron*, 31 October, https://alchetron.com/Annemarie-Jacir (accessed 19 April 2023).

Denes, Nick (2014), 'An Overburdened "Brand"? Reflections on a Decade with the London Palestine Film Festival', in *Film Festival Yearbook 6: Film Festivals and the Middle East*, ed. Dina Iordanova and Stefanie Van de Peer, St Andrews: St Andrews Film Studies, pp. 251–64.

Elassar, Alaa (2022), 'Palestinians Relive the Raw and Painful History of al-Nakba in Netflix's New Film "Farha"', *CNN*, 12 December, https://www.cnn.com/style/article/farha-palestinian-film-nakba-darin-sallam-reaj/index.html (accessed 19 April 2023).

Elphick, Jeremy (2017), '*Wajib* – An Interview with Annemarie Jacir', *Four Three Film*, 1 September, https://fourthreefilm.com/2017/09/wajib-an-interview-with-annemarie-jacir/ (accessed 19 April 2023).

Farhat, Maymanah (2008), 'Palestinian Artist Emily Jacir Awarded Top Prize', *The Electronic Intifada*, 15 December, https://electronicintifada.net/content/palestinian-artist-emily-jacir-awarded-top-prize/7859 (accessed 19 April 2023).

Ghazoul, Ferial, Annemarie Jacir, Moustafa Bayoumi, Hamid Dabashi and Mark Westmoreland (2011), 'I Wanted that Story to be Told (Interview)', *Alif: Journal of Comparative Poetics* 31: 241–54, Gale Academic OneFile, https://link.gale.com/apps/doc/A270810911/AONE?u=tel_k_cedgrv&sid=googleScholar&xid=f0221cea (accessed 19 April 2023).

Gilbert, Alia (2012), 'When I Saw You', Film Audience Network, Shrewsbury Film Society, https://bostonpalestinefilmfest.org/2014/04/25/interview-with-annemarie-jacir-award-winning-director-of-when-i-saw-you/ (accessed 19 April 2023).

Grant, Hugh (2014), 'Astonishing Palestinian Film', Twitter, 31 May, https://twitter.com/HackedOffHugh/status/472801201462185984 (accessed 19 April 2023).

Grisham, Ursula (2020), 'Annemarie Jacir', *Filmatique*, 27 March, https://blog.filmatique.com/all/annemarie-jacir (accessed 19 April 2023).

Hilwi, Rasha (2012), 'Romancing the Naksa Narrative', *Al-Akhbar*, 10 October, www.al-akhbar.com (accessed 19 April 2023).

'In Berlin: Filmmaker Annemarie Jacir Draws the Future of Palestinian Cinema' (2020), *Al-Bawaba*, 16 March, https://www.albawaba.com/editors-choice/berlin-filmmaker-annemarie-jacir-draws-future-palestinian-cinema-1345030 (accessed 19 April 2023).

Ismael, Aymann (2022), 'Inside the Making of the Year's Most Uncomfortable Scene', *Slate*, 13 October, https://slate.com/culture/2022/10/ramy-season-3-holocaust-congratulations-scene.html (accessed 19 April 2023).

Jacir, Emily (2007), 'Palestinian Revolution Cinema Comes to NYC', *The Electronic Intifada*, 16 February, https://electronicintifada.net/content/palestinian-revolution-cinema-comes-nyc/6759 (accessed 19 April 2023).

Lodderhose, Diana (2021), 'Filmmaker Annemarie Jacir on Her Journey to Preserve Palestinian Cinema for Future Generations', *Deadline*, 8 July, https://deadline.com/2021/07/annemarie-jacir-filmmaker-palestine-cinema-cannes-magazine-disruptor-1234787507/ (accessed 19 April 2023).

Mobarak, Jared (2012), '"When I Saw You" Writer/Director Annemarie Jacir on Jordan/Palestinian Relations and the Fadayee', *The Film Stage*, 13 September, https://thefilmstage.com/interview-when-i-saw-you-writerdirector-annemarie-jacir-on-jordanpalestinian-relations-and-the-fadayee/ (accessed 19 April 2023).

Morrill, Rebecca, Karen Wright and Louisa Elderton (2019), *Great Women Artists*, London: Phaidon.

Murphy, Maureen Clare (2013), 'Honoring Palestinian History: Filmmaker Annemarie Jacir on "When I Saw You"', *The Electronic Antifada*, 29 April, https://electronicintifada.net/blogs/maureen-clare-murphy/honoring-palestinian-history-filmmaker-annemarie-jacir-when-i-saw-you (accessed 19 April 2023).

Naficy, Hamid (2006), 'Palestinian Exilic Cinema and Film Letters: On Palestinian Cinema', in *Dreams of a Nation: On Palestinian Cinema*, ed. Hamid Dabashi, London: Verso, pp. 90–104.

Nicoletti, Chiara (2018), 'Annemarie Jacir – *Wajib*', Fred Film Radio, 22 April, http://www.fred.fm/uk/annemarie-jacir-wajib/ (accessed 19 April 2023).

Nusair, Isis (2018), 'Refusing the Separation: An Interview with Palestinian Filmmaker Annemarie Jacir', *Jadaliyya*, 6 September, https://www.jadaliyya.com/Details/37878 (accessed 19 April 2023).

Rastegar, Kamran (2006), 'On Palestinian Cinema', *Bidoun* 8, https://www.bidoun.org/articles/rashid-masharawi-buthina-canaan-khoury-nahed-awwad-hazim-bitar-annemarie-jacir-and-ahmad-habash (accessed 19 April 2023).

Romani, Rebecca (2014), 'Interview: Annemarie Jacir, Director of "When I Saw You"', *KPBS*, 13 June, https://www.kpbs.org/news/arts-culture/2014/06/13/interview-annemarie-jacir-director-when-i-saw-you (accessed 19 April 2023).

Rothe, E. Nina (2018), 'Why Cannes' Un Certain Regard Jury Member Annemarie Jacir is a Personal Favorite', 9 May, https://www.eninarothe.com/faces/2018/5/9/why-cannes-un-certain-regard-jury-member-annemarie-jacir-is-a-personal-favorite (accessed 19 April 2023).

Rothe, E. Nina (2022), 'Annemarie Jacir Sends her Palestinian "Postcard from the Future" to Locarno', *Moving Image Middle East*, 9 August, https://www.mime.news/posts/annemarie-jacir-sends-her-palestinian-postcards-from-the-future-to-locarno (accessed 19 April 2023).

Saadi, Dania (2018), 'The Arab Film Industry Needs More Support, Says Annemarie Jacir', *Arab America*, 16 December, https://www.arabamerica.com/the-arab-film-industry-needs-more-support-says-annemarie-jacir/ (accessed 19 April 2023).

Sinclair, Florence (2017), 'This Palestinian Filmmaker is Paving the Way for Middle Eastern Cinema', *Culture Trip*, 30 October, https://theculturetrip.com/middle-east/palestinian-territories/articles/this-palestinian-filmmaker-is-paving-the-way-for-middle-eastern-cinema/ (accessed 19 April 2023).

Vivarelli, Nick (2020), 'Palestinian Director Annemarie Jacir to Adapt Novel "Mornings in Jenin" for TV', *Variety*, 21 December, https://variety.com/2020/tv/global/annemarie-jacir-to-adapt-bestseller-mornings-in-jenin-for-tv-series-1234867707/ (accessed 19 April 2023).

NOTES

1. https://universes.art/en/nafas/articles/2012/emily-jacir-documenta (accessed 19 April 2023).
2. https://archive.vn/20130127050622/http://pivf.johnmenick.com/about.php (accessed 19 April 2023).

3. https://magazine.artland.com/female-iconoclasts-emily-jacir-and-the-politics-and-poetics-of-palestine/ (accessed 19 April 2023).
4. A video installation, accessible at https://www.artfund.org/supporting-museums/art-weve-helped-buy/artwork/10399/1-crossing-surda-a-record-of-going-to-and-from-work-2-from-texas-with-love-3-ramallahnew-york (accessed 19 April 2023).
5. https://bidoun.org/articles/emirates-now-emily-jacir (accessed 19 April 2023).
6. https://electronicintifada.net/content/photostory-retracing-bus-no-23-historic-jerusalem-hebron-road/6609 (accessed 19 April 2023).
7. Annemarie Jacir, interview with Alain Gresh, in the pressbook for *Salt of this Sea*.
8. These include the Chicago International Film Festival, Palm Springs International Short Film Festival, IFP/New York, Institute du Monde Arabe Biannual and Lenola Film Festival in Italy; it was the official selection at the New York Film Festival, Edinburgh International Film Festival, Telluride Film Festival and Locarno Film Festival. Other awards for this short film include World Premiere, Cannes Film Festival; Official Selection, Cinefondation, 2003; Recipient of Jerome Foundation Media Arts Grant, 2003; Best Films of the Year list, 2003 – *Film Comment Magazine*; National Finalist – Academy of Motion Picture Arts; Student Academy Awards, Best Short Screenplay; Nantucket Film Festival, Best Short Film; Palm Springs International Short Film Festival, Best Short Film (Emerging Narrative); IFP/New York, Silver Plaque; Chicago International Film Festival, Best Short Film; Institute du Monde Arabe Biannual, Best Screenwriting; Lenola Film Festival, Italy, Best Short Film Second Prize; Lenola Film Festival, Italy, Audience Choice Award; Polo Ralph Lauren Columbia University Festival, Special Jury Prize; Ramallah International Film Festival, Audience Choice Award; San Diego Women Film Festival 2006, Luis Trenker Award for Best Short Film; 4Film Festival, Borderlands, 2006; Locarno Film Festival, Official Selection; Edinburgh International Film Festival, Official Selection; Telluride Film Festival, Official Selection; New York Film Festival.
9. http://www.philistinefilms.com/sots (accessed 19 April 2023).
10. Including the Best Film at the Sguardi Altrove Film Festival Italy; FIPRESCI Critics Award at the Osians Arab & Asian Film Festival; Best First Film at the Traverse City Film Festival; Audience Choice Award at the New Orleans International Human Rights Film Festival; and the official selection at the London BFI Film Festival, Pusan International Film Festival and Tribeca Film Festival.
11. When called the first Palestinian director of international repute, Jacir names various Palestinian directors who have gained fame for their impressive work. When called the first woman Palestinian director of international repute, she resists the title by saying that she does not believe in women's cinema. It is true that each of her feature films has focused on a different gender, age and experience.
12. http://www.philistinefilms.com/wisy (accessed 19 April 2023).

13. Including the Best Asian Film at the Berlin International Film Festival; Best Arab Film at the Abu Dhabi Film Festival; World Cinema Best Picture at the Phoenix International Film Festival; UNICEF Award at the Olympia International Film Festival; and the Best Children's Film at the Asian Pacific Screen Awards.
14. Among others, the Best Film awards at the Dubai International Film Festival, Mar Del Plata International Film Festival, SIGNIS Prize, Amiens International Film Festival and Casablanca Film Festival in Morocco.

CHAPTER I

Experimenting with Realities in Jacir's Short Films

Stefanie Van de Peer

While Annemarie Jacir is best-known for her award-winning feature fiction films, before we focus on these famous works we want to have a closer look at the short and experimental films she has made. These announce some of the central themes in Jacir's work, such as the place of memory, the politics of space, the transvergence of transnationalism, and the role of aesthetic experiences, which will return in our analyses of the feature films in later chapters. These early short experimental films announce these topics with a directness that enables us to delve deep into the aesthetic and thematic complexities linked to being a Palestinian filmmaker. They present the particular intellectual and self-reflexive politics of Jacir as a writer and filmmaker, and a subjective, personally felt element to the role of the artist. Scholars tend to discuss Palestinian film culture in terms of its outright politics and context, but in Jacir's short films we see a global connection between the history of the land and its people, however dispersed geographically and far removed temporally they are from their homeland. Jacir's focus on personal lived experience has resulted in a particular type of realism, which opens space for historical and contemporary trauma to intimately connect to the roles of people involved in the production, distribution and exhibition of these films.

The traumas of 1948, 1967 and both Intifadas, as well as countless other devastating political and cultural shocks, have caused Palestinian films to become associated with revolutionary cinema. In addition, scholars have noticed that in the early 2000s, the era of the Second Intifada, filmmakers seem to have had a sustained interest in the representation of reality. Kamran Rastegar radically states that 'documentaries play a large, perhaps disproportionate role in Palestinian cinema, an understandable phenomenon given the political and social conditions within Palestine' (2002: 275), followed up by Nadia Yacub's assertion that the 'overwhelming majority of Palestinian films are documentaries' (2011: 232). Kay Dickinson nuances this somewhat and shows that the realities of the Second Intifada, together with the increased availability of lightweight equipment, the home video aesthetic for editing, and an increase in private funds resulted in a heightened 'refusal to dichotomise fact from fiction in the quasi-documentary' and that 'the whimsical looms large' (2016: 89–90). Seeing that reality in Palestine is, in and of itself, stranger than fiction, a documentary explanation of Palestinian life and politics is impossible and a full understanding unachievable. As such, we follow Laura Marks in her concept of experimental films as works that 'experiment with the relationship between fiction and documentary, in questions about truth, presence, index and performance. Indeed, some of the richest experimentation works with performativity, treating cinema as an event, from the pro-filmic act to the act of reception' (2015: 2). It is within this notion that we want to frame Jacir's short films: they are experiments with genre, with form, and most of all with performance, both on the part of the filmmaker and her crew, and on the part of the Palestinians she films. In all the works we discuss in this chapter, there is an element of the filmmaker's presence in and around the film, her performance, and her responsibility towards her subjects. The intricacies of Jacir's films and their effectiveness as activist works stems from the self-awareness that surrounds her presence as a creator in a destroyed landscape.

In this chapter, we look in detail at five of Jacir's short films, most of which are activist experimental shorts dealing with the difficulty of being a Palestinian inside *and* outside of the Palestinian territories. From her first internationally successful film, *Like Twenty Impossibles* (2002),[1] to an experimental short documentary set in New York at her alma mater, *An Explanation (and then burn the ashes)* (2005),[2] and collaborations such as *A Few Crumbs for the Birds* (2005)[3] with Nassime Amaouche, *A World Apart in 15 Minutes* (2006)[4] with Enas I. Al-Muthaffar, as well as *Sound of the Street* (2006),[5] all these films experiment with reality, lived experiences, the surrealism of Palestinian life, and the absurdity of being a Palestinian in the world. In these short experiments, Jacir questions artistic responsibility and the politics of filmmaking. Our attention here goes to the different ways in which she approaches the crossing of borders and boundaries: in these short films she addresses in experimental terms the concepts of limitations and im/possibilities. As different types of checkpoints and roadblocks prevent border crossings and halt journeys, the immobility of the roadblock movies of the Second Intifada gains expression in specific jerky aesthetics and fragmented voice-overs and sound design. Poetry, soundscapes and music emphasise unease, as speakers are not often seen in the act of speaking, and artistic interventions such as poetry and music serve as immaterial, ephemeral protests against the static and material nature of the roadblocks. This chapter lays out how these early works have shaped Jacir into the feature filmmaker she has become.

Jacir made a body of short films in the early 2000s, during the Second Intifada. As Dickinson explains, 'the Second Intifada heralded a particularly fresh, urgent and experimental approach to filmmaking, in tune with the uprisings to which they contributed' (2022: n.p.). This prolific period led to an artistic oeuvre that, purely by its existence, defies Israeli oppression and occupation. Indeed, the films of the Second Intifada give shape to a cinema of resistance, just as revolutionary as the early films of the PLO-funded Palestine Film Unit. Yacub observes that many of the films made in this era 'bear witness to and communicate the violence associated with occupation' (2011: 233) and the filmmakers do this in an embodied way, by inserting their own physicalities and experiences into those of the subjects of their films. Collapsing the personal and the political in these films results in a refusal to take on the identity of victimhood, and instead foregrounds an agency perhaps not seen before in Palestinian films, an agency that is both highly personal and shared among the community.

This cinema of resistance of the Second Intifada resulted, according to Dickinson, in anarchic films that showcase lawless spaces and aim for proper freedom, where limits are tested in the service of creativity. Jacir's work of this period experiments with the concepts of space and time in a way that is more visceral, more direct than in her feature films. In 2002, as the Israelis started building the Separation Wall, the increasing number of roadblocks, the checkpoints and the interrupted car journeys became central in the films as well. Dickinson explores the importance of roads, cars and journeys in detail. She describes how roads 'haunt' the films from the Second Intifada (2016: 97), as most of them are travelogues, descriptions of journeys and road movies. The actors and subjects of these films are groups of people working and travelling together and participating in conversations about travelling, the origin of the journey, and the plans at the destination. These journeys include hold-ups at checkpoints and critiques of the transit infrastructure, describing the Wall through symbols of condensed, limited and tightening spaces full of obstacles, and the paradox of a small, potentially easily traversed country where it takes forever to arrive at your destination because of prolonged interruptions. As such, the car journeys describe the land and create it, and the act of travel shows the immanent connection to the land and its interrupted geography, visualised in still images as well as handheld camera movements, brutal edits and the use of hidden cameras (Dickinson 2016: 100).

The embodiment of the defiance against blockages and limitations is evident in the topic of most of the films from this period, enacting and thematising the restrictions on movement and halted mobility through the exploration of expulsion, failures at border crossings and the constant interruptions of journeys and life, both symbolically through the rejection of permit applications and literally at checkpoints. This is what led Gertz and Khleifi to play on words with the genre of the road movie, and call Palestinian films of the period of the early 2000s 'roadblock movies', in which journeys through time and space remain unfinished, changed and compressed or extended endlessly, with no view of a (realistic) destination. Though Dickinson references the idea of the roadblock movie, she does not go quite far enough in expressing the lack of access to destinations, the complete disruption caused by checkpoints and the inability to travel even to a town only six miles away. Ultimately, cars and minibuses take up the main spaces in the films (Dickinson 2016: 106), which – as in the road movie genre elsewhere – present a freedom of movement, but in Palestine come to represent the fragility of a protective casing, where films are now shot through the window because Israeli soldiers demand that you stay inside. Shots of dashboard decorations and rearview mirrors abound. And we propose that it is these frames of halted journeys, or the embodiment of these borders, that give expression – literal (external) and symbolic (internal) – to the failure of the act of travel in Second Intifada films. The experimental films of Jacir illustrate this painfully.

In her short films, in fact, Jacir takes this further than Dickinson admits: she not only expresses the interruptions that these obstacles cause to the journeys, but also emphasises their absolute nature, their extreme upset, and the visceral violence they represent. The short films speak of anger in a form somewhere between fiction and documentary, being neither and both at the same time. Playing with the edges of realism within the experimental form becomes a ground for giving shape to a personal and perhaps individual working-through of the trauma of interruption and expulsion. Because such atrocious limitations are put on filming permits for certain locations and travel within the territories, the filmmakers have to be not only pragmatic about who they work with and what type of identity cards their crew members have (so that they are able to cross checkpoints), but also how they work and how they can bypass the limits of their permits. Jacir testifies to her own defiance in several interviews, when she points out that permits are constantly rejected, 'so either you give in and you do not make a film, or you find ways around the limitations' (Younis and Younis 2014). The sheer importance of the element of *choice* here shows Jacir's defiance of Israeli limitations put on her movements and acts as a filmmaker.

The paradoxical collapse of absurdity and reality is conceptualised by Hamid Dabashi as 'traumatic realism' (2006: 11). He describes the constant presence of an absence: a geographical and political absence as seen in the lack of leadership or, indeed, land. However, instead of the word 'absurdity', Dabashi uses the word 'madness' in his exploration of the Palestinian films' limits of representation of reality. This may reflect his directness of expression, but it also shows an acute awareness of the links between almost a century of trauma being perpetrated on the Palestinian people, and the impact such a prolonged oppression has on communal mental health. Dabashi explains how there is both an urgency and immediacy inherent to the need to testify – in film or other art forms – which stands in stark contrast with the time it takes to reflect and analyse, or make sense of traumatic instances. If such a traumatic instance is endless, as it is in the Occupied Territories, then individual testimonies become impossible, and so the Palestinian subject becomes his or her own (silent) witness. As such, Dabashi shows, reality is difficult, if not impossible, to represent in Palestine, and fictionalisation becomes a necessity, where the 'aestheticization of the political' reveals that representations of reality, its absurdity and its madness, are impossible. He calls this the Palestinian crisis of mimesis, which for Dabashi is the main element that makes Elia Suleiman's famous films so successful as depictions of a Palestinian 'reality', and it also makes experimental films so much more realistic than documentaries.

As mentioned before, Jacir made most of her experimental short films in the early 2000s, the era of the Second Intifada, or the al-Aqsa Intifada as it is more accurately called. We have been unable to see her earliest shorts made between the end of the 1990s, after she set up Philistine Films, and 2002: films such as *A Post-Oslo History* (1998), *The Satellite Shooters* (2001), *Palestine is Waiting* (2001) and *A Revolutionary Tale* (2002). From the online Columbia database of Palestinian films, we can glean that *A Post-Oslo History* deals with the disappointment of the Oslo Accords, represented through a moment at the Bethlehem checkpoint five years later. *The Satellite Shooters* experiments with the conventions of the Western genre and critiques the stereotypes inherent to its idealisation of masculinity and freedom. *Palestine is Waiting* is about the Palestinian Right to Return, made by a collective of Palestinian filmmakers based in the United States. From these brief synopses it is clear that even these very early experimental films champion collaboration, defiance and a critical mind about the role of filmmakers in their own work, something that returns explicitly in the more widely seen and accessible films discussed in what follows.

Like Twenty Impossibles (17 minutes long) is the most widely seen and discussed of Jacir's short experimental films. When it came out, it was the first Arab short film by a woman to be selected for Cannes, and it also made it through to the nomination list for the Oscars. It deals with the cruelty of Israeli checkpoints, both the static kind and the so-called 'flying' checkpoints, in Palestine. In the film, a Palestinian film crew and actor are making their way to Jerusalem, but a closed checkpoint makes them decide to take a remote side road. This decision is, once again, a *choice*, albeit a failed one, as we will see later. A male driver, soundman, cameraman, actor and a female director (a fictional Annemarie) are on a schedule but need to practise patience within the space of their minivan. As in any road movie, the camera captures the landscape and records snippets of the discussions in the car, where practical matters at hand mingle in quick succession with memories of driving around more freely in the family car and previous film projects. A female voice-over remembers how, as a child, on car journeys with her parents in Palestine, she used to lean out of the window, looking at the landscape and smiling with happiness. Meanwhile, the actor worries that he will not be good enough, and questions why she chose him for her film. She says he has an attractive face.

These relatively carefree moments stand in stark contrast with what happens next. When they arrive at an unexpected checkpoint on the side road, the camera keeps rolling and captures the ways in which the crew's relationships disintegrate and responsibilities are negotiated under the pressure of the Israeli soldiers' brutal behaviour. Choice-making is itself an act of emancipation and liberation in Palestine. When the crew members decide to take another route to Jerusalem, they attempt to make a choice; however, they are stopped by a flying checkpoint. Flying checkpoints are stark reminders that these choices are risky and indeed sometimes futile. These flying checkpoints rid Palestinians of the spirit of defiance to spatially manipulate and disrupt Israel's checkpoint system. The crew cannot get to Jerusalem. In 2003, the year the film was made, 734 such flying checkpoints existed (Dickinson 2016: 97).

The observational detail in the film shows nuances in different (in-)human interactions: we witness the differently coloured Palestinian ID cards and permits; we see the diversity of the landscape in terms of its beauty and its cruelty; people's straightforward solidarity is expressed when a man taps on the window of the minivan and tells the crew with a simple gesture that the checkpoint is closed; a young Israeli soldier says he was born in Florida. These details give shape to the tensions that come to a head when the crew disintegrates in front of the rolling camera. The soldiers repeat that the camera must be turned off, but it defiantly continues to roll and record the treatment they receive from the soldiers, an older and a younger man. Indeed, Dickinson observes that a lot of the Second Intifada films make interference from soldiers with the camera a cinematic feature of the treatment of both their crews and cast, and their documentaries. Soldiers are filmed as they forbid filming and often close scenes with the shutdown or covering with their hand of a camera's lens. Yet many of these films contain raw and covertly captured footage of brutal checkpoint encounters, or the dramatisation thereof (Dickinson 2016: 94). These disruptive instances are edited into the film, and lay bare the 'arrested movement' (Dickinson 2016: 102) within and into the territory. The scene that unfolds at the checkpoint, where the camera keeps rolling and captures the brutal treatment of the Palestinian crew by the Israeli soldiers, defying their calls to stop recording, illustrates the end of the choice, but also the stubborn refusal to let the soldiers take away all agency. The gaze here is a Palestinian gaze, a female Palestinian gaze that has attempted to create a counter-space of resistance. There is, in other words, at this flying checkpoint, a confirmation of Palestinian agency and of its absence.

Far from the aesthetic smoothness of the road movie as we know it, these roadblock movies use jerky, handheld, clandestine camerawork as a feature in their build-up and explanation of the tension and the impossibility of filming in the Occupied Territories.

This tension in the act of filming, and the defiance that typifies the roadblock movie in *Like Twenty Impossibles*, is strengthened by the soundtrack as well. As in many of Jacir's films, composer Kamran Rastegar contributed the original music, and the oud in his composition gives expression to the haunting, nostalgic atmosphere. This classical music is combined with ambient sounds of conflict, non-diegetic recordings of army jeeps, walkie-talkies and drones. This jarring combination elevates the discomfort the viewer feels when watching the film, as not only is the director embodied here in the fictional Annemarie, but the spectators' implication in their ignorance or neglect of the reality of Palestinian film crews' experiences is reflected in these sounds as well. This indictment of the global viewer is likewise present in the film's title, and in the poem it originates from, 'We Shall Remain' by Tawfiq Zayyad (1965), which is included in the end credits and includes the lines: 'Like twenty impossibles / we shall remain.'

The poem expresses both the defiance of Palestinian artists (and people) in their steadfast act of remaining, and the implication of the 'you', whose lives are so much simpler and so much more straightforward than any aspect of life is for Palestinian people. Jacir includes herself in the 'you' as well as in the 'we' – she acknowledges that she is both an insider with privileges (which expired in 2007, about which more later) and an outsider who remains ignorant of the everyday experiences of the Palestinian people. At the flying checkpoint, Annemarie can pull back and say she will 'get help'. The actor and soundman, held at gunpoint, do not have this option. As Nadia Yacub reasons, this very personal perspective on the situation expresses Jacir's questions, and the lack of answers to them, about artistic integrity and responsibility: even as she drives away and shouts that she will come back with help, there is 'no authority she can bring to bear on the situation' (Yacub 2011: 243). Jacir's awareness of her own privileged position as a Palestinian with an American passport, with a camera and with a certain amount of intellectual and political weight, is expressed here through the fictionalisation of Annemarie as film director dealing with very difficult ethical questions of responsibility and powerlessness. As an American outsider she is rash, but as a Palestinian insider she also possesses a clarity about the long-term traumas and consequences of 1948: she needs to balance the fragmentation of a society and country with the knowledge of her own privilege. Jacir herself accepts these as partly her responsibilities towards her compatriots under occupation.

If *Like Twenty Impossibles* asked difficult questions and left them unanswered, *An Explanation (and then burn the ashes)* tackles them head-on. In this 6-minute experimental film, Jacir collates voice messages received by Columbia University faculty members that threaten, insult and blame them for simply being Arab, or presumed to be of Arab and Muslim heritage. One person says, 'I know from your name that you are Islamic', illustrating the ignorance inherent to such assumptions. We can link the recordings to the organisation and curation of the Dreams of a Nation project that took place at Columbia University in New York in 2003 (see a detailed engagement with that event in Chapter 6), as well as to the public role that some professors such as Edward Said and Hamid Dabashi have in their commentary on US foreign policy. Jacir has testified about the threats that she and her colleagues received in the run-up to and during that film festival. Likewise, Columbia University was where Edward Said worked for most of his academic life, and where he wrote his most influential books. From the fragments in the voice-overs in *An Explanation* we can infer that some of the phone calls are aimed at him, as he is called a professor who writes about 'America and the complaints of the Islamic world'. This can be read as an attack on Said's book *Covering Islam* (1981), in which his criticism of US foreign policy and its continued support of the state of Israel as well as his analysis of the media's representation of Islam are scathing. In 2003, the same year Dreams of a Nation took place, Said followed up this book with an analysis of the Iraq invasion, which he labelled 'ill-conceived' and based on 'out of date' and 'wildly speculative' information and knowledge. However, the strength of the film is of course that it does not identify the speakers nor the addressees, and as such it reveals the universality of the attitudes expressed by the speakers. Indeed, they speak in diverse accents and dialects. One thing they have in common is that they are all male voices, and that they all resort to swearwords, threats and insults. None of them are reasonable or even well-informed. In contrast with the intellectual location and profession of the faculty members of Columbia University, they not only sound dangerous and out of control but also ignorant and pitiful.

These recordings are accompanied by static shots of fences, grates, chains, closed windows and doors, walls and gates in and around Columbia University. By juxtaposing the recordings with these images, the filmmaker asks where the freedom of expression is when people voluntarily phone up an educational institution that ostensibly safeguards learning, intellectual stimulation and thinking beyond the norm, and threaten the educators' lives. Filming the mostly deserted university squares from unusual angles that obscure the full view of the buildings where the learning happens again illustrates Jacir's half-insider, half-outsider point of view, a multiple perspective, and a slanted interpretation of what it means to be affiliated with such a liberal centre of learning. This multiple, slanted perspective is perhaps most evident in the static images of windows through which nothing can be seen because of the angle and the light. We only see shapes and reflections of clouds or the buildings opposite. This palimpsestic looking in and out simultaneously obscures the attempt of the camera to see what is inside and blocks the 'insight' learning can provide. It results in a confusing image of what is not there: clouds, tree branches, buildings and squares instead of people, learning or dialogue. With its focus on obstacles, reflections and a tangle of tree branches and bushes, the film expresses the confusion and frustration that a lack of education can cause, especially when it comes to ill-informed opinions on the Arab world in general and Palestine in particular. The film, as such, draws out the impact of symbolic walls and a lack of access to understanding.

A Few Crumbs for the Birds (2005) was co-directed by Annemarie Jacir and Nacim Amaouche, a French filmmaker with roots in Algeria. Jacir also contributed to the script, and did the cinematography and editing of the film. The setting is the Jordanian–Iraqi border, in a small town called Ruwayshed, furthest east in Jordan, where the Al Karamah border crossing is located. The village mainly serves as a rest stop for truckers in the oil business, and is, for the rest, a no man's land: desert, highway and a single hotel amid a few empty houses, ruins and car wrecks. In the film, the sound is dominated by the thundering noise of the lorries travelling at high speed along the highway or parking up to spend a night at the hotel. It is a loud but quiet place, where no one says a lot in words, and where a knowing look means more than words could. The staff at the hotel consist of placeless people too: Amer is a Syrian waiter, Sami is a Jordanian oil smuggler, and there are also Ruba, Hala, Yasmine, Ula and Maha, five very young Palestinian sex workers. Apart from them and the occasional lorry driver who stops over for food or a night's entertainment, the place is deserted.

In mostly static shots, the camera observes the emptiness of the place, highlighting this with several shots of car wrecks and garbage moving in the desert wind. One or two travelling shots interject the static nature of the place when the filmmakers show – as they are shooting from a driving car – the emptiness of the village with its abandoned houses, closed-up shops, shutters drawn. Exactly like in *An Explanation*, we see nothing but vaguely defined buildings, represented through reflections in windows, closed doors and shutters, solitary walls. At the hotel, the staff are introduced in documentary style: Amer is asked in voice-over by Amaouche what the song playing on the radio means to him, and he emphasises its nostalgia. He says it is the most beautiful song in the world, it is very old and everybody knows it. It is about exile, he says: the singer mentions that he is in prison, asks if anyone can sense his presence, but nobody knows he exists. He sends a message to his friends by pigeon. The filmmaker asks what he would say to his loved ones if a pigeon could carry his message, but Amer rejects the idea as impossible. It is much easier and quicker by telephone. The camera then cuts to one of the Palestinian girls on the phone but does not register what she says. The girls explain to Jacir that they are Palestinians from Amman. She asks them if they know their country and they say of course, questioning who would not know their own country. Jacir asks for more details, but they leave to get ready for work. Sami is putting oil into endless numbers of jerrycans, when Amaouche explains to him that his T-shirt reads 'Long Live America'. Sami pulls a face and looks visibly uncomfortable as he admits that he did not know this and is now embarrassed by the slogan; he quickly goes inside and changes into a neutral shirt. The anti-American sentiment is established.

Indeed, Amer explains that when the journalists covering the Iraq war were still there, the hotel was busy, but since they left after the downfall of Saddam Hussein, it is now just a place for passers-by. The Palestinian girls are skittish, hardly speaking to the camera, observed from a distance standing on the terrace of the hotel, bored and gazing into the void of the desert, or doing their make-up in their room and entertaining guests in the café. The camera keeps its distance, except when they apply their make-up, when it goes into extreme close-ups and explains, without words, what the girls' occupation actually is. The distanced camera enacts respect for their privacy, taking care not to explicitly implicate or judge them in their profession yet showing concern for them, remaining subtle and always nuanced. This distance is emphasised in the darkness of the images, under-lit as they are, while the girls dance to music that is not heard on the soundtrack. The detachment between the music and the dancing and singing of the girls is a representation of the refusal to acknowledge a commodification of their bodies. Their facial expressions become the focus as the melancholy oud music connects their identities to the spirituality of Arab Palestinian culture. In addition, it is the daily gestures – Amer sweeping up in the café, listening to music on his headphones, Sami transferring oil from a lorry to several jerrycans, the girls putting on make-up, the darkness and vagueness of their movements and interactions with the anonymous lorry drivers – that establish the fragile and melancholic aesthetics of the images and sounds in the film. At this border crossing, the hotel is a place where time stands still for the long-distance drivers, and where the daily slog of repetition and vagueness bears down on Sami, Amer and the young women: the soundtrack highlights a Palestinian song bathed in nostalgia, recounting the realities of people in exile experiencing solitude and isolation away from their families and lovers.

The slow, repetitive nature of life at the hotel and the way it is represented on screen in mostly static shots is interrupted when the local authorities develop an interest in the filmmakers. Towards the end of the film, on-screen text clarifies that:

> The Jordanian intelligence service Mukhabarat forbade us to film the diesel vendors and came to see what we were filming at the hotel. At the police station they helped us to think up other subjects in other regions [they propose a visit to Bourka, which is beautiful, they have camels and

you can visit archaeological sites, or Petra etc.]. We decided to stay in Ruwayshed.

This is followed by black and white still photography of empty houses and an empty hotel without the girls on the roof terrace and with closed doors and windows. The still photograph in black and white illustrates that what little life was left in this outpost in the deserted waste land is now in the past. The place is deserted, dead. More text explains the violence that followed the film crew's decision to stay and the responsibility they feel towards the people they have been filming:

The next day, Sami and the other diesel vendors had to close up shop at the demand of the police. During the night, three men ransacked the hotel. Frightened, the girls vanished into thin air. The film shoot was over. In the space of one day, the diesel traffic was stopped, and the hotel was closed down by the authorities. We spent ten days at the Iraqi border with a few passing birds who survive on forgotten leftovers . . . And we filmed them without knowing that our camera would sweep away the last few crumbs.

The very last images of the film are a set of black and white photographs of the damage done to the hotel, and then a single frame of pigeons in flight. When the image transforms back to moving colour there is an image of a flock of pigeons in the sky, interrupted by the deafening sound of an aeroplane engine which disperses them, so that the frame presents an empty image of clear blue sky divided in two by a fighter jet above. The parallel between the pigeon from the song and the pigeons at the end of the film aligns with the idea of the people in this outpost being birds in exile, surviving on a few crumbs left behind by the infrastructure that used to be in place before the invasion of Iraq. The crew's awareness of the impact their presence has had on the reality of these exilic birds becomes, in the end, an observation of the war machine and the West's infiltration into the oil business in Iraq.

A World Apart Within 15 Minutes (co-created with Al-Muthaffer, 2006), also titled *Palestine, Summer 2006 (I)*, is only three minutes long, and repeats what it says in a seeming loop, but really brings home the message of how absurdly difficult it is to make one's way from Jerusalem to Ramallah, two places that are, in fact, only 15 minutes apart. The Wall makes it almost impossible to get there, and there is a resistance (also a wall) in Israeli people to even attempting to imagine the other city or a way to access it. In this very short film, Jacir is filmed in her car, driving south in Jerusalem city, stopping at regular intervals to ask Jewish men and women, in English, the way to Ramallah. In fact, Ramallah lies 10 km (6.3 miles) north of Jerusalem, a fact that several of the interlocutors point out to her, and yet she continues to drive south and ask more people. The camera is on the right-hand side of the car, in the passenger seat, and Jacir is driving with her window open, stopping and asking passers-by of all ages and genders whether they know the way to Ramallah. Jacir plays the foreigner card and uses the (false) naivety of the tourist to compel people to deal with this unexpected question in earnest. There is no narrative, just an at times sped up and slowed down repetition of the same question posed by Jacir, with varied but similar answers from everyone she asks: Ramallah is north, but no one knows or can explain how to get there, probably because they have never tried and because they know it is quasi-impossible due to the many roadblocks and checkpoints.

The feigned ignorance, the use of American English, and her insistence on driving south are three tactics that reveal the irony of the situation and legitimise her questions and behaviour, convincing the respondents to answer. The element of surprise when a car stops by the side of the road to ask for directions adds to the willingness of people to try to answer, even if they do not know or are flummoxed by the nature of the question. All of this leads to the irony of the situation becoming read as sarcasm, as we know well that Jacir knows the way to Ramallah. The car here acts, as we showed before, as a safe space from which she can innocently 'ambush' people on the road and in which she can drive off in case it is necessary; but it also functions as a reference to the trope of travel, starting and stopping, recognising the interrupted movement of car journeys within Palestine or between cities in the Occupied Territories. Dickinson points out that people are 'so culturally and politically estranged from their neighbouring town' that loss of knowledge, or loss of willingness to engage with the reality of their nearness 'manifests psycho-geographically on both sides, rendering it yet another site of conflict'; as such, Ramallah to the inhabitants of Jerusalem, 'might as well be another planet' (Dickinson 2016: 100). The blank looks on the faces of the people on the street when Jacir asks for directions speaks volumes about the huge gap between the protected illusion of a Jewish Jerusalem and the reality of protracted occupation and geopolitical conflict the city represents.

Sound of the Streets or its alternative title *Palestine, Summer 2006 (II)*, is another three-minute experimental short that plays with simple camera movements and combines these with recordings from street life in an unnamed Palestinian city. Overall, it provides an aural portrait of life on the street where people discuss everything, from complex political leanings and opinions, to finding work and gossiping about one another. The camera is aimed at a small patch of floor in a courtyard, focusing on ants hurrying back and forth across the surface. This is synched with a soundtrack of dialogues, making possible a reading of these ants as busy and hard workers like the Palestinians. It is as if the ants are discussing politics and gossiping with one another. On top of the voice-overs is also a familiar tune, 'Expensive Shit' by Fela Kuti, a jazzy afrobeat track that gives expression to the initial playfulness of the film and foregrounds the quirky effect of aligning the speed of the ants with the wit of the recorded voices. It starts with a woman's voice explaining how 'Kundara Rice' – referring to Condoleezza Rice – visited Mahmoud Abbas, the President of Palestine, in November 2006; she ostensibly came to solve the problems in the Middle East, but she loves problems too much to actually solve them. The woman plays with words here, as Kundara means shoe, and 'she wears him [Abbas] like a shoe', suggesting that Rice (and thus America) always takes the lead and patronises Abbas (or Palestine), not properly understanding what the priorities on the ground are and how the politicians themselves are not in touch with their people.

The snippets of conversation include a man asking for a job; he says he can do gardening or cleaning windows. There's also a conversation about football and in particular French-Algerian striker Zinedine Zidane, but the conversation soon returns to politics, and things start to become linked that at first sight might not seem connected: Martin Luther King would be disappointed with Black Americans fighting in the Middle East. Mubarak from Egypt and Abdallah from Jordan as well as the Saudis sold themselves to the Americans. Even Abbas is trying to get as much personal wealth as possible before he loses his seat, it is suggested. Lastly, the conversation turns back to the situation in Palestine, where it is said that the international community only cares about the Jewish people because of the history of the Holocaust, but in fact there is a Holocaust happening in Palestine as we speak. These are tough opinions, controversial in nature, but they are linked together for the Palestinians speaking. In the final moments of the film, Palestine is compared with South Africa, where the oppressed fought for their freedom and managed to gain 'their own independent country, without occupation' – which was apparently also what the Palestinian president, Abbas, wanted to gain from an alignment and conversation with Condoleezza Rice, who – together with President Bush at the time – said she was in favour of a two-state peaceful solution to the conflict. The actions of the Second Intifada do not go far enough for the person in the voice-over: he says he wants 'a real uprising against the Wall, not this fake one'. Someone then brings Hugo Chavez into the conversation, but the connection remains implicit, and in the final seconds of the film someone shouts 'They're all crooks!', thus giving voice to the utter frustration with the way in which the national and international communities and politicians have dealt – or not, as the case may be – with the political and humanitarian situation in Palestine.

It is at this moment that the camera follows a trio of ants to the left side of the frame where suddenly a thick block of wood is placed in front of them so that they can no longer follow their path or pass through. The music has stopped, there is no more voice-over, and all the ants are scurrying back and forth by the block of wood to find a way through, unsuccessfully. For the ants the block of wood is a cruel surprise and a threat, just as for the Palestinians the Wall is an insurmountable obstacle that disrupts the peace talks. Ousmane Sembène, the Senegalese filmmaker, once said that outsiders making films in Africa 'are looking at us like insects', pointing out the distance between filmmaker and object of interest. It is also a reference to Spivak's theory of the representation of the subaltern, who does not have a voice. In contrast, this experimental short centralises the voices of Palestinians, and clarifies that they can speak: they have always had voices and opinions, but outsiders do not listen or cannot hear them, drowned out as they are by the distance from the outsiders filming them. An interesting parallel here can be drawn with Azza el-Hassan's film *News Time* (2001), in which she deals with this exact issue: that Palestinians are so used to Western cameras observing and disrupting their lives and their political actions that they have become used to performing a specific role preferred by these outsiders. This has, according to her, resulted in a very specific discourse on Palestine, a 'single story' that is far removed from the traumatic reality which, as she and Jacir and other Palestinian filmmakers have shown, can only be represented fairly and in its full complexity by specific types of filmmakers with knowledge and experience.

In our view, the ants in Jacir's film refer to those ideas and are a vehicle through which to amplify the voices of the Palestinians speaking: their sarcasm, bitterness and deep understanding of the multiple layers of the national and international political discourse illustrates that they know much better than so-called political observers do. The voice-overs and ants also poke fun at the way in which Palestinians are usually observed from a great distance by politicians who claim to but do not actually do anything useful for them, and Western journalists or observers who do not understand the full complexity of the problem and their implication in it. In combining the sound recordings with the image of the ants and giving the film the title *Sound of the Street*, Jacir ironises and decolonises historical, Western and colonial attitudes to the Palestinian people, showing that the Palestinians have voices and opinions, and that they can speak, and that both the West's refusal to listen to these voices and the construction of the Wall are the problem, not the Palestinian people.

From looking at these five short films, it becomes clear that Jacir's experimental work develops a deep concern with the post-Oslo Accords era. From an exploration of roadblocks and checkpoints on a road trip to Jerusalem, where she asks unanswered questions about art, power and responsibility, to the exploration of a centre of learning and freedom of expression subjected to a campaign of threats; concerns with those temporarily making a living on the Jordan–Iraqi border after the ill-advised invasion of Iraq; the absurd impossibility of travelling six miles and the ignorance of Jerusalemites; and, finally the cruel placing of a block so that ants cannot follow their instincts – these films reveal an increasing preoccupation with borders, obstacles and the absolute impossibility of movement. Where scholars such as Dickinson assert that Palestinian cinema of the Second Intifada focuses on road(block) movies, movement and interruptions, we would say that in this oeuvre, the emphasis is rather on an absolute rejection of the genre of the road movie; instead a representation emerges of the absoluteness of borders as endings, insurmountable obstacles and indeed full stops. Jacir became a part of the common Palestinian experience of exile in November 2007, when she was prevented from entering the country after the release of her feature film *Salt of this Sea*. These stories therefore illustrate the reality of exiled Palestinians while they also all implicate the artist herself in her personal experiences of privilege and devastation.

REFERENCES

Dabashi, Hamid (ed.) (2006), *Dreams of a Nation: On Palestinian Cinema*, London: Verso.
Dickinson, Kay (2016), *Arab Cinema Travels: Transnational Syria, Palestine, Dubai and Beyond*, London: BFI.
Dickinson, Kay (2022), 'The Second Intifada – Twenty Years On', *Unpacking the ArteArchive, ArteEast*, 9 June, https://artearchive.eventive.org/schedule/627d5fe db4675a00308806c4 (accessed 19 April 2023).
Marks, Laura U. (2015), *Hanan al-Cinema: Affections for the Moving Image*, Cambridge, MA: MIT Press.
Ramamurthy, A., and P. Kelemen (2020), *Struggling to be Seen: The Travails of Palestinian Cinema*, Wakefield, Québec: Daraja Press.
Rastegar, Kamran (2002), Conference Report, 'Dreams of a Nation: A Palestinian Film Festival', *Edebiyât* 13.2: 273–6.
Said, Edward (2003), 'Resources of Hope', *Al Ahram*, 27 March, https://web.archive.org/web/20150221221020/http://weekly.ahram.org.eg/2003/631/focus.htm (accessed 19 April 2023).
Yacub, Nadia (2011), 'Dismantling the Discourses of War: Palestinian Women Filmmakers Address Violence', in *Gender and Violence in the Middle East*, ed. M. Ennaji and F. Sadiqi, Abingdon: Routledge, pp. 231–46.
Younis, Usayd, and Jumanah Younis (2014), 'Interview with Annemarie Jacir: "I'm not interested in showing the West that Palestinians are humans, too"', *Ceasefire Magazine*, 29 August, https://ceasefiremagazine.co.uk/film-annemarie-jacir-im-interested-showing-west-palestinians-humans-too/ (accessed 19 April 2023).

NOTES

1. *Like Twenty Impossibles* is available to buy on DVD from mec film (https://mecfilm.com/), and can also be viewed on Netflix.

2. *An Explanation (and then burn the ashes)* can be viewed on YouTube: https://www.youtube.com/watch?v=6UHg15TeL9s (accessed July 2022).
3. *A Few Crumbs for the Birds* can be found on Philistine Films' Vimeo channel, accessible through their website: https://www.philistinefilms.com/shop (accessed 19 April 2023).
4. *A World Apart in 15 Minutes* can be found on Philistine Films' Vimeo channel, accessible through their website: https://www.philistinefilms.com/shop (accessed 19 April 2023).
5. *Sound of the Street* can be found on Philistine Films' Vimeo channel, accessible through their website: https://www.philistinefilms.com/shop (accessed 19 April 2023).

CHAPTER 2

Heterotopias and Thirdspaces: Construction of Space in Jacir's Films

Iqra Shagufta Cheema

Space is central to the Palestinian experience and thereby remains central to Palestinian cinema.[1] It serves as an archive and a marker of memories and histories.[2] But it also remains the site of personal, communal and political crises as well as the potential site of resolution of these crises – and that is the conundrum that Jacir's films dwell upon. The strength of Jacir's films resides in the fact that she assigns primacy to everyday spaces and banal life experiences, simultaneously exploring the way historical locations impact the characters' psyche and their quotidian experiences.

In this chapter, we deliberate on Jacir's feature films *Salt of this Sea* (2008), *When I Saw You* (2012) and *Wajib* (2017) to examine both the geographical and cinematic role and representation of place and space in her cinema. *Salt of this Sea* tells the story of a woman who inhabits multiple conflicting spaces and whose identity is shaped by these non-monolithic geographies and their formative impact on her subjectivity. *When I Saw You* represents politicised geographical spaces where the characters are suspended between variegated formations and conceptions of home while simultaneously attempting to (re) locate themselves in the spaces available to them. *Wajib* explores Nazareth, an Arab city in northern Israel with communities of diverse faiths, as Shadi and Abu Shadi drive around its alleys and crossroads to deliver wedding invitations, thus literally exploring the Palestinian spatial experience in contentious geographies while tracing and relocating the personal, familial, political and national ties and identity markers in Nazareth.

Reading these everyday spaces in Jacir's oeuvre through a spatio-analytical lens establishes that these seemingly innocuous spaces are multifaceted and multivalenced. Concepts such as the social production of space (Henri Lefebvre), thirdspace (Edward Soja) and heterotopia (Michel Foucault) help analyse these spatial complexities and the relationship of spatiality, sociality and subjectivity in Jacir's films. Lefebvre (1991) views everyday spaces as complex social constructions that interact with social values and the production of meaning. Foucault (1986) defines heterotopias as discursive, institutional spaces that are othered, but that are transformative and exist within other worlds. Influenced by Lefebvre and Foucault, Soja (1996) argues that thirdspace is always a fluid lived space: it contests and (re)negotiates geographical boundaries and cultural identities. Since our focus is transnational and multicultural, we mainly deploy thirdspace in its postmodern political geographical context to understand the cinematic representation of the multiple constructions and representation of spaces and heterotopias in Jacir's feature films.

Instead of grand events or defining historical plots, Jacir's primary focus is everyday life which, inadvertently, is influenced by political and historical events of the past and the present. Conceptually, Foucault, Lefebvre and Soja all contest the focus on time and history, instead of lived spaces, when studying human beings. Foucault emphasises that the lived space is 'not an innovation', but it 'itself has a history'. Therefore, it is 'not possible to disregard the fatal intersection of time with space' (Foucault 1986: 22). Contending that the 'anxiety of our era has to do fundamentally with space more than with time', he asserts that time has been desanctified, but the 'practical desanctification of space' has not occurred (1986: 23). He exemplifies the sanctified 'oppositions' that are taken as a simple given: 'private space and public space', 'family space and social space', 'cultural space and useful space', and 'the space of leisure and that of work' (1986: 23). Foucault wrote his essay on heterotopia, 'Of Other Spaces' (1986), after the Nakba, and presumably the Palestinian situation informed this essay. These same anxieties and uncertainties about functions of spaces, inhabiting spaces, losing and asserting one's right to space are at the heart of Jacir's films.

Jacir's films break down these sanctified oppositions exemplified in Foucault's essay. Perception of time and space is different in all three of her feature films. Both time and space are animated, organic and fast in *Salt of this Sea*, as the characters move through various social, political, religious and cultural spaces, both geographically and ideologically. Though the day-to-day time is filled with activity and passes quickly, the characters' lives or their lived spaces remain stagnant and transfixed. In the end, the characters end up in the same situation where they started: Soraya is deported to the US to return to her life in Brooklyn; Emad's chances of a Canadian student visa or a positive change in his life increasingly diminish as a Palestinian man under restrictions and surveillance. In *When I Saw You*, time, space and human lives remain frozen. The characters slowly move through spaces and struggle to break free of the spatial and temporal restraints as they construct and reconstruct their residential and affective spaces. Tarek, like Soraya, is fixated on the past, and that fixation determines his social, spatial and affective life.

Unlike these two films, *Wajib* offers a messy resolution to the spatial questions. Shadi seems to have reached a new comprehension of space and his place within it which causes friction with his father. Space becomes a character, a mediator for Shadi and Abu Shadi as they employ the closed space of the car, the narrow spaces of the residential homes, and the open spaces of Nazareth to smooth out their bumpy relationship. *When I Saw You* and *Salt of this Sea* open with a focus on space: *Salt of this Sea* shows panoramic shots of buildings being bulldozed while *When I Saw You* opens with a low-angle shot of Tarek's feet on a road. Both films portray characters struggling to return to a home or reconstruct the space of the home in the image of the places their ancestors inhabited. As opposed to these films, *Wajib* opens with Abu Shadi sitting in a car waiting for his son, who is not too keen on living in his ancestral home in Nazareth.

SPACE AS A CONCEPT

Before elaborating further on space in Jacir's cinema, let us first discuss the concepts of thirdspace and heterotopia. Building on Lefebvre's work, Soja coined the terms firstspace, secondspace and thirdspace. Firstspace, in Lefebvre's terms, is the 'perceived space' or spatial practice perceived, which represents 'the practical basis of the perception of the outside world' (1991). Soja comments that firstspace focuses on the 'real' material world and has two aspects: a description of the surface appearance, and a spatial explanation in sociopolitical and other processes (1996: 6). Secondspace, which Lefebvre terms conceived space, is mental. It is 'the representation of power and ideology, of control and surveillance' (Soja 1996: 67). Secondspace is also the 'primary space of utopian thought and vision, it's the semiotician or decoder, and the purely creative imagination of artists and poets' (Soja 1996: 67). Thirdspace is an 'efficient invitation to enter a space of extraordinary openness, a place of critical exchange'. In thirdspace, 'geographical imagination can be expanded to encompass a multiplicity of perspectives that have heretofore been considered by epistemological referees to be incompatible, and uncombinable'. In this space, 'issues of race, class, and gender can be addressed simultaneously without privileging one over the other' (Soja 1996: 5). Thirdspace is 'a creative recombination, extension', which is 'built on a firstspace perspective' and 'a secondspace perspective' and 'interprets the reality through "imagined" representations of spatiality' (Soja 1996: 6).

Thirdspace comes into being because of the people that come together to inhabit a space and interact in it, without any restrictions. Thirdspace, then, is the space where time and history mingle with humans' social lives in a spatially accommodating environment. It offers a combination of 'spatiality-historicality-sociality' and their 'inseparability and interdependence', which is a 'simultaneous and interwoven complexity of the social, the historical, and the spatial' (Soja 1996: 3). Soja enumerates the following 'defining qualities' of thirdspace: 'a knowable and unknowable, real and imagined lifeworld of experiences, emotions, events, and political choices' that is 'shaped by generative and problematic interplay between centres and peripheries, the abstract and concrete, the impassioned spaces of conceptual and the lived, marked out materially and metaphorically in spatial praxis' (Soja 1996: 31). Thirdspace historicises everyday spaces and infuses them with radical subversive possibilities to blur the boundaries between centre and periphery, or between the powerful and the disenfranchised. Prior to Soja, Foucault also critiqued the treatment of history and space wherein history takes precedence and space is neglected. He considers the problem of space not only in demographic terms but also in relations of 'propinquity'. He terms lived sites 'heterogeneous space[s]', which are defined by 'the relations of proximity between points or elements' (Foucault 1986: 23). These lived sites 'designate, mirror, or reflect' the relations of proximity, but they can also 'suspect, neutralize, or invert' these relations (1986: 23).

In his theorisation, Foucault describes two types of sites: utopias and heterotopias. Utopias are sites with no real location, whereas heterotopias are the 'counter-sites' or 'effectively enacted utopias' in which all the other real sites are 'represented, contested, and inverted' (1986: 24). He offers a 'systematic description' or 'heterotopology' to note that heterotopia is 'a sort of simultaneously mythic and real contestation of the space in which we live' (1986: 24). This heterotopology has some principles: heterotopias exist in every culture, albeit with widely varied forms and functions; they juxtapose multiple incompatible places within one single space; they open to 'heterochronies' that 'function' after people experience an 'absolute break with traditional time'; they 'presuppose' specific rites of 'opening and closing that both isolate them and make them penetrable'; they have a 'function in relation to all the space that remains'; societies, as their histories change, reassign new functions to old heterotopias (Foucault 1986: 24–6). Functions of heterotopias shift as does the social fabric that informs the initiation and operation of these heterotopias. Both heterotopias and thirdspace serve as liminal spaces that exist outside of the normative conceptions of temporality/historicality, spatiality and sociality.

Thirdspace also emerges as an important concept in the work of Homi K. Bhabha, who describes the 'structure of meaning and reference' as ambivalent (1994: 37). Bhabha's thirdspace represents both the 'general conditions of language and the specific implication of the utterance in a performative and institutional strategy' (1994: 36). While Soja writes it as thirdspace, Bhabha writes it as third space. Despite the spelling and conceptual differences, thirdspace ultimately serves as the liminal, interstitial, subversive space of multiplicity, heterogeneity and hybridity. In Jacir's films, thirdspace or heterotopia serve as disjunctive frames, which Arjun Appadurai conceptualises as 'deeply perspectival constructs inflected very much by historical, linguistic and political situatedness of different sort of actors: nation-states, multinationals, diasporic communities', 'subnational groupings and movements', and 'intimate face-to-face groups', which ultimately construct 'imagined worlds' that are constructed by the 'historically situated imaginations' of people (1990: 296–7). Using thirdspace and heterotopia as primary frameworks, we read the fedayeen base in *When I Saw You* and the car in *Wajib* as the heterotopic thirdspace of simultaneous spatiality-historicality-sociality. We simultaneously discuss the affective and political ramifications of the spatial boundaries and urban spatial structures in Jacir's films.

HETEROTOPIC SPACE: FEDAYEEN BASE AND REFUGEE CAMP

The fedayeen base in *When I Saw You* is complex to read from a firstspace perspective because of its elusive existence or non-traceability.[3] From a secondspace perspective, it remains a space where multiple subjects gather to form a community for a shared cause, a shared fight for liberation and their right to a land. But from a thirdspace perspective, the fedayeen base is a space of 'extraordinary simultaneities' (Soja 1996: 57). Because of the constant fear of attack, the fedayeen base becomes a space that accommodates multiple incompatible political and affective sensibilities. It is a space where fedayeen build a community in which to live on their own terms, share a collective past, figure their future, but also inhabit their present more fully and intentionally.

Figure 2.1 *When I Saw You*: Ghayda and Tarek in the refugee camp after a tense moment when Ghayda is unhappy about Tarek's performance in school and Tarek is upset about his father's absence. Credit: Philistine Films

When Ghayda and Tarek live in the refugee camp, their life is a cycle of constant waiting for Tarek's father. History and time gain precedence in the refugee camp, delimiting the possibilities of living a full life in the present. Refugees wait not only for their families but also for their everyday supplies, all the while clinging on to the hope of a more agential life. They long for residential, emotional and culinary comforts. In contrast, the fedayeen base is intentionally defined and constructed by people who project a kind of vitality, a life that is absent from other spaces portrayed in the film. The fedayeen base is a space of hope where inhabitants choose to protect their independence *as* agential subjects, even when they are unable to sustain themselves as national subjects inhabiting a national space. The fedayeen base is a thirdspace because it is materially untraceable, it disappears when necessary, and its location is neither perceived nor represented.

This untraceability and invisibility of the base is also the key to the fedayeen protecting their agency and operations from the Israeli military as well as imperial interventions. In one scene in the film, the fedayeen learn of an attack. They instantly pack their tents and disappear, erasing all material marks of any human existence in that space. They stand hidden inside a cave with its entrance blocked with tree branches and eventually come out when the sound of aeroplanes disappears. In a panoramic shot of the base's previous location, a tent is raised and the base returns to life. Fedayeen reconstruct their communal space as a thirdspace of resistance and resilience. Soja comments that Lefebvre:

> opened a new domain, a space of collective resistance, a thirdspace of political choice that is also a meeting place for all peripheralized and marginalized 'subjects' where they may be located. In this politically charged space, a radically new and different form of citizenship can be defined and realized. (1996: 35)

While fedayeen citizenship is unacknowledged because of its invisibility and its political positionality, it locates the fedayeen in a self-regulating community that serves the same purposes as a state.

A state is a 'conceptual abstraction' (Patrick Dunleavy cited in Cudworth, Hall and McGovern 2007: 2). The modern conception that states 'possess legal and administrative unity within well-defined borders' is not the 'inevitable consequence of universally present principles' (Cudworth, Hall and McGovern 2007: 20). Overall, the functions that states perform arguably include but are not limited to forging alliances, creating cohesion among communities, resolving conflicts among members of society, streamlining and institutionalising labour processes and productivity, maintaining and safeguarding order, deciding punishments for deviant members or for disorderly activities, and monitoring any subversions or deviations (Cudworth, Hall and McGovern 2007). But these functions do not necessarily require state intervention or territorial limitations.

Since the fedayeen base performs the functions and the regulatory roles of a state, it serves as a non-state or a self-regulating state for fedayeen and other disenfranchised community members such as Ghayda and Tarek, without the oppressive tendencies of a formal political state. But since the fedayeen base exists outside of the recognised and accepted spatio-political territories, it turns into a heterotopia of crisis and deviation that is functionally state-like and affectively home-like – but simultaneously more equitable than both.

The fedayeen base, as a heterotopia of crisis and deviation, accommodates those who are evicted from their homes and homeland and who are also misfits in temporary housing alternatives such as the refugee camp in Jordan. But to be accepted into the heterotopic community of fedayeen, they must submit to the rites of entrance and closing, which 'isolates' the fedayeen base but also renders it 'penetrable' (Foucault 1986: 26). Fedayeen act as inhabitants and organisers of this space, but they are deviants and aggressors in the popular imagination. Beverley Milton-Edwards notes that the fedayeen were 'modern revolutionaries fighting for national liberation, not religious liberation' (1999: 94). Fedayeen movements 'spawned heroic idealised images of male and female commandos attacking the enemy' (Milton-Edwards 1999: 94).[4] While the term fedayeen was used for Palestinian guerrillas in the mid-twentieth century, it later became a 'link of support between Palestinian communities who were forced to flee their country during the Arab–Israel War (1948–1949)' (Seddon 2013: 165). *When I Saw You*, rather romantically, maintains the same idea and posits that fedayeen primarily live their daily lives, while the fight for liberation and right to the land remains in its background.

This fear of irreversible loss of the actual national space or site of home recurs in *When I Saw You*. This fear informs and constructs the fedayeen base as a heterotopia of crisis. It is a result of a collective traumatic experience in which the inhabitants of the base have lost their homes and families. One female fedayee's family is unaware of her presence in the base. They are all fighters, but strategically they cannot retaliate to every attack, which frustrates some fedayeen. Majed (Firas W. Taybeh) resents the restless passivity in the face of attacks on refugee camps. Even Abu Akram (Ali Elayan), their commander, is upset when he sees fedayeen singing, dancing, lounging or enjoying themselves. Some fedayeen feel resentful towards Abu Akram because he does not permit them to attack the enemy. Despite minimal material and political support and the impossibility of 'defeat[ing] an army as sophisticated as the Israeli Defence Forces (IDF)' (Milton-Edwards 1999: 95), they spend most of their time training for the fight to reclaim their home and homeland. As a peripheral space, the base accommodates the lonely, the abandoned, dreamers, dilettantes, deviants and revolutionaries. Because of the presence of the deviants and revolutionaries, the fedayeen base turns from a heterotopia of crisis into a heterotopia of deviation.

In multiple ways, the absences of home, past, family, traditional society, social expectations and national territory also makes the fedayeen base into 'the space of radical openness, the space of social struggle' (Soja 1996: 68). While the fedayeen's active attacks on the enemy signify their armed resistance to the settler forces, their quotidian lives and everyday artistic and communal activities also constitute resistance. Settler forces, in evicting them from their homes, also destroy the possibility of a stable life, family and community. They face the threat of complete erasure because of their refusal to secede or accept defeat. In the face of such danger, they enjoy the simple artistic, communal and culinary pleasures of human life in the heterotopic thirdspace of the fedayeen base, thereby sustaining their agential selves, communal belonging, and their intent to return to their homeland. In the fedayeen base, fedayeen enjoy what is present in their lives: friends, community, dreams, hope and a shared goal.

But in the refugee camp, refugees live in the shadow of what is absent from their lives: their homes, husbands, sons, friends. Ghayda is the lonely wife of an absent husband and the frustrated mother of an angry son. She is hit on by Tarek's schoolteacher, Mr Nasser (Anas Algaralleh), who believes that Tarek is a difficult child because of his father's absence. 'A house without a man can be difficult', he avers. He proposes to become that man in their life. However, in the heterotopic fedayeen base, in the thirdspace of possibility, Ghayda and Tarek find their community. Tarek finds father figures, role models and companions in the base. Fedayeen pretend to shave Tarek's non-existent beard, give him a cigarette to pretend-smoke, and jokingly comment that it is 'time to become a man'. After one of Layth and Majed's spats about wanting to attack the enemy, Tarek goes so far as to ask 'When will I have a gun? Everyone has one except me.' Despite feeling happier in the base, Ghayda doesn't want Tarek to become a fedayee. One morning when Tarek combs Ghayda's hair (something he never did in the refugee camp), she suddenly scolds him for even thinking of becoming a fedayee. More than being fighters, fedayeen and the fedayeen base present and preserve models of positive masculinity for the young Tarek.

Instead of being portrayed as 'traditional, conservative or rural figures', fedayeen were popularly portrayed 'in a vanguard role' as 'educated, urban, worldly and sophisticated' (Milton-Edwards 1999: 95). Despite being trained fighters, their community appears harmless. They spend their time washing their clothes, listening to music, and talking Marxism and politics. The fedayeen base reflects a 'growing awareness of the simultaneity and interwoven complexity of the social, the historical, and the spatial and their inseparability and interdependence' (Soja 1996: 3). Their songs and conversations also reflect this as they sing of love, home, mountains and gardens. They paint, sing, dance, talk, share and express their emotions. In one scene, a white photographer does a photoshoot of fedayeen. With their keffiyeh, their curly hair and their guns, they squint their eyes and gaze at the idyllic landscape in the distance, striking different poses for the photos. They have lean bodies and chiselled faces, which are usually portrayed as feminine in Western media. This shot is meta-cinematic in this commentary, as we show via a comparison of Azza el-Hassan's film *News Time* (2001) with Jacir's *Sound of the Streets* in Chapter 5. The fedayeen training here is disrupted and invaded by the Western photographer who, instead of asking their seasoned commander Abu Akram about their fight or goals or recording their voices, prefer to shoot photos of young, handsome, long-haired quiet fedayeen posing with their guns. This shot highlights this paradoxical portrayal through their dialogue with Abu Akram. The young fedayeen believe that their photos show their enemies that they are strong fighters, but their feminine bodies make them appear non-threatening despite their guns. Abu Akram comprehends the futility of these representational exercises and that, unconsciously, young fedayeen are performing a specific role preferred by the Western outsiders. This photoshoot highlights their desire to be visible to the world but also shows that they do not control the way they are represented. Others control their visibility and the manner of their presentation. Their portrayal as romantic young men extends also into their personal relationships. Even the romantic scene between Layth and Ghayda in the base is consensual and results from them spending time together, instead of Layth trying to exploit her loneliness in her husband's absence, like Mr Nasser in the refugee camp did.

The torture of separation from a lover or a life-partner is not exclusive to Ghayda. Fedayeen are either away from their beloveds or have sacrificed their love lives for the greater cause – but longing for romantic companionship and love underwrites their characters. However, this loneliness engenders different communal responses for different genders. While Ghayda's husband's absence results in insecurity, instability and unwanted sexual approaches by other men, a male fedayee's separation from his wife emasculates him. His fellow fedayeen poke fun at him, implying that his wife sleeps with other men in his absence. In one scene, two fedayeen exchange the following dialogue during a seemingly jovial argument:

> First fedayee: Your wife is glad you're gone. I saw her last night, her red lipstick smeared.
> Second fedayee: At least I have a woman who loves me. And my heart is full, unlike you, easy as the streetwalkers, and yours, empty.
> First fedayee: Heard you had to pay a prostitute to look at your face.

The target of this retort, interestingly, remains unnamed and sometimes absent from the screen when he is insulted, which universalises this experience in the fedayeen base. During these spats, they continue their daily activities as if this is a recurrent, normal conversation. This conversation highlights that fedayeen miss their lovers and their touch, but at its centre remains men's inability to build a strong love rather than women's disloyalty to their lovers. It comments on fedayeen's choice between love or agential life, but it suspends judgement on women finding companionship with other people in their lovers' absence, and provides nuance in the idealistic portrayal of fedayeen, who function in a patriarchal Palestinian culture.

The fedayeen base is a place of equitable gender relations and an inclusive and democratic model of a community. Though the film does not indulge in the question of gender relations among fedayeen beyond women's participation in the armed struggle for liberation, these questions underwrite the plot and inform the portrayal of the refugee camp versus the fedayeen base. Most of Ghayda's shots in the refugee camp are either inside her tent, outside looking for her husband or her son, or interacting with people only when necessary. In the fedayeen base, in contrast, she socialises, smokes, sings with fedayeen, and does not perform any traditional domestic chores. The fedayee uniform also blurs the gender binary by making female fedayeen such as Soraya look androgynous. Fedayeen have a more communal and collective conception of life. When Tarek meets the young girl outside the toilet in the refugee camp, he tells her how he misses his home, his bed, his toilet. But she does not share the same sentiments about her own home in Palestine. She, on the contrary, tells Tarek that her brother and her cousins are fedayeen and she also intends to become a fedayee once she grows up. When Tarek asks, 'Don't you want to get married?', she responds that she'll marry a fedayee. She also tells Tarek that her fedayee cousin went to Palestine and saw his house. This conversation and Tarek's stay in the fedayeen base inspires a shift in his perception of home and homeland.

It is due to this sociality and spatiality that Tarek and Ghayda eventually join the fedayeen. The film highlights their assimilation with the fedayeen via mirroring: Tarek mirrors the fedayeen's training and their lives; he mirrors Abu Akram as they drink from similar cups, sitting in the same posture, raising their cups, sipping from the cups at the same time, and watching other fedayeen train. In the refugee camp, Tarek longed for his home. But in the fedayeen base, he wants to go to the homeland. Or as they postulate in the film: 'We're fedayeen. We're preparing ourselves to return', wherein the Palestinian Right of Return always implies a return to the homeland.

In the pursuit of reclamation of the space of the homeland, fedayeen bases serve as self-fashioned heterotopias of crisis and deviance. This renders it possible for fedayeen to live non-normative agential lives despite their limited means, and simultaneously to fight for their home. This agential life is only possible for the refugees and other exiles in a thirdspace of possibility where the incompatible or paradoxical elements can cohabit. This heterotopic thirdspace is the 'discursive space organized around different discursive terms' that question the 'sheer contingency of the established order of gender, spatial, political, and social relations' (Dikeç 2009: 7). Hence, the idea of 'spatial justice' or reclamation of space is 'mobilized as a critique of systematic exclusion, domination and oppression, which are reproduced, among other things, by the police order that has been consolidated' (Dikeç 2009: 7). The fedayeen base, then, as heterotopic thirdspace, offers alternative forms of citizenship to those who are excluded from the regular models of citizenship.

URBAN SPATIAL STRUCTURES AS HETEROTOPIC THIRDSPACES

In *When I Saw You*, these heterotopic thirdspaces emerge only after the loss of the homeland and out of the desire to emulate the past life to create a community, or a family inside or outside the national borders. But the construction of a heterotopic thirdspace does not always follow the same model in Jacir's films. Sometimes, these heterotopias develop because of temporal transition and resultant friction between family members, whereupon they renegotiate their lives and their relationships. For example, in *Wajib*, the car seemingly serves as a means to travel and deliver wedding invitations. But in actuality it simultaneously serves as a heterotopia of conflict and a thirdspace of possibility, negotiation and openness where Shadi and Abu Shadi relocate and re-establish the foundations of their tense relationship. The narrow confines of the Volvo force Shadi and Abu Shadi into the necessary conversations. During their arguments in the car, the characters and the audience gradually witness the multiple layers of their relationship, both with each other and with other community members. The houses they visit function as reservoirs of the small, albeit significant differences between the son and the father. In each of the houses, they unearth a new friction or contradiction in their desires and goals, which are then negotiated or resolved in the car. The car then becomes a 'new discursive space' that is 'organized around different discursive terms' (Dikeç 2009: 7) in their personal, familial and social relationships.

Just like Foucault's boat, the car in this case serves as a heterotopic space. Like the boat, the car also serves as a 'great reserve of imagination' and memory. It is a moving 'piece of space, a place without a place, that exists by itself, that is closed in on itself, and is also given over' to the modern infrastructure of roads and urban landscape (Foucault 1986: 26). *Wajib* depicts the most striking, casual, reflective and uncontentious exploration of Nazareth. In the drive around Nazareth, the car follows various principles of heterotopology enumerated by Foucault. Space, according to Foucault, is 'more than a given and static container of politics' (1986: 23) and is instead 'causal, transformative, and is itself always in the making' (Dikeç 2009: 1). Space is not an empty signifier; rather it is consistently imbued with meaning and signification through emotions and functions – that is what renders the car in *Wajib* a heterotopic thirdspace.

Figure 2.2 *Wajib*: Shadi and Abu Shadi driving by the Star of David in Nazareth. Credit: Philistine Films

The car as a secondspace serves only as a means to transfer people from one place to another. However, Shadi and Abu Shadi's dialogical exchange transforms the car into a thirdspace 'where geographical imagination can be expanded' in order to 'encompass a multiplicity of perspectives' (Soja 1996: 5). In this thirdspace, Shadi and Abu Shadi exchange their differing opinions, which range from the banal to significant familial decisions to state persecution. Abu Shadi disapproves of Shadi's fashion choices, his profession, his partner, his partner's family, his connection with his mother and his decision to live in Italy. Shadi is resentful of Abu Shadi for his decision to send him away to Italy at a young age, his taste in music, his architectural choices, his grudge against his ex-wife who is Shadi's mother, his desire for Shadi to work in a more prestigious profession such as medicine, and his attempts at pleasing the state's spies. Abu Shadi perceives Shadi to be selfish, snobbish and stubborn, whereas Shadi believes Abu Shadi to be timid, submissive and complacent. While Shadi as 'an outsider puts emphasis on the recreational values including aesthetic values' in a city, Abu Shadi as 'the local' highlights its 'everyday functional values' (Haapala 2005: 44). Shadi views the city as a tourist, a guest, a visitor, whereas Abu Shadi views it as a resident, a host, an owner. Abu Shadi values the city as a reservoir of his lived life, memories and community, and for a sense of familiarity, whereas Shadi views the city from the affectively detached perspective of an artist or museumgoer.

Many of Shadi's negative emotions and his unwillingness to live in Nazareth manifest in his affective and verbal responses to the city's architecture and the exterior decor of homes. While he appreciates the history of the city, he is unable to embrace it in its ancient form. He wants to contemporise history and its spatial markers. As an architect, he views everyday objects as art, as aesthetic phenomena. He wants these objects to comply with his Europeanised aesthetic judgement, because that symbolises progress, novelty and unorthodoxy for him. Residents such as Abu Shadi view Nazareth as a space of familiarity, security and stability, whereas Shadi wants novelty, defamiliarity and newness. While newness and 'strangeness is temporally prior to familiarity', it is not a 'continual state' (Haapala 2005: 44). People start noticing the familiar things anew only when their 'familiarity has been broken by something new' (Haapala 2005: 45). Shadi's familiarity has been broken by his experience of living in Italy. However, Abu Shadi, who has spent his entire life in Nazareth, is only able to experience this defamiliarity second hand – via Shadi's defamiliarised perspective. But encountering the same architecture daily remains an assurance of stability in his life.

For Abu Shadi, the architectural constructs such as houses and buildings 'do not denote – that is, do not describe, recount, depict, or portray'. Rather, they 'mean, if at all, in other ways' (Goodman 1985: 642) – they usually have a 'practical function' (Goodman 1985: 643). A building's 'daily dedication to a practical purpose often tends to obscure its symbolic function, and usually most buildings might not have a symbolic function at all' (Goodman 1985: 643). Abu Shadi is aware of the practical functions of a house but is not attentive to its artistic or symbolic functions. When Shadi insists that they do not use ugly green tarp in their house for Amal's wedding, Abu Shadi tells him that tarp is practical. He recognises the 'nonaesthetic practical rightness' of art (Leddy 2005: 9) in the residential buildings.

Residential spaces in *Wajib* exemplify the personal, communal and urban histories of Nazareth. The architecture or organisation of a space symbolises historical, cultural, religious and environmental factors that constitute its style. For Abu Shadi, these houses mean or symbolise via their accessibility, stability and comfort for their residents. Most of the houses that Abu Shadi and Shadi visit appear claustrophobic and dimly lit, with heavy curtains separating the outside urban space from the residential spaces of old people. By contrast, Abu Rami's house is well-lit with open windows and curtains, because 'Rami had triplets', who are sitting on the table, on the floor and on their mother's lap. Houses with happier families and younger family members are spacious, bright and welcoming.

A house or home 'is by definition of utmost familiarity' to a human being (Haapala 2005: 46) and Abu Shadi wants to retrieve the familiar home of his past. He desires familiarity, especially since many of the permanent members of his family are not part of his everyday lived life any more: both Shadi and Shadi's mother have migrated out of the country and have chosen to form relationships with people whom Abu Shadi dislikes for personal or political reasons. Marriage, generally considered a lifetime commitment, proved temporary for Abu Shadi. His son, the offspring who is traditionally tasked with taking care of older parents, lives far away in Italy. These displeasing changes make Abu Shadi feel emasculated and weak, even though he has a good reputation as a teacher and as a community member.

In the thirdspace of the car, Shadi and Abu Shadi comprehend the rationale behind each other's life choices. They recognise and resolve their lingering differences that had 'heretofore been considered by epistemological referees to be incompatible, and uncombinable' (Soja 1996: 5). Contrary to Abu Shadi's perception of Shadi as a Europeanised young man, Shadi is person who upholds traditions and protects his family just like Abu Shadi did when Shadi was a child. Shadi has come from Italy to perform his duty of delivering invitation cards for his sister Amal's wedding, and their car ride makes Shadi's respect and dutifulness visible to his father. Though Shadi, after a particularly heated argument, leaves the car and starts walking on foot, he eventually has to reconcile with his father and get back in the car. Thus, the car becomes the thirdspace of 'extraordinary openness' (Soja 1996: 5) where they acknowledge and reform their contentious relationship. While commenting on the urban architecture and landscape during their drive, they also confront the emotional landscape and the uneven architecture of their relationship.

Urban and residential spaces are assigned different affective and quotidian functions in Nazareth than in Italy. Shadi, reminiscing about Italy, tells Fayda, 'the whole city is like a museum' – a museum, a space that contains a linear memory of a time, or that preserves the images of history as objects to be looked at and marvelled at. Shadi, both as an architect and as a resident of a tourist city, is unable to value the practicality of assigning functions to urban spaces or decorating a space for a sense of stability and comfort. This variegated conception and construction of public and private spaces and their affective ramifications is a recurring theme in Jacir's films. This construction is particularly intentional in *When I Saw You* since the space in the film is constructed around transitoriness, assuming that people will either find permanent homes (like refugees in the refugee camp) or that the construction of a space is illegal and erasable (like the fedayeen base). But the affective and occupational spatial politics and its ramifications in *Salt of this Sea* are different than those in *When I Saw You* and *Wajib*.

THE RIGHT TO INHABIT SPACES IN *SALT OF THIS SEA*

Salt of this Sea presents a diverse engagement with Palestinian space. It evocatively portrays the issues of spatial (in)access for Palestinian residents and for the diaspora. In a circular opening, the camera symbolises the loss of access to

Figure 2.3 *Salt of this Sea*: Soraya and Emad sitting on top of a hill while Soraya shares her grandfather's memories. Credit: Philistine Films

the space of the homeland as well as the return of the next generations to revisit and recover the spatial and financial losses of their forefathers. Soraya, the granddaughter of Palestinians evicted from their homeland during the Nakba, travels from Brooklyn to Ramallah. The airport personnel reluctantly grant her access to her ancestral homeland. From then on, the film turns into a whirlwind of events where residents-forcibly-turned-tourists explore various public and private spaces to evoke the sociopolitical and personal histories of spaces across what was and what remains of Palestine.

Soraya's motivation for visiting Palestine stems from her grandfather's description of the Palestinian spaces he had inhabited. Her inheritance of memories contains a 'personal or autobiographical component', which is 'typically keyed to particular spaces and places' (Malpas 1999: 176). Her grandfather remembered his past by associating it with 'specific places and surroundings' or 'in characteristic poses or moods that imply a certain situation' (Malpas 1999: 176), which becomes clear when Soraya narrates his memories to Emad. Malpas terms this connection 'the binding of memory to place' whereby subjectivity is 'embedded in place, and in specialised, embodied activity' (1999: 176). This memory–place binding and the construction of subjectivity solidifies 'the connection of a sense of identity with a past' (Malpas 1999: 179). Soraya's return to Palestine and her desire to visit Ramallah is not merely a desire to touch her grandfather's past life but also to grasp the constituents of her own subjectivity and her sense of identity as an immigrant in the US.

Her affective investment in a visit to the spatial markers of her ancestors' lives is also her attempt to locate herself in the embodied planes of identity housed within these spaces by personally navigating them. This 'ordering of experience', which is also 'the ordering of the mental self', is 'both temporal and spatial' (Malpas 1999: 180). The ordering of self occurs 'through an agent's active engagement within a concrete spatiotemporal, intersubjective frame' (Malpas 1999: 180). This ordering relies on grasping the past, and hence a sense of identity, which 'cannot be grasped independently of location in place' but is graspable solely via the 'spatio-temporal ordering of things' (Malpas 1999: 180). The process of establishing one's identity via spatiotemporal links across generations is blocked by material and bureaucratic barriers. Soraya is told she cannot get a Palestinian identity card based on her ancestral ties to the land. When she attempts to access the locations of her ancestors' memories, she has to pass through barricades, checkpoints and iron gates. By the end, her presence in Palestine becomes a paradox in itself: she returned to establish and reclaim her identity as a Palestinian, but throughout her stay in Palestine she had to resort to lying about her identity in order to navigate the spaces that were supposed to grant her an identity.

This spatiotemporal access to Palestinian spaces is challenging both for Palestinian residents and non-residents. Because of her accent and her clothes, Soraya passes as a young Jewish American woman and gets access to spaces. However, Emad as a Palestinian man is unable to access domestic or international places. He must strip naked at a security checkpoint in front of an Israeli officer while Soraya looks on. He is asked to prove his identity multiple times, but Soraya rescues him every time by intervening and introducing herself as a Jewish American tourist either explicitly through verbal statements or implicitly via her linguistic and sociocultural capital. Emad is awarded a fully funded scholarship to pursue his studies in Canada, but is refused the study visa four times. They are even investigated by ordinary citizens when they are staying in the national park in Dawayima. Thus, the exclusionary construction of spaces requires ordinary people to work as guards, who stop the entry of unwanted people into private and public spaces both domestically and internationally. As a Palestinian man, Emad is refused entry into Western spaces. As a Palestinian woman, Soraya is refused entry into Palestine. But they are accepted and allowed into all spaces when they pose as Americans or Jews or Jewish Americans.

Hence, public places such as the national park, sea, roads, airport and bank, and private spaces such as Soraya's grandfather's home and the temporary home they make in the national park in Dawayima, are multipurpose spaces that simultaneously serve as spaces of comfort and as spaces of risk, as spaces of safety and as spaces of threat. These contradictory functions are automatically assigned to a space as soon as some communities are barred from accessing it. These simultaneous spatial functions become visible in the national park when a Jewish professor, who is on an educational tour with his students, starts aggressively interrogating Soraya about who she is and what she is doing in the park.

Upon learning that she is from Brooklyn, he further asks her how she knows of Dawayima. She claims that nobody told her and that they just visited Dawayima because they are going everywhere. He then inquires if she is Jewish, and upon confirmation he excitedly shares that he has brought his students to show them 'these ancient ruins, their roots. How [they] turned these biblical ruins into life again.' He beckons his students, 'Guys, come meet someone from Brooklyn.' Soraya, when asserting her ancestral links to the land, never receives a favourable response. However, as soon as her Americanness shows in an explicit or implicit form, she is instantly offered room in each space. Soraya does not even know how to pronounce Dawayima, but it is Emad – who not only pronounces it but also finds his father's friend to guide them there – who remains invisible in this exchange between Soraya and the professor. Had Emad shared anything, it would have incriminated him as a resident, a local who had a claim to these spaces but whose presence there is declared illegal. In contrast, Soraya is identified as a Jewish-American tourist who has a right to these places but whose fascination with these places will eventually exhaust, which will thus eventually prompt her to return to the comfort of her residential space abroad.

The 'eulogized space' – graspable and defendable 'space [Soraya] loves' – turns into a 'hostile space' – a 'space of hatred and combat' in the 'context of impassioned subject matter' (Bachelard 1994: 19–20) through her ancestors' right to it. Had Soraya shared her actual attachment to Jaffa and her intention behind visiting Dawayima, her interaction with the Jewish professor would not have been cordial. But she gradually learns to navigate these spaces by mobilising her experiences and observations. After her initial failed attempts to reclaim her rights to the spaces her ancestors inhabited, she resorts to alternative surreptitious ways to gain access by hiding her ancestral right. She switches her identity as an international subject to present the Jewish-American subjecthood that is most venerable and trustworthy to her respective interlocutors. Thus, the exclusionary construction of different social spaces in Palestine compels her to switch between her different subjective experiences and identities.

When Soraya and Emad cross into Jaffa 'disguised' as Jewish Americans, she exclusively relies on her American self to save both herself and Emad – except when they visit Soraya's ancestral home, where her ancestral connection to the house gains her entry in the house. A house, as a repository of the most intimate parts of human lives, is the most vital space for stabilising a subject's identity and their sense of belonging. This is especially true for young people who are figuring out the constituents of their subject formation and identity construction. The memory–space binding (Malpas 1999: 176) is rooted in the fact that 'subjectivity as a structure' is 'embedded in a world of other subjects and of multiple objects' – particularly 'the mental life of the subject is dependent on the subject's active engagement with the surrounding environment'. Hence, this relation to space is both 'intricate and inevitable'

(Malpas 1999: 177). We remember people by their presence in certain spaces or 'in characteristic poses or moods that imply a certain situation' (Malpas 1999: 176). Mostly, this endowment of identity and belonging also comes from other community members who share the same values and the same linguistic, religious, ethnic, racial or national identity, and whose identities are also attached to their association and presence in these shared spaces.

This binding of identity to a space consistently finds expression in Jacir's oeuvre. In *Wajib*, Shadi finds a community in Italy that shares the same language, nationality, history and values, so he loses interest in returning to Nazareth. In *When I Saw You*, Tarek, along with his family, is evicted from his house and his familial community of care breaks down, which leads to his fixation on the house. In *Salt of this Sea*, Soraya also loses access to any sites or artefacts of her family, which destabilises her sense of belonging and motivates her to go to Palestine to access these memories and locations that contain her ancestors' life histories. All human migration, voluntary or forced, is essentially a struggle to seek and establish a stable home and supportive community. Soraya finds her supportive community in Emad and Rayan, with whom she immediately builds such strong ties that they risk their lives to help her access her grandfather's money.

She keeps attempting to build a home with Emad till the end of the film. Soraya, Emad and Rayan visit her ancestral house, a journey filled with difficulties both literally and metaphorically. They break laws, take different identities and risk their lives to get access to Soraya's house and to see the sea in Jaffa. After crossing multiple legal and geographical borders and emotional ups and downs, Soraya also traverses architectural ups and downs in the form of multiple flights of stairs leading up to the house. The Israeli artist, who is the current resident of the house, condemns the Israeli occupation of Palestinian land and Israeli violence against Palestinians. She invites Soraya to spend the night there. But her invitation to Soraya to stay in the house further implies that Soraya is a stranger there, a guest who can visit the space that now belongs to the artist, not to Soraya's family. The artist, sitting in Soraya's ancestral home as its owner, condemns the politics that evicted her ancestors from that house, while Soraya tries to recover and rediscover the traces of her family's memories in the house that now brims with the artist's and her family's memories. This scene raises critical questions about the power relations and imbalances between civil subjects and their responsibilities in contested spaces.

While the artist who resides in Soraya's ancestral home is more gracious and kinder than everyone else Soraya meets in Jaffa, she is still implicated in the spatial and affective violence by virtue of her occupation of the home and her implicit assertion of that fact. In a way, the artist has treated the house in the same way that the Israeli state treated Soraya's family during the Nakba: they have both emptied a space and then repurposed it. While the state emptied the

Palestinian residential space and assigned it to new people, the artist emptied the house of its history and assigned it a new character. This new character requires the erasure of its previous histories and any remnants of the presence of previous characters in this space. The artist, then, involuntarily turns into a civic tool in the larger political project of the state. So, this visit and the artist's graciousness serve as the final stamp of denial in Soraya's reclamation of her ancestral memories and spaces. This eviction from her ancestral house inspires an affective and then physical reaction. She vomits in the ocean after leaving the house. It is the final act of rejection, the failure to contain unwanted objects in physical spaces. Soraya, the unpalatable subject in the house, and her vomit, the indigestible objects in her body, both finally find their way out of the spaces of their containment. The human body houses the food it eats and needs for nourishment, just as the house is endowed with life and character through the people that inhabit it.

These physical responses to spatial eviction and unbelonging incite affective responses in the subjects who undergo these experiences. Humans are 'thinking, remembering, experiencing creatures' only due to their 'active engagement' in a space. Human 'identities are, one can say, intricately and essentially [space]-bound' (Malpas 1999: 177). These spaces embrace innumerable categories, such as private, familial, public, communal, national, international, and often serve multiple intersecting purposes. For example, home as a familial or communal space also contains private spaces such as bedrooms and bathrooms. Similarly, public and communal spaces such as parks also contain spaces that can serve as reclusive private spaces, albeit briefly. Soraya's physical response to her eviction from the house, the location of her family's intimate memories, sets in motion the larger cycle of eviction from communal and then national spaces.

After leaving her family house, Soraya and Emad stay in a national park in Dawayima. After their eviction from both the personal and communal spaces of Soraya's house and the national park, they return to the city, where Soraya goes into a shop to buy cigarettes. While the news of Israeli attacks on refugee camps and the demolition of Palestinian homes runs on the TV in the shop, Emad is confronted by two police officers outside. By the time Soraya comes out, the police officers have pulled Emad out of the car and are investigating him. They ask Emad for his ID, which he fails to produce. They ask him where he is from, whereupon he responds, 'Jerusalem'. The police officers refuse to believe him. When Soraya attempts to intervene, the officers, instead of asking Soraya, ask Emad three times if he knows Soraya. Despite his refusal to retaliate, he remains the centre of their investigation and aggression. After consistently failing to incite the desired response from him, one officer pulls Emad by his ears. Soraya and Emad attempt to wrestle out of the police officers' grip, but eventually the threat of an unwanted Palestinian man is eliminated from the Israeli space to be put in a jail. Soraya, on the other hand, is taken to the airport for deportation after they learn that her visa has expired. She answers the same series of questions that she had to answer when entering Palestine – the purpose of her visit, her birthplace and her family's whereabouts – and they search her luggage. But this time Soraya's answers are different: she tells them that she was born in Jaffa on Al-Nuzha Street. This perturbs the police officer who rhetorically comments, 'Do you think this is some kind of a joke?' The scene ends with a shot of the airport, leaving vague the certainty of Soraya's return to the US.

Soraya and Emad are eliminated from the personal, communal and national spaces. These spaces are socially and legally reconstructed and restructured, with layers of formal and informal checkpoints and barriers to keep unwanted bodies out. After successfully crossing many formal and informal checkpoints, barricades and restrictions, they are eventually assaulted, arrested, investigated and evicted for the crime of their presence in the spaces that were inhabited by their ancestors.

CONCLUSION: SPATIAL IDENTITIES, EVICTIONS AND THE RIGHT TO RETURN

The production and construction of space receive attention in Jacir's films because her characters' subjectivities and identities are primarily formed and informed by their locations and their voluntary or involuntary eviction from personal, communal and national spaces. The politics of space, through access and inaccess, leads to the affective complexity of these characters. Because of the spatial, familial and communal support after eviction, characters' responses to their eviction differ. In *Salt of this Sea* Soraya constructs a new home for herself in Brooklyn despite her family's eviction and exile caused by the Nakba, but she never finds a community that shares her values, heritage and memories. This lack of community and an unstable sense of self leads her back to Palestine. There, despite her eventual eviction, she (re)locates herself inside a understanding community, familial spaces and ancestral history. Her responses to the border control officers encompass her new-found certainty that she is a Palestinian from Jaffa, despite not having the right to reside there.

In contrast to Soraya, Shadi, after his voluntary eviction from Nazareth, finds a community of people who carry a similar history, values, memories and emotions about their homeland. This allows him to shape a stable sense of self as an immigrant in Italy and engenders a lack of interest in relocating to Nazareth. During their slow spatial exploration of Nazareth, the car serves as an affectively contained heterotopic thirdspace for Shadi and Abu Shadi to resolve his childhood trauma of eviction and reach reconciliation.

Unlike these two films, where the characters navigate their (in)access to spaces that are already socially, geographically and politically constructed, the characters in *When I Saw You* build their own heteropic thirdspace, the fedayeen base. They form a community, despite the temporary nature of their residential heterotopia. Unlike Soraya and Shadi who both leave Palestine to return to America and Italy respectively, Ghayda, Tarek and the fedayeen have no official access to any space to root themselves or to locate their identities. This crisis of identity, which is intricately tied to space, is most visible in young Tarek who is undergoing the process of identity construction – a challenging task amid the affective violence, uncertainty and instability of the refugee camp. In all three feature films, Jacir highlights the interconnection of private, illegal, urban and official spaces such as cars, refugee camp, fedayeen base, Jaffa, Ramallah and Nazareth with the characters' identities and lives. In doing so, she explores everyday, historical and national spaces and the affective, familial, communal, financial, and national ramifications of these spaces. The (re)construction of these spaces as heterotopias, thirdspaces or imagined worlds of intimacy, interaction, interrogation, argumentation, residence and reconciliation informs both the development of Jacir's characters in her films and the audience's attachment to these characters.

REFERENCES

Appadurai, Arjun (1990), 'Disjuncture and Difference in the Global Political Economy', *Theory, Culture, and Society* 7: 295–310
Bachelard, Gaston (1994 [1957]), *The Poetics of Space*, Boston: Beacon Press.
Bhabha, Homi K. (1994), *The Location of Culture*, London: Routledge.
Casey, Edward (2013 [1997]), *The Fate of Place: A Philosophical History*, Berkeley: University of California Press.
Cudworth, Erika, Tim Hall and John McGovern (2007), *The Modern State: Theories and Ideologies*, Edinburgh: Edinburgh University Press.
Dikeç, Mustafa (2009), 'Space, Politics and (In)justice', *Spatial Justice*, https://www.jssj.org/wp-content/uploads/2012/12/JSSJ1-6en1.pdf (accessed 19 April 2023).
Foucault, Michael (1986), 'Of Other Spaces', trans. Jay Miskowiec, *Diacritics* 16: 22–7.
Gertz, Nurith, and George Khleifi (2008), *Palestinian Cinema: Landscape, Trauma, and Memory*, Bloomington: Indiana University Press.
Goodman, N. (1985), 'How Buildings Mean', *Critical Inquiry* 11: 642–53.
Grosz, Elizabeth A. (1995), *Space, Time, and Perversion: Essays on the Politics of Bodies*, London: Routledge.
Haapala, Arto (2005), 'On the Aesthetics of Everyday. Familiarity, Strangeness, and the Meaning of Place', in *The Aesthetics of Everyday Life*, ed. Andrew Light and Jonathan Smith, New York: Columbia University Press, pp. 39–55.
Leddy, T. (2005), 'The Nature of Everyday Aesthetics', in *The Aesthetics of Everyday Life*, ed. A. Light and J. M. Smith, New York: Columbia University Press, pp. 3–22.
Lefebvre, Henri (1991 [1974]), *The Production of Space*, Oxford: Blackwell.

Lefebvre, Henri (1996), *Writings on Cities*, Chichester: Wiley.
Malpas, Jeff (1999), *Place and Experience: A Philosophical Topography*, Cambridge: Cambridge University Press.
Milton-Edwards, Beverley (1999), *Islamic Politics in Palestine*, London: I.B. Tauris.
Saito, Yuriko (2012), 'Everyday Aesthetics and Artification', *Contemporary Aesthetics* 4, http://hdl.handle.net/2027/spo.7523862.spec.405 (accessed 19 April 2023).
Seddon, D. (2013), *A Political and Economic Dictionary of the Middle East*, Abingdon: Routledge.
Soja, Edward W. (1996), *Thirdspace: Journeys to Los Angeles and Other Real-and-Imagined Places*, Cambridge, MA: Blackwell.

NOTES

1. Elizabeth Grosz describes place as 'a territory that is mappable, explorable' and place as an 'occupation, dwelling, being lived in' (1995: 123). Edward Casey also distinguishes space and place in terms similar to Grosz's, but simultaneously highlights the interrelation or connection between space and place (2013). Jeff Malpas notes that Foucault in his 'Of Other Spaces' refers both to 'the concept of space as a system of locations ("a network that connects points") as well as to spatial notions that involve concepts of locality and position ("the near and far . . . the side-by-side") that might suggest connections with broader notions of place' (1999: 20). On the contrary, Henri Lefebvre is dissatisfied with the use of space and spatiality, especially in Foucault's work, and develops concepts of space and spatiality and the ways they relate to both the occupation and dissemination of space (1996: 3–4). While Malpas acknowledges the difference between place and space along similar lines as those proposed by Grosz, he also warns against the temptation of a clear separation or distinction between them. He highlights the interconnection and interdependence of both concepts: 'place is inextricably bound up with notions of both dimensionality or extension and of locale or environing situation. The exploration of the concept of place, and its elaboration as a philosophically significant concept, must do justice to, and take cognisance of, the complexities of the notion and its necessary implication of concepts of both dimensionality and locale . . . the investigation of place cannot be pursued but in conjunction with an investigation of the notion of space' (1999: 26). Malpas further contends that 'organisation of mental states is analogous to the ordering of subjective space' (1999: 96). He maintains that 'the structure of the mind, and of mental content' cannot be 'severed from the structure of the world in which the subject is necessarily located' (1999: 100). This chapter uses space and place interchangeably, except a few times when their difference is clearly delineated.
2. Nurith Gertz and George Khleifi (2008) identify the intertwined relationship of space, place, time and memory in Palestinian cinema. They highlight that lack of access to a place sanctions the idea of a temporality constantly informed by an 'enduring and unchanging' trauma. While Gertz and Khleifi discuss space from a historical and collective experience, this chapter focuses on everyday space.

3. Though the word fedayeen etymologically means 'one who sacrifices himself' (Seddon 2013: 165), Milton-Edwards describe fedayeen as those who are 'willing to make the ultimate sacrifice in the struggle for Palestinian liberation' (1999: 95). For further reading, see Seddon (2013).
4. Their sacrifice and struggle for nationhood and a nationalist movement was 'well-rewarded by the religious establishment'. But despite the religious translation/root of Jewish–Palestinian conflict, calling these fedayeen mujahideen 'would have been political as well as religious blasphemy' (Milton-Edwards 1999: 95)

CHAPTER 3

Locations of Memory: Home and Homeland

Iqra Shagufta Cheema

'Memory is everywhere' (Radstone and Schwarz 2010: 1). Allow me to describe three scenes from Annemarie Jacir's three feature films:

Salt of this Sea: Emad and Soraya climb to the top of a hill. In a moving panoramic shot, the camera lens indolently captures the hills, the sea and the distant foggy sprawl of Jaffa. Longingly gazing at the ocean in the distance, Soraya shares her grandfather's memories with Emad: 'My grandfather swam in the sea every morning, then he'll walk to the Al-Helwa street to reach al-Tawfiqia library then on to al-Nuzha. He always talked about al-Madfa café. Umm Kulthom and Farid al-Atrash sang there. My grandmother loved Farid. Sometimes, they'd go to the cinema.'

When I Saw You: Standing in the long queue outside a toilet in the refugee camp, Tarek turns to the old man standing behind him. 'We have our own toilet at home', he says. Later, he joins the grave-looking young girl sitting on the ground:

Tarek: Do you miss your house?
Girl: Yes.
Tarek: Your bed?
Girl: (*confused*) My bed?
Tarek: I miss my bed. Your bathroom?
Girl: No idea.
Tarek: I miss my bathroom. My dad's towel has a hole in it but mine doesn't.

Wajib: The resentment and bitterness between Shadi and Abu Shadi surface when they get into an argument:

Abu Shadi: You're afraid of telling your PLO girlfriend that one of our guests at the wedding is Jewish?

Shadi: Not because he's Jewish, but because he's a spy.
Abu Shadi: Does that mean I'm not patriotic enough? We're forced to live with them.
Shadi: This isn't living. Living is choosing how you want to live.'
Abu Shadi: Everywhere else is worse.
Shadi: Have you ever left this place in your life? Ever lived anywhere else?
Abu Shadi: I don't want to go to Europe and wear fancy shirts and sit in the parlour with Nadia and her daddy, talking about the liberation of Palestine. What's this Palestine you keep talking about? Where is it? I'm living it here.
Shadi: You call this living? To become headmaster, you need a loser like Ronnie to approve you. What a school! It's forbidden even to mention our own history. Forbidden to think. I grew up watching you beg them to recognize you, asking permission to exist, permission to breathe. You learned their language better than them, but you're invisible to them. Fuck this life.
Abu Shadi: I had a family to raise, you've no idea what I had to do to make sure you had a nice life. God damn you, boy.

These scenes, despite being widely variegated, share one commonality: the impact of memories of home and homeland on characters' affective, social and political lives. These films capture the innumerable ways in which characters' personal, familial and geographical memories of the past shadow their present lives and inform their future decisions.

Jacir's films manifest two curious tendencies: first, the characters are not afforded unbroken, unified or functional family lives, hence, they are always chasing a memory of their ideal of a family in a house; secondly, familial memories of characters are intricately intertwined with locational or spatial memories. Both of these convergent elements cathect Jacir's characters. Edward Said, commenting on the relationship between memory and geography, notes that it is only by understanding a 'special mix of geography generally and landscape in particular with historical memory', along with 'an arresting form of invention', that we can 'grasp the persistence of conflict and the difficulty of resolving it, a difficulty that is far too complex and grand than the current peace process could possibly envisage, let alone resolve' (2000: 183). Jacir's films can be read as the form of invention that is pivotal in providing an understanding of geographical and historical memory in the Israeli–Palestinian conflict.

While scholars have commented on collective memory and trauma in Palestinian cinema caused by the Nakba and Naksa (Gertz and Khleifi 2008), Said highlights the further 'importance of constructing a collective history as a part of trying to gain independence' (2000: 184). Susannah Radstone and Bill Schwarz observe that 'memory has become the site of, or the sign for, many intersecting issues: the temporal imaginings of the past, present, and future; sensitivity and identification; the passage from the inner life to the outer world; even the politics of being in the world and of recognition' (2010: 2). Similarly, Said comments that 'perhaps the greatest battle Palestinians have waged as a people has been over the right to a remembered presence and, with that presence, the right to possess and reclaim a collective historical reality' (2000: 184). Therefore, this chapter focuses on Jacir's renderings of the impact of personal memories in these films via an analysis of the characters' quotidian lives and banal activities, to ultimately accentuate the ways these films construct and contribute to a collective memory.

By zooming in on characters' personal memories, we explore the various ways in which Palestinian subjects grapple with their past, present and future in the absence of political agency and freedom of mobility amid consistently contested historical memories. Furthermore, we examine how Jacir's feature films construct an affective historical memory by sequentially tracing the familial and spatial memories of Palestinian subjects along temporal lines to examine how past traumas cathect and permeate their present and future. In doing so, these films maintain temporal continuities in portraying the role of memory in Palestinian subject formation: Palestinian-American Soraya in *Salt of this Sea* (2008) is motivated to visit Palestine because of her past memories of her grandfather's Palestine; Tarek and his mother Ghayda in *When I Saw You* (2012) reconcile with their past and find jouissance in their present life in the fedayeen base in Jordan; and the past of Shadi and Abu Shadi in *Wajib* (2017) cathects their present and (in)forms their future. Despite their different locations and lives, these characters' memories are shaped and informed by the same shared histories of affective, material and ideological violence.

These shared historical realities are, first and foremost geographical. Hence, their collective shared past, despite the variegated impact of deterritorialisation and violence on personal lives, is tied to the Palestinian land: Soraya, an expatriate, returns to her grandfather's homeland to rescue his memories and money; Tarek, a refugee child, grapples with the loss of his small home and his broken family in the grand geopolitical plot; and Shadi, a migrant against his father's desires, resides in two places with two irreconcilable families: with his sister and their divorced father in Nazareth, and with his girlfriend and her father, whom Shadi respects but Abu Shadi dislikes in Italy. Memories 'explain the past', connect the past to the present, and 'foresee a more desirable future' (Gertz and Khleifi 2008), and Jacir's cinema affectively captures these functions and motivations of memory. Historical memories of the violent past (that led to these characters' and their ancestors' eviction and deterritorialisation) render their personal memories into markers of stability amid the chaos in their present lives and the uncertainty of their future. Hence, these films focus on characters' personal struggles to reclaim their right to a family, a home and a life without violence. Jacir's cinematography depicts and inscribes characters' quotidian lives and everyday spaces as markers of familial memories and reservoirs of past histories. Employing her characters' different affective responses to their own or their families' displacement, Jacir constructs a collective Palestinian memory. Since these films maintain temporal continuities, we also attempt to sustain this temporal sequence in our discussion to highlight the topology of Jacir's cinematic oeuvre.

PAST: PERSONAL, COLLECTIVE AND CONTESTED MEMORIES IN *SALT OF THIS SEA*

If we consider this 'an era of the search for roots' where people want to 'discover the collective memory of their race, religion, community and family, a past that's entirely their own, secure from the ravages of history and a turbulent time' (Said 2000: 177), then Soraya's journey to and within Palestine in *Salt of this Sea* is an attempt to find her roots, her community and her place in Palestine. She is so embroiled in her ancestors' memories in Palestine that she centres both her present and her future around reclaiming the sites and markers of her familial past. As a result of the traumatic memories of past events, her 'past replaces the present and the future is perceived as a return to the past' (Gertz and Khleifi 2008: 3). But when she attempts to (re-)connect with the Palestinian land to retrieve that past via material artefacts, such as her family house and her grandfather's money, she learns that the past is irretrievable both temporally and materially. This film, then, renders the relationship between memories of the past and their relationship with the land simultaneously critical and unstable.

This unstable and unrestorable relationship between Palestinian subjects and Palestinian land manifests from the very opening of the film. The opening documentary footage foreshadows the film's major concerns, that is, separation from the land of one's origin, resulting rupture in the subject's identity, and the affective problematics of the subject's (dis)loyalty. This documentary footage was shot from one of the boats that took refugees away from Haifa in 1948 and was obtained from the military archive in Jerusalem to be used in this film (Armes 2015: 276).[1] The opening monochromatic long shot shows houses being bulldozed and an aerial shot of an aeroplane dropping bombs. The succeeding claustrophobic close shot shows tens of people, with bewildered, shocked and resigned faces, scrambling into a boat in the water. The camera zooms out to capture the city skyline with a widening shot of dark, tumultuous waters that further distort the increasingly farther city skyline – while sombre music continues in the background. The next panoramic shot transitions on to blue, calm waters with pleasant, upbeat background music and then on to a close-up of Soraya's excited face at the airport with the sound of announcements in the background. This transition shot from monochrome to the chromatic blues of the water captures the temporal and affective transition of memories that transpires among Palestinian exiles and refugees across generations.

This generational transfer and exchange of memories is foregrounded in Jacir's oeuvre. In the absence of access to the sites of these memories or as a result of the absence of any marker of identity and belonging, Jacir's characters rely heavily on their memories to establish a stable identity, which is inevitably associated with locations. This construction of subjecthood/self is more markedly attached to memories for those who no longer belong to a community where they can locate their identity. In order to restore their sense of self and belonging, the reclamation of those sites of traumatic memory and reconstruction of the ideal life as preserved in the memory becomes affectively necessary.

This 90-second-long opening documentary footage locates the narrative in shared collective memory by capturing the forced deterritorialisation of a people from their land, and therein situates Soraya's memory-driven personal narrative. Soraya's face appears hopeful and expectant in her introductory close-up at the airport security check. However, the ensuing aggressive investigation by the security personnel quickly makes her look confused, discouraged and, by the end of the scene, appalled. The airport security personnel question and ridicule not only the components of her identity but also her relationship to Palestine. The camera moves from the close-up of the airport officers' faces as they ask increasingly invasive questions to a close-up of Soraya's face while she responds: Soraya repeats the purpose of her visit, her name, her parents' names, her grandfather's name, her family members' birth locations, her religion, her profession, her source of income and the place of her stay. In an over-the-shoulder three-shot, where the camera looks over a female and a male officer's shoulders on to Soraya's face, the male officer mockingly asks the questions that Soraya has already answered twice. These security officers physically block Soraya's entry into Palestine in a scene that is foregrounded by their broad shoulders. While her visit to Palestine is motivated by her grandfather's pleasant memories, her own memories become both physically and emotionally traumatic at the point of entry: the female security officer inserts her fingers in Soraya's curly hair, commands her to spread her legs, directs her to remove her trousers, and even tells her to take her bra off. They rummage around in Soraya's suitcase and flash her books and her lingerie in front of the camera. As a *coup de grâce*, the male officer grimacingly waves a man's photo in front of Soraya's face: 'Boyfriend?', he asks. Disgusted, she responds: 'My father.' In examining her body and her material possessions one by one, they disintegrate each component of her identity. They explore her as a sexual object that must be stripped in front of the audience, and whose perceived perversity must be rendered visible.

Just like the Israeli narrative of historical Jewish memory, Israeli officers receive disproportionate camera visibility in this scene, while Soraya's counter-memory of her ancestral relationship to the land receives less visibility and acknowledgement. These officers interrogate, invade and dismiss Soraya's personal and familial, intellectual and affective, and even physical memories. This airport scene not only foreshadows the upcoming events but, more importantly, it turns Soraya's entry into Palestine into her entry into a site of perpetual confrontation, rejection and expulsion.

Gradually, the audience learns that this experience is hardly uncommon, when Soraya's friend, upon learning that she told the airport personnel that she was going to Ramallah, comments: 'You're lucky they let you enter.' The camera, in a moving shot, captures scattered images of the grey landscape, sparse green trees, tall city buildings, military checkpoints, military vehicles and barricades, as well as images of a dancing constable, men lounging, ogling, standing and sitting in various positions. This first introduction to Palestine shows images of both Israeli settler presence and Palestinian citizens' persistence. Soraya's image of Palestine is formed by her grandfather's memories. But on her first visit to the bank, she learns that those memories are no longer reliable. When she takes her grandfather's financial documents to the bank to claim his money, the British bank manager informs her that the whole financial record after the Nakba has been erased and 'the country is gone'. Memory is a 'social, political, and historical enterprise' available to be 'used, misused, and exploited' to build the desired view of the past (Said 2000: 178–9). In this case, the erasure of the personal financial records of Palestinian exiles is a part of the larger figuration and invention of historical memory of Palestinian land.

Since the official memory has been erased, rewritten and reconstructed, Soraya is only left with the memories that were transferred to her orally. Oral storytelling, or the transfer of personal memories in a family, is the 'necessary constitutive influence of the past–present relation as the basic retrospective condition' (Popular Memory Group 2012: 244). People such as Soraya's grandfather who were 'forced into a marginal position in the economic, cultural and social life of a society' and who were 'fearful of an absolute oblivion', had 'little to lose but their memories' (Popular Memory Group 2012: 243). Therefore, they mobilise their memories as tools of preservation of their heritage and history. Countering the ruptures in their life, they employ these memories as 'continuities' of their past to 'relive certain past events imaginarily, often with peculiar vividness' (Popular Memory Group 2012: 243). Memory and the transfer of familial memories is, therefore, 'a profoundly complicated construction' and an immensely 'active process' wherein complex past events are 'worked and reworked' (Popular Memory Group 2012: 243). Orally transferred memory of past histories is 'inherently democratic' because it provides 'an alternative viewpoint' (Popular Memory Group 2012: 243) to the professional and official accounts of history. These memories 'deprofessionalize history' by giving common people a chance to disseminate their experiential memories and countermemories (Popular Memory Group, 2012: 223).[2] The effect of undemocratic processes behind the professional reconstruction of Palestinian/Israeli memory and the demarcation of Palestinian land manifests in Soraya's futile attempts at reclamation or, at least, recognition of her family's history in Palestine.

As part of this attempt, she tries to get an identity card to prove her relationship to her ancestral homeland, Palestine. But she is refused both the official acknowledgement of her ancestral relationship and access to her ancestors' sites of memory. In the scene described at the start of this chapter, Soraya shares her grandfather's memories, an ordinary citizen's account of pre-Nakba quotidian life, with both Emad and the film's audience. As shown by her reveries, Soraya's memories, her identity, her family and the Palestinian land are intertwined. So vividly preserved are familial memories and the sites of her memories that when she asks Emad if he had ever been to Jaffa, he responds: 'Are you sure you haven't?' For Soraya, these inherited memories are 'the sedimented form of past events' that are 'dead and gone' (Popular Memory Group 2012: 241). All her memories, despite not having lived in Palestine, are rooted in and associated with various spatial identity markers in the Palestinian landscape.

Since her memories and her sense of belonging are tied to the sites of her grandfather's memories, excavation and reclamation of these sites is challenging but necessary. Sites, such as Soraya's grandfather's house, serve as 'points of reference not only for those who survived traumatic events, but also for those born long after them' (Radstone and Schwarz 2010: 313). She faces the threat of erasure of her identity in losing access to those locations. People who visit these sites of memory, or 'commemorative sites', 'inherit earlier meanings attached to the event as well as add new meanings' to these sites (Radstone and Schwarz 2010: 312). Soraya's family house serves as a 'site of memory',[3] albeit a 'site of second order memory', that contains the memories of those family members who survived the traumatic events that forced them to abandon their house (Radstone and Schwarz 2010: 313). However, to gain access to these sites of second-order memory means taking up secondary identities. Soraya is only able to enter Jaffa in the guise of a Jewish American woman. This false identity enables her to pay the commemorative visit to her grandfather's house, which is now occupied by an Israeli artist.

The current occupant of the house, though not hostile, is unable to comprehend the emotional meaning that the house carries for Soraya. While for the artist the house is a place to live, for Soraya it is a place of affective, familial and historical identity and (in)stability. Luscombe and Green contend that a house is the 'single most important aspect of material culture' because of the

Figure 3.1 *Salt of this Sea*: Soraya and Irit, the Israeli artist, in the middle of their heated exchange in Soraya's ancestral home. Credit: Philistine Films

'significance attached to home ownership in public and political discourse' (2019: 651). The building of a house 'exercises performative agency' in terms of its cultural meaning, and the dialectical relationship between memory and these markers of memory in the context of orally transferred family histories (Luscombe and Green 2019: 656). Even the house that is 'no longer in family ownership' remains a 'visible material marker framing family trajectories across the generations' (Luscombe and Green 2019: 652). Walking towards the house, a visibly distraught Soraya caresses the walls. She slowly ascends the stairs to the house via a dark tunnel, literally walking into light as she nears the marker of her grandfather's memory, the reservoir of her family history.

The house can be read as a smaller archive of the common Palestinian political history within the larger archive of national Palestinian history. The house has iron bars on its doors and windows just as Palestine has checkpoints and barricades to control the entry of the Palestinians, the previous residents. Emad knocks at the door and the current occupant of the house comes to the barred gate, oblivious to the history of the house. Upon learning that the house belonged to Soraya's ancestors, she invites her to come in. Then she goes on to comment:

> Artist: It's terrible, this situation. All this violence . . . I think everyone wants peace, except for the leaders.
> Your grandfather left in 48? It's so sad. I wish they had stayed.
> Emad: They were not allowed.
> Artist: They were treated so poorly everywhere they went.
> Soraya: What happened to all the furniture?
> Artist: I don't know. I guess my family got rid of it at some point.

The house, as a site of memory and as a material marker of family trajectories, does not carry the same affective value for the artist as it does for Soraya. The new occupant of the house answers Soraya's and Emad's question in a matter-of-fact way, without any semblance of recognition of Soraya's emotional devastation in the house. She recognises the historical violence, acknowledges the expulsion of Palestinians from their houses, and desires peace; she even has 'Peace now. End the Occupation' mugs in her kitchen cabinet. She tells Soraya and her friends that they are welcome to stay in the house as long as they like. But in doing so, she establishes that she is the rightful owner of the house even if she recognises that it originally did/does belong to Soraya. This individual-on-individual material and affective violence exhibits itself multiple times in Soraya and Emad's interactions with state officials or employees, such as the banker, the police and the security officers. It's not the Palestinian subjects who they fight or target, but any claim to Palestinian historical memory.

The house now carries two discordant, clashing familial memories; two narratives that don't carry the same weight in the collective political memory. A house is a signifier of clashing historical realities, a site of 'radical irreconcilability' (Said 2000: 183). Palestine 'instances an extraordinarily rich and intense conflict of at least two memories, two sorts of historical invention, two sorts of geographical imagination' (Said 2000: 182–3). These two contested memories in Soraya's house are the Palestinian memory that Soraya's grandfather transferred to her, and the Israeli memory – an overwriting of the Palestinian memory – that the artist carries. Both Soraya and the artist acknowledge these affective personal memories: the current owner laments Israel's eviction of Palestinians from their homeland while being a beneficiary of that settlement; Soraya leaves her grandfather's house and thereby acknowledges that her family has lost its official right to these sites of memory, irrespective of how unpalatable this reality is.

Although Soraya no longer has a claim over the house, her visit remains 'crucial to the presentation and preservation' of this 'contested site' of memory and identity not only for her but for all exilic subjects because of the symbolic weight that the house carries (Radstone and Schwarz 2010: 312–13). The collision of these contested memories recurs at the bank in conversations between Soraya and the bank officer, in Soraya's narration of her memories and Emad's attempts to cross borders, and in the exchange between Soraya and the Israeli artist in the house. If Soraya, as a carrier of her grandfather's memories, 'disperses or disappears', then the house 'lose[s] [its] initial force, and may fade away entirely' (Radstone and Schwarz 2010: 312) – which is why this collision of contesting memories, though unpleasant, remains crucial for the commemoration, if not reclamation, of collective history and memory.

Family memories include a 'material dimension' that reflects 'a narrative peripeteia' (Luscombe and Green 2019: 657). Symbols such as a house 'enable an individual to hold onto a cherished sense of self-worth in the face of family adversity or instability by grounding their personal identity in family circumstances prior to the pivotal event' (Luscombe and Green 2019: 657). Soraya is never shown leaving the house; the camera cuts to her vomiting on the beach. This expulsion of contents from the body is similar to Soraya's expulsion from the house, a site that can no longer contain her despite the fact that they sustain each other. An inherited house, in this case the house that Soraya could have inherited, means a 'more secure past' (Luscombe and Green 2019: 652). The lost house serves as a 'symbol of personal and family identity and status' which is derived not 'from the present but from memory or genealogical knowledge of past generations' (Luscombe and Green 2019: 657). Hence, a lost house, for Soraya, is a reminder of 'what-could-have-been' (Luscombe and Green 2019: 652). This positioning of personal memories of past events against the collective political narrative highlights the often-neglected cost of nationalistic or state politics. These places, then, help 'evaluate particular sites and types of memory as they invoke the past in specific ways and for specific ends' (Grainge 2003: 1). *When I Saw You* reflects a past that remains materially irretrievable, but that maintains its affective hold in Soraya's present life via the sheer power of orally transferred memories of her family's past in pre-Nakba Palestine.

HOMES AND HOMELAND IN *WHEN I SAW YOU*

While loyalty and attachment to past memories marks and advances *Salt of this Sea*, *When I Saw You* is permeated with a sense of disloyalty to the past. *When I Saw You* is contemplation, a slow deliberation on the static present and unpredictable future. *Salt of this Sea* contains sites of affective familial and national signification. But these sites remain so inaccessible in *When I Saw You* that even the new sites of residence such as the refugee camp and the fedayeen base, which ultimately turn into sites of memory, remain nondescript and generic.

Cinematically too, the urgency and expedited events in urban spaces in *Salt of this Sea* contrast with the recurrence and slow rumination in the idyllic setting in *When I Saw You*. *Salt of this Sea* relies on the force of personal and familial memories and motivations, but *When I Saw You* mainly invokes the collective historical Palestinian memory. So, in a way, *When I Saw You* inverts the sequence of memories of *Salt of this Sea*. *When I Saw You* contemplates memories to 'forge' the past in order to 'serve present interests' (Radstone and Schwarz 2010: 4). Nevertheless, the characters don't seek urgent reclamation or a reassertion of the sites or markers of their memories.

Characters hold on to the hope of a return to the homeland, but the vision of this return is collective and never individual – and mostly remains on hold.

Maybe that is why Roy Armes describes *When I Saw You* as a 'positive, idealistic film' that 'unashamedly romanticiz[es] the struggles of the late 1960s' (2015: 280). Armes notes that the film focuses on the 'viewpoint of its constantly positive and optimistic 11-year-old protagonist' in a way that 'contains no hint of the wider issues or subsequent disappointments and failures' in the Palestinian struggle, so the audience never witnesses the 'violence of what has happened and the violence that refugee families have escaped from' (2015: 278–9). But we posit that the film, though idealistic and distant from the immediate, visceral effects of violence, is far from positive/optimistic.

The film, on the contrary, is tragically realistic. While it does not explicitly employ historical violence as its defining impetus, this history underscores the film's setting and its affective utterances. The film is set in a refugee camp and a fedayeen base. These living conditions render it impossible for characters to not reminisce about the past when they lived in their houses in Palestine. *Salt of this Sea* remains idealistic in the way Soraya imagines her return to the sites of her memories in Palestine and then robs the bank, but *When I Saw You* is more realistic in the way the characters, though yearning for home in the homeland, recognise the difficulty and improbability of that aspiration. The focus of the film is not Tarek's life but the characters' perception of and reactions to their trauma, which results in repetition of regimented routines of fedayeen and Tarek's elopement to the border. Much of the film's force resides in the quotidian inaction and recurrence of events.

Time stays static in *When I Saw You*. In a way, the movie is a rendition of the Beckettian imagination: the characters' lives do not move anywhere. They are stuck in time. They repeat the same motions, sit around the same fire, sing similar songs. They train for the fight but actually never fight the enemy on screen, longingly looking at Palestine but never going there. Tarek, the young protagonist of the film, becomes the vehicle that conveys the gradual recognition of and reconciliation with the tragic reality of the lives of Palestinian refugees and exiles. Tarek is played by a non-professional actor, which 'allows the film to elide most of the tensions, rivalries, antagonisms, and daily humiliations that must be present in such a camp which keeps filling up after the devastating Arab defeat in the 1967 Six-Day War' (Armes 2015: 279). While Tarek's hopeful insistence and conviction of return to his house read naively to the film's audience, this also invites a more empathetic viewership: the audience is forced to recognise the affective intensity of this recurrent realisation of the difficulty of return on Tarek's psyche. The trauma of sudden expulsion from their home and homeland and the difficulty of return is familiar to everyone in the refugee camp and the fedayeen base, and even to Jacir herself.

When I Saw You is set in 1967, the year when Jacir's family was 'expelled from Bethlehem' (Armes 2015: 279). Besides that, Jacir's 'personal situation' in Amman was the secondary motivation for this film. Jacir was 'forbidden, for the first time, to enter Palestine'. She said that her 'whole world collapsed and [her] heart broke'. She 'could only see Palestine across the Jordan Valley', but couldn't enter it. This experience and lack of access made her realise that 'the most difficult thing' these 'possessed Palestinians' are forced to do is 'stand somewhere in the valley and look at Palestine without being able to go back' (Jacir 2012). This difficulty exercises an affective hold on 11-year-old Tarek and others throughout the film. The film opens with a truck full of incoming Palestinian refugees.[4] A group of jubilant children runs after the truck as it inches closer to the refugee camp in Jordan and farther from Palestine. Tarek and his mother, like many others, expectantly run towards the truck to welcome his father, who doesn't arrive. Tarek's memories mostly remain affective, wherein he reminisces about the comforts of a house and the security of a family in Palestine. Tarek hates his teacher, his school and his life in the camp; his notion of a happy life is attached to the presence of his father and his house in Bayt Nuba. Through his recurrent confrontation with the implausibility of a return to an ideal past, the audience is also repeatedly exposed to the disillusionment and trauma resulting from this undesired realisation.

Tarek does not possess enough cognitive memories to measure the gravity of this trauma. Jacir portrays the complex relationship that traumatic memories share with perceptions of time and space. Despite his mathematical competency, Tarek perceives the loss of his house beyond a temporal perception – and then even without a spatial conception. One of the early scenes in the film is a wedding in the refugee camp. Everyone dances, sings and claps. Suddenly, Tarek asks an older woman how long she has been in the refugee camp. She responds, 'Twenty years.' While Ghayda remains unresponsive, Tarek is incredulous: '1300 days?', he exclaims. 'Twenty years, these are 175,320 hours.' This is a new realisation for Tarek, who expects to return home soon. The dismal living conditions in the refugee camp compel him to draw comparisons with his home. While waiting in the long queue outside the bathroom in the camp, an old man tells Tarek, 'Palestine's gone.' But this realisation is lost on Tarek. Later, he talks to a young girl sitting in the dirt outside the camp. He asks her, 'Are you staying here?' She responds, 'Where else can we go?' In another scene, Tarek repeatedly asks his mother: 'When are we going back?', 'What are we waiting for?', 'What if dad can't find this place?' and 'Why don't we go home?', until his mother snaps. But living in constant trauma and anxiety, these affective memories start to recede. Later, he sobs that he can't remember where or in which direction their home is. Living in limbo, in a transitory state, as non-agential refugees, Tarek and his mother cling on to 'the anticipation for the return to the homeland' as the 'only permanency' (Sanbar et al. 1997: 24, cited in Gertz and Khleifi 2008: 2). While Soraya invests her financial, affective and legal capital in retrieving and reliving her past familial memories, *When I Saw You* encourages forgetting and relinquishing those memories in favour of building new memories and affective experiences in the present.

Figure 3.2 *When I Saw You*: Tarek in the fedayeen base playing with the fedayeen just before Ghayda stumbles in looking for him. Credit: Philistine Films

In an attempt to imitate the inaccessible ideal life, characters perform seemingly incongruous roles as fighters and artists, as warriors and lovers, and as teachers and caretakers. These roles, despite being necessary, also highlight the affective rupture. When Tarek's teacher, Mr Nasser, complains to Ghayda about Tarek's disruptiveness in school, he goes on to add, 'I know a house without a man can be difficult.' Ghayda, waiting for his father's return, flirts with Layth when in the fedayeen base. Fedayeen are portrayed painting and singing more frequently than they are shown fighting. Instead of strategising a return to Palestine, they are often captured listening to music and songs about Palestine. But these artistic, joyful activities are constantly disrupted either by their leader, news of an Israeli attack, or an attack itself. They consistently reconcile their opposing desires: the desire for a peaceful home and the necessity of armed resistance to fulfil the desire to return home; the desire to fight the violator and the desire to perform art; the desire to fulfil their duties as men and wives and the desire to find companionship to alleviate the loneliness in their lives.

The film also consistently attempts to reconcile the violent memories of the past and the current realities of the present, which could also be read as an attempt to reconcile personal desires and collective goals. Unsettling the subjective erasure of refugees' memories, the film consolidates them with collective desires. In the refugee camp, Tarek wanted to return to his father and his home. But in the fedayeen base, Tarek trains with other fedayeen for the return to home. It is at this defining narrative shift that Jacir invokes the idyllic agricultural chronotope. Mikhail Bakhtin describes the idyllic chronotope as a 'little spatial world', which is 'limited and sufficient unto itself, not linked in any intrinsic way with other places, with the rest of the world' (Bakhtin 1981: 225). These 'chronotopes are mutually inclusive, they coexist, they may be interwoven with, replace or oppose one another, contradict one another, or find themselves in even more complex relationships' (Bakhtin 1981: 251). Jacir's camera leisurely explores the idyll around the refugee camp, with Palestine in the distance.

These idylls represent the 'unity of an ancient complex and a folkloric time, which is expressed in the special relationship that space and time have within the idyll' (Naficy 2001: 155). As idyllic symbols of collective memory, places such as pasture, hill and plain become 'important symbolic sites in the Palestinian cinema's rhetoric of the land, home, and identity' (Naficy 2001: 167). Exposure to the agricultural idyll, along with his visit to the fedayeen base, eventually incites a shift in Tarek's character. Chasing a memory of his lost home, Tarek saunters past a shepherd and his flock of sheep, a group of lost travellers, and a range of dusty hills beyond which lies Palestine. From his mother's reaction and his (lack of) sense of direction, it appears that it is his first exposure to this idyll. In this crucial moment, Tarek reorients his memories and the audience witnesses him exploring the world outside the refugee camp. This exposure to the agricultural idyll and his interactions with Jordanian residents – a woman who hands him pomegranates, travellers who rebuke him, and the sheep that he plays with – shift his perception of the loss of his home, thereby fusing the personal with the collective.

Tarek walks the light brown landscape for the whole day until night falls, when he falls asleep under the sky, only to be discovered by a fedayee, Layth (Saleh Bakri), who takes him to the fedayeen base. His personal memories of the house gradually dwindle and merge into the collective national traumatic memory that inspires the fedayeen base. Tarek is instantly happy being there among a group of different people. He shadows the trainer, Abu Akram, working as his assistant, counting the number of push-ups, shots fired and other activities that fedayeen perform. But he soon tires of the routine and says to Layth, 'You are all boring', and that he's going home.

Layth: where is home?
Tarek: Palestine, we will live with my father. My school, Ms Hala.

Layth assures him that they are 'preparing [themselves] to return'.

Despite the fedayeen's daily training to return to Palestine, they appear content with their present life, albeit there are affective expressions of their trauma in art and singing. Fighters are

> depicted as idealized figures, attractive young men and women, living together as equals and without tensions. They play music, sing, smoke,

and train but never discuss the details of the war they are planning or express political opinions about the Israelis or the limited support coming to them from their fellow Arabs. They accept without question the brutal training regime to which they are submitted. (Armes 2015: 279)

When Ghayda traces Tarek to the fedayeen base, she also, despite her initial reluctance due to her official registration at the refugee camp, ultimately joins them. The fedayeen base, then, can be read as a joyful site of relief and pleasure where fedayeen are free to pursue their artistic interests and do not have to wait for international aid or the arrival of their loved ones. Their lives are not on hold. They live a more autonomous life, which seems to be the purpose, despite their pronouncements of preparation for the reclamation of Palestine. Instead of the fedayeen, their training and their planning of their attacks, the camera focuses on their banal routines that provide hope, a structure and sense of purpose to their quotidian lives.

But Abu Akram, their commander, signifies an invocation of the national memory, a reminder of their original goal – to reclaim their homes and homeland. At one point Abu Akram, upon seeing them playing cards and listening to music, sarcastically reminds them that 'playing cards is a bourgeois activity, for a bourgeois people'. He turns the music off and rotates the radio dial to the news, where the newscaster, coincidentally, announces the bombing of the refugee camp by the Israelis. The radio announces: 'Israeli aircraft have hit the Harir refugee camp with missiles and napalm bombs in an effort to target the fedayeen bases scattered throughout the country as cross border operations have shown a steady increase.'[5] This shocking news accentuates the traumatic clash between memories of the past exile and the pull of a harmonious life and the necessity of resistance in the face of violence.

For younger fedayeen, this stirs memories of lost homes and loved ones. But for older fedayeen, it's not the time to get emotional. Their aspiration for the reclamation of Palestine appears to be an illusion that gives them the strength to live their daily lives. Unable to face their betrayal of familial memories and the surrender of their homeland, they forge connections with each other, they make new families. In this state of transitoriness in the camp and with diminishing hopes of the success of their resistance, the agricultural idyll and Tarek emerge as symbols of stability and hope.

The film invokes the idyll as a means of bodily and affective sustenance and nourishment. When in the refugee camp, Ghayda and Tarek stand in line to receive rations that are distributed to the refugees. In the fedayeen base, Tarek gains an agency unknown to him before. He chooses to eat rice and sits wherever he wants. He finally finds the community that he desired. As he joins the group of fedayeen in the base, his need for his father translates into a stronger need for a return to his home in the homeland. Tarek, whenever he speaks about home, mentions the objects that provide the comforts of the house, and his father who ensures the safety and provision of those comforts. Ghayda, though she keeps saying that she is going to take him back to the refugee camp, seems emotionally unwilling to go back to the desolate and lonely place. Upon receiving the reassurance of companionship and a joyful community, both Ghayda and Tarek gradually relinquish the memory of the father and submit to the concept of the nation and the homeland as the dominant affective memory.

The film fills the gap between the past and the future via its employment of the agricultural idyll and art. This idyll works as a bridge between past memories and their collective push towards a future. Surrounded by green shrubs in an otherwise grey and brown landscape, Tarek plays the oud. The sound of his music resonates as the sound of hope in the isolated fedayeen base. Even Ghayda experiences a rare moment of joy. That is what Jacir does best in her films – she excavates the horrific memories of the lost homes and families and gives her characters moments of pleasure and peace amid the chaos that has historically only worsened.

Despite the surface serenity and collaboration between the fedayeen, the past is present between them, like a ghost whose presence they feel but which they can neither eliminate nor fully embrace. Fedayeen, who are often wilfully portrayed as terrorists in the West, receive a more complex portrayal in this film. In portraying them as artists, painters, singers and fighters, Jacir attends both to the softer and tougher sides of their personalities. The desire for a community and a family underscores their motivations. When the teacher complains about Tarek's disruptive behaviour to Ghayda in the refugee camp, he comments on the difficulty of running a house without a man. Considering the fedayeen's frustration at not attacking the Israelis to reclaim their land, this desire to be desired by a woman can be read as their need for reassurance about their heteronormative masculinity. Though Armes comments that 'attractive young people liv[e] together as equals and without tensions' in the fedayeen base (2015: 279), it quickly becomes clear that frustration and anxieties underlie this equality and peace. These anxieties are not limited to the (im)possibility of a return to the homeland but also the (im)probability of access to the lives and loves that these exiles, fedayeen and refugees left behind. In one of the scenes, two fedayeen, sitting far apart, quibble with each other:

> First fedayee: Your wife's glad you're gone. I saw her last night, her red lipstick smeared.
> Second fedayee: At least I have a woman who loves me and my heart is full unlike you. Easy as the street walker, and your heart empty.
> First fedayee: What's in the heart is in the heart and what's gone is gone. All that counts is who remains.

This exchange, initiated as banter, quickly transitions into resignation and acceptance of a bygone past. In another episode, Layth and Ghayda briefly flirt: she asks him if he had a lover and he says that his lover's hair was as black as Ghayda's. He asks Ghayda if she wished she had not met her husband; she responds that she wishes she had met him sooner, so she could have spent more time with him. These moments provide rare respite from the woes of monogamous romances and subsequent separations.

Amid this uncertainty, the consolidation and confrontation of personal desires and political intentions appears more jarring when viewed from Tarek's perspective. He notices Ghayda, his mother, eagerly listening to Layth's memories, stories of his past and anecdotes from his childhood. He witnesses their flirtatious laughter – this is the most Ghayda has laughed in the film. Tarek, enraged, asks Ghayda: 'You going to do your hair like that in twenty years?' She is suddenly reminded of her lost husband, and her increasing age. In a close-up of Layth holding Ghayda's hand, Tarek starts yelling: 'Liars, liars, you are all liars. You made him sad. You're always unhappy. You think you're always right. You made him leave. Now he's lost. You lost him.' Tarek, in two scenes, blames his mother for his father's absence. Though Tarek's comment hints at the friction in Ghayda's marriage, the audience never learns the details. This lack of specificity in her marriage details makes it a prototype for other familial relationships in *When I Saw You*.

All familial relationships in the film are sustained through memory, which consistently lingers in the background. Even when Ghayda flirts with Layth, her realisation that the moment is fleeting is visible. This soon concretises when she sees Layth with another fedayee woman in his tent, though Ghayda does not react. But witnessing his mother as a woman in these fleeting moments affects Tarek so strongly that he leaves in the night to go to Palestine. Ghayda, once again, starts looking for Tarek with help from Abu Akram and Layth, who gather a group of fedayeen to look for him. Ghayda wants to accompany them, but Layth points to her dress: 'Like this?' She reappears in a unisex fedayee uniform. With this, her incorporation into the fedayeen group is complete. After her arrival at the refugee camp, she experiences a split between her past and present while the future remains absent. This temporal conflict and the impossibility of its resolution sustain a paradoxical presence and absence throughout the film. In becoming a part of the fedayeen, she establishes her past relationship with her missing husband, her present relationship with Tarek, and her future relationship with the land or the struggle for its reclamation. While this restoration of relationships and convergence with the fedayeen resolves the temporal and ideological problematics, it also accentuates gendered questions contained within this resolution.

Though the signification of trauma and resistance remains gender- and age-dependent throughout the film, it culminates in these final moments. Tarek becomes the device that pulls both fedayeen and Ghayda to the border after the film suspends attention to the question of the fedayeen fighting for the land and the national memory that they regularly train to reclaim. In their attempt to save Tarek, they also attempt to save their future. Tarek disappears in the vast, empty plane stretching out before them, while the fedayeen cautiously and tactfully walk towards it. All previously unresolved contradictions and troubled relationships surface in this scene: Ghayda and Tarek, fedayeen and Israeli guards, and nature and military tanks. In alternating shots, the camera specifically focuses on the urgent resolution of the conflict between Tarek and Ghayda. The camera captures the moment of contention, a stalemate, between the mother and the son.

Teary-eyed Tarek looks at Ghayda pleadingly, helplessly; Ghayda looks at Tarek, uncertain and sympathetic. The Israeli tank slowly disappears behind the trees. Then she suddenly runs towards Tarek while Layth beckons her to stop. Despite the danger that lies ahead of her, she joyously runs and holds Tarek's hand. Both of them keep running towards the fence, nearing Palestine and the military tank patrolling the border. The camera freezes on the frame while they are still holding hands, just a little way from the fence, with Ghayda's hair flying in the air and Tarek's school bag on his shoulder. The film's final push erupts from Tarek's memories of his past and his house. Motivated by the urgency to find and protect their future in the figure of Tarek, they finally break the stagnation of their daily routine in the fedayeen base and refugee camp. These camps represent the Palestinian traumatic history 'through plotline' that 'documents present occurrences', but 'revives' the story of the past 'in a very abstract and symbolic manner' (Gertz and Khleifi 2008: 4). The film explores solely the quotidian lives of refugees and fedayeen, but their activities are charged and sustained because of past events and memories. The final freeze-frame punctuates the continuation, and simultaneously the uncertainty of the outcome of resistance. But it does establish that resistance is the only solution both for the resolution and convergence of personal and national memories.

DESIRES AND MEMORIES IN *WAJIB*

Wajib differs from *Salt of this Sea* and *When I Saw You* in its setting and its affective engagement with personal and national memories. Family and familial memories, more so in *Wajib* than in Jacir's other films, become a symbol for the nation and national memories. Therefore, familial memories also converge into national memory. The film is set in Nazareth, but essentially captures the constant mobility required to sustain relationships and perform duties, as most of the intimate moments between father and son occur inside the car. *Wajib*

Figure 3.3 *Wajib*: Shadi and Abu Shadi after delivering a wedding invitation to the house of one of their friends. Credit: Philistine Films

is the narrative of a Palestinian expatriate Shadi and his father Abu Shadi, who drive a Volvo around Nazareth to distribute invitation cards for Shadi's sister's wedding. Shadi visits from Italy to distribute the wedding cards, since it is *wajib* (a duty) for him as the bride's only brother. Abu Shadi enjoys a vast, interconnected network of family and friends in Nazareth. He is a respectable teacher and a dutiful father who is constantly split between the realistic and idealistic aspirations of life.

In portraying this split, the film accentuates the generational problematics of attending to and responding to affective memories. But this gap stretches far beyond the difficulty of living in Nazareth. Abu Shadi consistently expresses his disapproval of Shadi's choices: his clothes, hairstyle, profession, country of residence, marriage decision, and even his girlfriend. This friction between them emerges less from Shadi's decisions and more from Abu Shadi's desires. Despite being a respected teacher, he feels emasculated because his wife left him, he feels lonely because his only daughter is getting married, and he feels dismayed because his son lives in Italy. The multiple layers of the characters' lives are unfolded as they move from house to house, driving from road to road. Despite its focus on family and family drama, the film longingly explores the Palestinian land as Shadi and Abu Shadi drive along the long roads and narrow streets. The landscape itself emerges as a character in the film. This immobile character sometimes says more about the Palestinian past and its present than the characters themselves. Considering Abu Shadi's constant insistence that Shadi move back to Palestine and Shadi's repeated refusal to return, *Wajib* reads as Abu Shadi's long-drawn love letter and Shadi's goodbye to the land.

In tracing the progression of their distribution of invitations via their road trip, the film also reveals the progression of their relationship, temporally locating it in the past, present and future.

Their personal memories and conflicts rise to the surface in their interaction with other people or in conversations about them. The audience learns about Abu Shadi's dislike of Shadi's career when other characters comment on it; the audience learns about the details of the rift between Shadi and Abu Shadi through their disagreement about inviting Ronnie to the wedding. This incident leads to the disintegration of the illusion that the film initially sustains: the illusion of Abu Shadi living a safe and free life in Nazareth:

> Shadi: He is the reason you were interrogated. He is the reason you sent me away. I won't invite him to my sister's wedding. He is secret service.
> Abu: You have always been paranoid.
> Shadi: His job is to report to the ministry what the Arab schools do.
> Abu: I was the one who decided to send you abroad, not Ronnie. I did it for you. You found a girlfriend whose father is in the PLO.
> Shadi: What has that got to do with anything?
> Abu: Your hero, an intellectual, who has lived all over the world. At whose expense? He's a revolutionary. The palace he lives in? At whose expense? The price of this car can feed a refugee camp. And you want to talk to me about Ronnie?
> Shadi: Drive yourself.
> Abu: Get back in the car. You are more stubborn than your mother.

With the emergence of their past memories erupt their oppositional responses to the tragedy of separation, and the tragedy of the family split. *Wajib* could be read as a film of contradictions and illusions: both Shadi and Abu Shadi read the memory of Shadi's exile differently; the camera creates an illusion of access by following their ride through the city streets and their house visits, but it simultaneously remains claustrophobic, as the street view is mostly hidden behind the car and the houses are dimly lit or appear too small; their responses to Abu Shadi's divorce are contrary; their future visions of an ideal life collide; the camera is positioned in such a way on the car that it bars a complete view, inhibits the complete imaginary mapping of the streets. The affectively and materially chaotic after-effects of these contradictions and illusions invoke the Bakhtinian carnivalesque (Bakhtin 1984).

Bakhtin describes a carnival as a 'complex and varied' form that contains 'diverse variants and nuances depending upon the epoch, the people, the individual festivity' (1984: 122). He enumerates four categories of a carnivalesque sense of the world: 'free and familiar contact among people' resulting from the suspension of all hierarchies; 'eccentricity' of interaction and behaviour; carnivalistic mésalliances of all contradictions into a living form; and celebratory profanation (1984: 122–30). The carnivalesque consciousness and aesthetic in the film recurrently manifests in both private and public moments: the realisation that the wrong date is on the wedding cards after they have been distributing them all day; the brawl in the street which Abu Shadi gets out to resolve; Shadi leaving the car in protest; Amal learning that her mother won't come to the wedding while she is trying on wedding dresses. This carnivalesque chaos underscores the significant plot occurrences as the anticipation of happiness and resolution in the multiple frictions of memories between family and friends.

Here, we would like to reflect on the joyful memories in *Salt of this Sea* and *When I Saw You*. Soraya, though disappointed in the first half of the film, forms happy memories in the latter half. She remains constantly suspended between the traumatic and the joyful, the past and the present/future. Even in her conversations about her grandfather, she not only bears the traumatic memories of the Nakba, but also shares his happy memories of the land, of early mornings, of his walks to the café and to the library. Tea Sindbæk Anderson and Jessica Ortner highlight the significance of joyful memories, and challenge the dominant role that 'trauma and traumatic memories play within memory studies' (2019: 6). They contend that 'contemporary societies also need positive or hopeful memories in order to create alternative imaginaries for the future' (2019: 5). But memory studies 'ignores [these] important aspects of collective memory and eclipses group memories that differ from society's hegemonic discourse about the past' (2019: 5). Ann Rigney also invites others to 'think critically about the cost of this apparently natural link between memory and trauma'. She suggests that memory studies themselves 'have become implicated in perpetuating the idea' that 'violence is the primary subject of collective memory and a grievance the core identity' (2018: 369). Jeffrey Olick (2018) also points out that the connection between memory and the past is a 'way of underwriting identity and underwriting the future', but memory scholars have become 'traumatologists' by focusing 'exclusively on the dark side, necrology, victimology, trauma, atrocity' (Anderson and Ortner 2019: 6). Memories of the house and the homeland hold power for Soraya and Tarek, along with other characters, because they are reminders of the joyful periods before the traumatic events. Land and national sites of memory also contain the remembrance and the possibility of joy.

Even the traumatic and exilic periods are punctuated by joy, hope and stability – however ephemeral it might be. Tarek and his mother find friends in the refugee camp and companionship and happiness in the fedayeen base; Abu Shadi has his friends and family and his dutiful children; Soraya also finds joy and prospects of a new family with Emad. Against the backdrop of looming collective memories of chaos, violence, homelessness and instability live the personal memories of joy, hope and peace. Jacir, by paying attention to both traumatic and joyful memories in these movies, resolves, or at least allays, the clash between personal and collective memory, loss and happiness, trauma and recovery.

REFERENCES

Anderson, Tea Sindbæk, and Jessica Ortner (2019), 'Introduction: Memories of Joy', *Memory Studies* 12.1: 5–10.
Armes, Roy (2015), *New Voices in Arab Cinema*, Bloomington: Indiana University Press.
Aulander, Leora (2005), 'Beyond Words', *The American Historical Review* 110.4: 1015–45.
Bakhtin, Mikhail (1981), *The Dialogic Imagination: Four Essays*, ed. Michael Holquist, trans. Caryl Emerson and Michael Holquist, Austin: University of Texas Press.
Bakhtin, Mikhail (1984), *Problems of Dostoevsky's Poetics*, Minneapolis: University of Minnesota Press.
Bresheeth, Haim (2001), 'The Boundaries of the Palestinian Memory: Home and Exile, Identity and Disappearance in the New Palestinian Cinema', *Theory and Criticism* 18: 77–102.
Bresheeth, Haim (2002), 'A Symphony of Absence: Borders and Liminality in Elia Suleiman's *Chronicle of a Disappearance*', *Framework* 43.2: 71–84.
Byrne, Ruth M. J. (2005), *The Rational Imagination: How People Create Alternatives to Reality*, Cambridge, MA: MIT Press.
Foucault, Michel (1977), *Language, Counter-Memory, Practice: Selected Essays and Interviews*, ed. Donald. F. Bouchard and Sherry Simon, Ithaca, NY: Cornell University Press.
Gertz, Nurith, and George Khleifi (2008), *Palestinian Cinema: Landscape, Trauma, and Memory*, Bloomington: Indiana University Press
Ghosn, Faten, Tiffany S. Chu, Miranda Simon, Alex Braithwaite, Michael Frith and Joanna Jandali (2021), 'The Journey Home: Violence, Anchoring, and Refugee Decisions to Return', *American Political Science Review* 115.3: 982–98, http://doi.org/10.1017/S0003055421000344.
Grainge, Paul (ed.) (2003), *Memory and Popular Film*, Manchester: Manchester University Press.
Hirsch, Marianne (1997), *Family Frames: Photography, Narrative and Postmemory*, Cambridge, MA: Harvard University Press.
Jacir, Annemarie (2012), 'Romancing the Naksa Narrative', interview with Rasha Hilwi, *Al-Akhbar*, 10 October, www.al-akhbar.com.
Kansteiner, Wulf (2018), 'History, Memory, and Film', *Memory Studies* 11.2: 131–6.
Luscombe, Kayleigh, and Anna Green (2019), 'Family Memory, "Things" and Counterfactual Thinking', *Memory Studies* 12.6: 646–59, doi: 10.1177/1750698017714837.
Mandel, David R., Denis J. Hilton and Patrizia Catellani (2007), *The Psychology of Counterfactual Thinking*, Abingdon: Routledge.

Naficy, Hamid (2001), *An Accented Cinema: Exilic and Diasporic Filmmaking*, Princeton, NJ: Princeton University Press.
Nora, Pierre (2001), *Entre mémoire et histoire: Les lieux de mémoire*, 2nd edn, París: Gallimard.
Olick, Jeffrey (2018), 'The Horizons of Memory Studies: Roundtable Discussion', Memory Studies Association Conference 2017, http://www.memorystudies-association.org/copenhagen-conference-2017-program/#Intro_video (accessed 21 April 2023).
Popular Memory Group (2012), 'Popular Memory: Theory, Politics, Method', in *Making Histories: Studies in History-writing and Politics*, ed. Richard Johnson, Gregor McLennan, Bill Schwarz and David Sutton, Abingdon: Routledge, pp. 205–52.
Radstone, Susannah, and Bill Schwarz (eds) (2010), *Memory: Histories, Theories, Debates*, New York: Fordham University Press.
Rigney, Ann (2018), 'Remembering Hope: Transnational Activism beyond the Traumatic', *Memory Studies* 11.3: 368–80.
Roese, Neal J., and James M. Olson (2014), *What Might Have Been: The Social Psychology of Counterfactual Thinking*, New York: Psychology Press.
Rogan, Eugene L., and Avi Shlaim (eds) (2002), *The War for Palestine: Rewriting the History of 1948*, Cambridge: Cambridge University Press.
Said, Edward W. (2000), 'Invention, Memory, and Place', *Critical Inquiry* 26.2: 175–92.
Sanbar, Elias, Jean-Claude Pons, Farouk Mardam-Bey and Subhi Hadidi (1997), *Palestine, l'enjeu culturel*, Paris: Institut du Monde Arabe.
Schacter, Daniel L., and Michael Welker (2016), 'Memory and Connection: Remembering the Past and Imagining the Future in Individuals, Groups, and Cultures', *Memory Studies* 9.3: 241–4.
Tamm, Marek (2015), *Afterlife of Events: Perspectives on Mnemohistory*, London: Palgrave Macmillan.
Verovsek, Peter J. (2020), 'Memory, Narrative, and Rupture: The Power of the Past as a Resource for Political Change', *Memory Studies* 13.2: 208–22, doi: 10.1177/1750698017720256.
Young, James E. (2016), 'The Memorial's Arc: Between Berlin's Denkmal and New York City's 9/11 Memorial', *Memory Studies* 9.3: 325–31, doi: 10.1177/1750698016645266.

NOTES

1. Jacir repeats this technique in her other works. For example, *Like Twenty Impossibles* (2003) also opens with documentary footage shot at Kalandia checkpoint.
2. Counter-memory is a practice that counters the official accounts of memory and represents those memories that are excluded, suppressed or erased by the official, institutional accounts of history. For further reading, see Foucault (1977).
3. The term 'site of memory' was first introduced by Pierre Nora in *Les Lieux de mémoire*, a seven-volume work. Nora defines these sites as places where 'memory crystallizes and secretes itself' and must be defined in material, symbolic and

functional senses in varying degrees. An interplay of memory and history makes them into sites of memory. For further reading, see Nora (2001: 23–43).
4. The UN Relief and Works Agency reports that when it 'began operations in 1950, it was responding to the needs of about 750,000 Palestine refugees'. Today, their number has gone up to 'some 5 million'; 'one-third of these registered Palestine refugees, more than 1.5 million individuals, live in 58 recognized Palestine refugee camps in Jordan, Lebanon, the Syrian Arab Republic, the Gaza Strip and the West Bank, including East Jerusalem.' See United Nations Relief and Works Agency for Palestine Refugees in the near East, https://www.unrwa.org/palestine-refugees#:~:text=Nearly one-third of the,West Bank%2C including East Jerusalem (accessed 4 February 2021).
5. I quote this directly from a 20-second clip from the film, which is presumably taken from documentary footage. Jacir has not spoken about the origin of this clip in her interviews. Although this is, like many things in the Israel–Palestine conflict, contested, since this is documentary footage included in a fiction film, it could be seen in a fictional context while keeping in mind that Jacir has shared her use of documentary footage for her film.

CHAPTER 4

Transvergent Transnationalism: Borders, Homes and Humans

Iqra Shagufta Cheema

Despite being widely known as a Palestinian, internationalism characterises Jacir's life as well as her films. Experiences of exile and migration are foundational for the spatial, ontological and affective geographies of Jacir's characters: Soraya, in *Salt of this Sea*, is a Brooklyn-born Palestinian American, whose parents are Lebanon-born, and who returns to Palestine while Emad and Marwan, who live in Palestine, hopelessly seek to leave; Tarek and Ghayda, in *When I Saw You*, live in a refugee camp in Jordan, while fedayeen such as Layth train to reclaim their homeland, Palestine, but their plans for return are affected by transnational events and politics; and Shadi and his family in *Wajib* bring diasporic and resident experiences face-to-face to reveal sociopolitical anxieties and resulting interpersonal conflicts in Nazareth, the largest city in northern Israeli. Overall, Jacir's characters' ubiquitous and shared experiences of transnationalism are heterogeneous and diverse, both politically and personally. Because of the overwhelmingly exilic, diasporic and refugee experiences that underwrite these characters, Jacir's becomes a cinema of transvergent transnationalism. Transnationalism has been a debatable term since its early use in film studies. Mette Hjort rightfully critiqued its use as 'a largely self-evident qualifier requiring only minimal conceptual clarification' (2010: 13). Due to varying definitions and for the sake of conceptual clarity, we provide a brief overview of conversations about transnational cinema. Building on these conversations, we then propose the term transvergent transnationalism as a more suitable descriptor for Jacir's cinema.

CONCEPTUALISING TRANSVERGENT TRANSNATIONALISM

Krzysztof Loska credits Sheldon Hsiao-peng Lu and Andrew Higson for introducing transnational film studies as a category (Loska 2016: 1). Lu highlights the problematisation of the concepts of national cinema and nationhood against the backdrop of the 'globalization of mechanisms of film production, distribution, and consumption', focusing on Chinese transnational cinemas (1997: 3, 12).[1] Higson critiques cinema studies' proclivity to focus on films that portray nation as a 'finite, limited space, inhabited by a tightly coherent and unified community' (2000: 60). Despite this foundational observation, Higson's critique overlooks the exilic, diasporic, expatriate and postcolonial themes in transnationalism – themes that are of vital consideration in studying the increasingly expanding body of non-Western films.

Hamid Naficy's theorisation of accented cinema fills this gaping lacuna in transnational film studies. Naficy's accented cinema is simultaneously attentive to material (funding, production, distribution, reception), political (location, culture, religion, aesthetic) and personal (memory, desire, habits, affect) aspects of exilic, diasporic and postcolonial films and filmmakers. These films include 'open-form and closed-form visual style', and their subject matter and themes 'involve journeying, historicity, identity, and displacement; dysphoric, euphoric, nostalgic, synaesthetic, liminal, and politicized structures of feeling; interstitial and collective modes of production; and inscription of the biographical, social, and cinematic (dis)location of the filmmakers' (2001: 4).[2] Accented cinema, because of its primarily non-Western and inevitably political focus, is ultimately transnational, a term that Elizabeth Ezra and Terry Rowden further refine.

Ezra and Rowden define transnationalism as cross-national linkages between people and institutions that recognise 'the decline of national sovereignty as a regulatory force', 'dissolution of any stable connection' between a film's production location and the nationality of its crew and cast, and a shift in contemporary circulation of human, financial and epistemological sources motivated by neoliberal capitalist forces (Ezra and Rowden 2006: 1). Transnational cinema, then, includes both cultural globalisation and 'counterhegemonic' cinematic responses (Ezra and Rowden 2006: 1); it both 'transcends' and 'presupposes' the national (Ezra and Rowden 2006: 4); it is both local and global (Ezra and Rowden 2006: 40) because of its 'translocal understandings' (Vertovec and Cohen 1999: xviii); and 'digital distribution' works as a catalyst for it (Vertovec and Cohen 1999: 5). Transnational film is, then, a 'spectatorial object' with requisite 'epistemological and referential frameworks' that are increasingly devoid of any national and cultural specificities (Vertovec and Cohen 1999: 4).

Unarguably, Naficy's conceptualisation of accented cinema and Ezra and Rowden's of transnational cinema share discernible commonalities as manifested by similar terminological resonances in their diction. For example, both refer to audience expectation, spectatorial climate, resistive potential, political impact, mobility of commodities and capital, heterogeneity, fluidity, and its focus on interstitially, territoriality, rootedness and home, all of which is cathected by religious, cultural and national markers of subjecthood. While

Naficy's theorisation looks beyond Hollywood, Ezra and Rowden draw relatively more comparisons between Hollywood and transnational films. Similar terminological and theoretical references appear in other scholarly conversations about transnational cinema such as Kinder (1993), Crofts (1998), Marks (2000), Enwezor (2007), Higbee (2007), Bergfelder (2005), Bergfelder et al. (2007) and Durovičová and Newman (2010). Higbee and Lim propose a critical transnationalism that is discursive and generates a 'transnational, translingual dialogue' (2010: 18–19). Mette Hjort further categorises 'cinematic transnationalisms' by offering a typology: epiphanic, affinitive, milieu-building, opportunistic, cosmopolitan, globalising, auteuristic, modernising and experimental transnationalism (2010) – some of which we shall return to in succeeding sections of this chapter. In their individual speculations, Lim (2007) further stresses the connection between transnationalism and politics, whereas Higbee (2007), combining Marcos Novak's idea of transvergence with Deleuze and Guattari's idea of the rhizome, argues for a cinema of transvergence.

The concept of the cinema of transvergence serves to analyse films both on a global and local and a transnational and national level. It problematises and subverts the notions of nation and nation construction, and expresses a critical understanding of 'discontinuity, difference, and imbalances of power' among films and filmmakers and their 'interconnectedness' (Higbee 2007: 87). It assumes filmmakers' identity or location as fluid and serves as an 'interconnected (politicized) site of resistance' that 'foregrounds the experiences of the alienated, marginal other' (Higbee 2007: 87). Due to constantly shifting transnational relations and cinematic politics, these multiple definitions of transnational cinema remain contested. Hence in this chapter, we contend that relying on a singular concept or definition to study the variegated manifestations of transnational interactions and influences is disadvantageous. Therefore, reliance on any singular approach should be jettisoned in favour of a concept that honours the fluidity, heterogeneity, mobility, interstitiality and complexity of diasporic, exilic and immigrant cinemas, as well as acknowledging the political and material entanglement and ambivalence of these cinemas. While above-discussed concepts centralise these issues, they do not offer room for the convergence of conceptual multiplicities and future problematics related to transnationalism in films and film studies.

Therefore, we propose the term 'transvergent transnationalism' to attend to the fluid multiplicities of transnationalisms. Transvergent transnationalism, as a concept, first and foremost accommodates difference, multiplicity and fluidity between any people, ideas and/or commodities, while simultaneously acknowledging that affective, material, ideological and cultural problematics are inseparably intertwined. Cognisant of its own conceptual limitations, transvergent transnationalism offers room for fluidity and transitions that occur not only in transnationalism but also in people's transnational sensibilities and cinematic representation of these shifts. These concerns about transnationalism assume more importance when discussing Palestine and Palestinian cinema, where the issues of territoriality, mobility, rootedness and home are not only personal and political but almost existential. Through its interregional setting, funding sources, international distribution and authorial identity, Jacir's cinema is transnational on affective, material, cultural and political levels. Through her focus on Palestinian subjectivities, Jacir explores and portrays not only the question of the nation and nationhood but also issues of fundamental human rights and the various ways in which the Palestinian experience becomes an enabling or restrictive factor in obtaining these human rights to safety, security, privacy, respect and mobility transnationally. For a further exploration of the ways in which Jacir's cinema can be characterised as a cinema of transvergent transnationalism, an analysis of her feature films follows.

TRANSVERGENT BORDERS IN *SALT OF THIS SEA*

Salt of this Sea, starring Suheir Hammad and Saleh Bakri as Soraya and Emad, could be described as a collective affective manifestation of autochthonous, immigrant, exilic and diasporic Palestinians, all of whom share an affective affiliation with their homeland. *Salt of this Sea* was Bakri's debut Arab-language film. While Bakri has lived in Europe for brief periods (Barlow 2013), Hammad's life has been a combination of refugee, exilic and immigrant experiences. She was born in Amman, Jordan, to Palestinian refugee parents who later moved to New York. She inherited a reservoir of stories from her grandparents' life in Palestine, her parents' lives in Jordan, and then combined these stories with their experience as Palestinians in New York. Because of Hammad's activism and poetry, Gloria Steinem describes her as an 'embodiment of the global reach of feminism' (Nussbaum 2008). Along with Jacir's and her protagonists' transnational experiences, the film's shooting in Palestine itself invites attention to filmmaking, mobility and transnationalism.

Jacir prefers to hire local crew members to support local infrastructures (Lodderhose 2021), despite the challenges of mobility that this entails. In 2007, when *Salt of this Sea* was shot, Amnesty International reported '84 manned checkpoints and 465 unmanned blockades within the West Bank alone' (Woldt 2009). Lack of affordable film crew, unavailability of modern filming equipment, lack of funding and restricted mobility are only a few challenges faced by Palestinian filmmakers. The crew for *Salt of this Sea* comprised 'novices' who included a 'former ambulance driver, a jeweler and a radio DJ'. The film had 80 shooting locations – the greatest number of locations of any of Jacir's three feature films – so it was made possible mostly because of the determination of its crew and the support of local communities and police. The film crew needed permits to leave Ramallah, which were refused multiple times. The entanglement of people's lived experiences and cinematised film narrative becomes evident through Jacir's statement that 'in some cases we just filmed anyway. We put the actors in a real situation and we just did it guerrilla-style. That's how most Palestinian filmmakers are managing to do their work' (Woldt 2009). It comes as no surprise that Jacir thinks it's 'going too far to speak of a "national cinema" at this stage'. These challenges also explain some of the critique that the film received for its 'sermonizing', 'contrived' dialogue and scenarios, and underdeveloped characters (Farhat 2009; Buckwalter 2010). Despite these struggles, the film was an official selection at Cannes Film Festival 2008 and the Palestinian entry for the Best Foreign Language Oscar category (Mundell 2008), which evidences Jacir's mastery as a filmmaker.

The film contains multiple themes that invite speculation about transnationalism and its problematics; for example, its exploration of issues of mobility, familial and national belonging, and social and financial capital. The film is an exercise in transvergence because it operates at the intersections of multiple film genres, multiple languages, multiple colour schema, and fluid characters – converging many strands from cinematic transnationalism. The characters are constantly becoming, transitioning between hopeful immigrants, hopeless indigenous residents or exiles, travellers, workers, impostors, rebels, wanderers – all the while steered by what Hjort terms 'affinitive transnationalism' (2010: 17) based on their shared territorial, linguistic and sociopolitical affinities.

From its very beginning, the film explicitly delineates Palestinian history as it opens with a documentary scene of a standing wall that collapses as soon as

Figure 4.1 *Salt of this Sea*: Soraya, Emad and Marwan looking at the Al Aqsa in the distance after illegally crossing into Jerusalem. Credit: Philistine Films

the camera's eye falls upon it, thus anticipating the role of cinema in an exposition of Palestinian narrative. The collapse of this wall symbolises the collapse of stability and security that most humans find in a home and in their homeland. Houses are bombarded, bulldozed and razed. The first shot of human faces is from boats on a tumultuous sea, longingly looking at a receding skyline. People are not shown evacuating their houses, but already in the boats, marking the futility of any attempt at reclamation, return or resistance. The next shots of the sea against the backdrop of music signify people's temporal and geographical movement across territories. The close shot transitions from monochromatic to polychromatic seawater; this transition shows the progress of both time and cinematic equipment, symbolising not only the transnational lives of Palestinian exiles but also the advanced technological means of bringing their narratives and history to transnational audiences. This initial, albeit forced, movement of people and seawater foreshadows the trope of constant movement in the film. The film could be described as an exploration of mobility and its discontents. This mobility is the *raison d'être* of transvergent transnationalism. Below, we further explore this concept via a close reading of a few scenes from the film.

Soraya is interrogated and frisked by the airport personnel, who ask a series of repetitive questions about her grandparents' and parents' lives and their professions, her religion, the purpose of her visit, and her accommodation in Ramallah. In this scene, both the film's audience and Soraya witness the reality in contrast with Soraya's idealised version of Palestine. She informs the security officers that her grandparents were from Jaffa, that her parents lived in Lebanon, and that she was born in Brooklyn. When she tells the security officer that her grandparents were 'from here', he rhetorically asks: 'In Israel? From where?' to remind her that the Palestine her grandparents left doesn't exist any more. To claim her relationship to Palestine, Soraya tells the second officer: 'Here, [my grandfather] was born here.' But the officer refuses to acknowledge this relationship by asking 'here, where?' He not only rejects Soraya's relationship with Palestine, but also dismisses and undermines her identity by rhetorically asking 'What kind of a name is [Soraya]?' Despite her ancestral connection to Palestine, it is her connection to America that makes her admissible. This interrogation, despite the officers' recurring facetious assurances that the questions are for Soraya's safety, is employed as a rhetorical tool to dismiss and question her right to visit Palestine. The third officer's investigation turns the whole affair into an outright humiliation. They ask her to 'spread [her] legs' and take off her trousers and her bra, in the presence of the male security officer. The audience does not see Soraya's face when she strips. She disappears as a human being and is reduced to a symbolic Palestinian body to be invaded.

After this thorough body search, the female officer invades Soraya's suitcase and scans various items, ranging from her underwear to a book. Soraya's suitcase carries her specific identity and serves as 'a contradictory and multi-layered key symbol of [Soraya's] exilic subjectivity: it contains souvenirs from the homeland; it connotes wanderlust, freedom to roam, and a provisional life; it symbolizes profound deprivation and diminution of one's possibilities in the world' (Naficy 2001: 261). Through the body search, dismissive and invasive questions, and the scanning of her personal belongings, the security officers not only strip Soraya of her idealised construction of the homeland but also of her dignity as a human being. Some variation of these invasive incidents occurs every time Soraya and Emad try to cross any geographical, religious or linguistic borders. But gradually, she also realises her border-crossing privileges as an American.

It is largely due to her American passport that she is allowed to enter Palestine. She employs her Americanness in order to cross borders in the film multiple times. When she enters Palestine, it is as barricaded and restricted as the airport was. These borders are 'increasingly deterritorialized and reterritorialized in transit spaces' such as airports, seaports, checkpoints and barricades that 'function as strategic nodes within our transnational network of control' (Bayraktar 2016: 3) or 'empirical border places' (Naficy 2001: 238). Depending on one's possession of documents and conditions of departure from the homeland, these borders invoke 'intense emotions' such as 'fearful escapes, tearful departures, sudden entrapments, devastating rejections, joyful arrivals, and euphoric sense of liberation' (Naficy 2001: 238). Soraya and Emad cross these borders when going into Jaffa to visit her grandfather's house, riding in Emad's car at night in Ramallah, staying in the national park in Dawayima, and shopping in Jaffa. These border-crossings are 'cathected with affect', and serve as 'portals to other places and times' (Naficy 2001: 238). While Emad remains vulnerable and entrapped throughout these border-crossings, Soraya's sociopolitical capital – her proficiency in English, her American passport, her ability to pass as Jewish – afford her the freedom and agency that is unavailable to Emad, Marwan and other residents of the West Bank.

Soraya 'visits Ramallah with two projects in mind: to recuperate the money her grandfather left in his bank account when he was expelled from Haifa in 1948 and to establish her Palestinian citizenship' (Armes 2015: 277). But as soon as she enters, she is 'essentially marginalized in occupied Palestine' (Armes 2015: 277). Soraya faces challenges when she admits her Palestinian identity, but Emad is humiliated and dehumanised everywhere. To exemplify this, we can compare two instances of passing through checkpoints: first when Soraya and Emad are driving in Ramallah at night, and second when they drive into Jaffa after their bank heist. In the first instance, Emad's car is stopped at a security checkpoint. Under the patrol car's headlights, his face is partially invisible when the Israeli soldier orders them to get out of the car. Emad and

Soraya step out and walk towards the officer slowly. The officer orders them first to raise their hands and then take off their shirts. Emad responds: 'She is a woman', upon which the officer tells him to take off his shirt. Emad complies. Soraya only becomes visible to the camera after Emad raises his hands because, as a young Palestinian man, he is ultimately the bigger territorial and security threat. The Israeli officer now orders Emad to pull his trousers down; before lowering his trousers, Emad turns to a bewildered Soraya and says: 'Don't worry, this is normal.' After the officer waves at him to go, Emad returns to the car, while an incredulous Soraya stands in indignation and disbelief for a few seconds. This affectively charged incident takes place within the span of a few seconds on camera but summarises a historically long complex of experiences.

In this scene, Soraya is reduced to a witness of Emad's humiliation. Most of this episode occurs on the affective plane. Emad's face remains partially or completely invisible throughout this scene, while the complex of Soraya's emotions at this horrific treatment is frequently visible. The film's audience and the characters never see the security officer; the interaction takes place on an auditory sensory plane where Emad and Soraya just hear the reverberation of commands from the loudspeaker, which renders the sound almost (non/in)human. In the darkness, the patrol car's headlights appear like a preying animal's eyes. The Israeli security officer has the authority to make Soraya and Emad visible through his headlights on an otherwise dark road. This authority to endow visibility and identity on Palestinians or acknowledge their rights recurs throughout the film.

Soraya experiences the disadvantages of her Palestinian identity and quickly adapts – she starts passing as a Jewish and/or American woman, which makes navigating life in Palestine and the Occupied Territories instantly smoother. Soraya, as a Palestinian, is refused services or accommodation. She is denied a Palestinian passport or residential identity card based on her parents' birth in Palestine. The Palestinian officer inquires if she has family from the West Bank or Gaza. When Soraya says that her family is from Jaffa, he rhetorically comments: 'Where are you from?' – turning places such as Jaffa into non-places. She incredulously asks: 'So you agree that they decide if I am Palestinian or not?' The officer confirms: 'I'm afraid that's the case on paper.' While the Israeli state refuses to acknowledge her Palestinian identity, the citizenship laws become increasingly lax for both practising and non-practising Jews who want to reside in Israel.

Palestinian identity appears in the film as a facilitative tool to be used or discarded as convenient. Soraya was subjected to interrogation because of her ancestors' links to Jaffa, but the state will not officially acknowledge those links in the form of a passport or identity card. Hence, she is denied the material tools and official documents required for a legal Palestinian identity. But her American identity grants her access to the spaces and services that Emad is denied as a Palestinian. Soraya was stripped at the airport because of her ancestral connections to Palestine, Emad goes through the same treatment because he himself is a Palestinian. Soraya claims her right to America multiple times by merely speaking English or saying that she is from Brooklyn, mostly without even having to prove it by showing her American passport or a valid visa. Out of necessity and convenience, she consistently switches between her Palestinian and American identities. This arbitrariness and absurdity become visible when Soraya and Emad cross into Jaffa after claiming her grandfather's money from the Ramallah branch of the Palestinian British Bank at gunpoint.

Soraya, Emad and Marwan employ a combination of Jewish and American religious and cultural signifiers to cajole Israeli security guards to let them cross into Jaffa. While previous scenes of border-crossing were aggressive and rapid, this scene is contemplative and slow as if everyone is safe and calm at the checkpoint. They change their car's numberplate to an Israeli one. As their car creeps up to the checkpoint, Emad and Marwan put kippahs on their heads; Emad also changes into a graphic T-shirt. Soraya covers her head with a mitpahat and hangs a star of David on the rearview mirror. While they wait in the queue of vehicles being searched, a Jewish woman confidently drives through the checkpoint. She smiles at Soraya when driving past their car. More than being a mere contraction of muscles, her smile is an expression of her cognitive awareness of access to safety and freedom of mobility. Upon noticing her drive through the security check without any questions, Emad directs Marwan to change lane and follow her car. These few seconds in the film are moments of heightened anxiety for both the audience and the characters. As the car approaches, a security officer saunters in front of them, crossing over to the other side, and inquisitively looking at their car. Emad greets him and says 'Shalom' while Soraya smiles and says 'Hey' in a distinctly American accent – the camera brings into focus Emad's T-shirt which reads, 'America, don't worry.' It turns out that they didn't need to worry as the security guard waves them through security. They employ language and appearance to accentuate or hide features of their identity to cross the border. On the opposite side of the road, young Palestinians squat in a queue as a punishment. As soon as they cross into Jaffa, they are euphoric with a childlike joy and overcome the 'crippling sorrow of estrangement' (Said 1990: 357) from the homeland. This scene manifests the markers of religious, cultural and political identity as arbitrary and manipulable to highlight the problematics of official procedures for establishing identities and nationalities.

These three incidents of mobility and border-crossing – Soraya's entry into Palestine, Soraya and Emad driving in Ramallah, and Soraya, Emad and Marwan entering Jaffa – reflect transnational, transcultural, translingual and transreligious sociopolitics. The impact of these scenes is heightened by their duration. The first scene of border-crossing in Ramallah is 1 minute 15 seconds long, but the second scene from Ramallah to Jaffa is three minutes long – almost three times longer than the first but more minimal in action and motion. The first scene is textured with both emotional and physical intensity and violation. In this case, Soraya and Emad are the people 'whom [religious and sociopolitical] capital circulates' across borders (Slavoj Žižek, cited in Ezra and Rowden 2006: 8). Their ability to show possession of the right linguistic, religious and cultural capital turns them into desirable subjects for this border-crossing. While these various borders 'continue to be heavily policed and entry often comes with a price tag', Soraya gets the price tag waived because she 'possesses the right papers' and cultural capital (Higbee and Lim 2010: 17). By contrast, she fails to retrieve her grandfather's money despite possessing the pre-Nakba financial documents. To claim material possessions or territorial rights, one does not only need capital – one needs the right kind of capital, capital that has currency, recognition and acknowledgement. In this case, Soraya's US citizenship and her linguistic and religious performance serve as the right kind of capital – an American passport, an American accent and an American outlook.

After entering Jaffa, Soraya mobilises this transcultural and transnational capital to save Emad, who is more vulnerable to state violence. Emad, with little exposure to the world outside Palestine, is unable to consistently perform a different national or religio-cultural identity convincingly. Even with an expired visa, Soraya has more freedom and power than Emad because her capital is unquestioningly accepted. Emad can explore Jaffa and Dawayima only because Soraya employs her capital to save him. When they go into a restaurant, even the server recognises Emad as an illegal presence. He asks Emad if he is from Ramallah. Emad assures him that he is from Jerusalem; upon which, the server comments, 'We're both in the same boat, I'm illegal too.' Soraya smiles, Emad doesn't. This smile is similar to the Jewish woman's smile when Emad and Soraya crossed the border into Jaffa. That woman's religio-political identity helps her conveniently navigate the border that was dangerous for Emad and Soraya. In Jaffa, Soraya has the resources to perform a Jewish American identity, which affords her safety and mobility but leaves Emad vulnerable. Another more multilayered example of religio-cultural passing is Soraya and Emad's stay in the national park in Dawayima that we discussed previously. The Jewish professor is perceptibly friendlier when he learns that Soraya is a Jewish woman from Brooklyn. He calls to his students, 'Guys, come and meet someone from Brooklyn. Come on, move quickly.' The professor's different reactions towards the presence of Palestinians, Americans or Jewish Americans in the national park reflect the various ways in which transnational sociopolitical and linguistic capital is mobilised and received.

The film's examination of belonging and mobility inside and outside the homeland is further complicated via the genders of its protagonists. Soraya's sociolinguistic capital serves to protect both her and Emad. But Emad feels emasculated by her willingness and ability to protect him. He also envies her

American nationality as he asks her, 'If you had a baby, would he get an American passport?' Soraya, as an American, can afford to take risks when border-crossing but she fails to consider the impact of her choices on Emad's life. Her transnational capital enables her to access her ancestral home, the sites of her grandfather's memories, and to journey to the places that are inaccessible even to indigenous residents such as Emad.

Journeys serve a means of transnational or trans-communal border-crossing both for people and commodities, and are an important part of Jacir's films. Starting on a journey assumes that a person has physical or intellectual ability and spatial access to one point and can move on to the next point. While these journeys are quick and fuss-free for monetary capital, they are cumbersome and complicated for humans and sometimes for commodities. Transvergent transnationalism encompasses these journeys and their complexity. These can be journeys of seeking, escaping or founding a home, or of homecoming, homelessness, lostness or quest. These journeys shift and alter as do their goals. But the people on these journeys do not always have the agency to make decisions about their nature and direction. For example, Soraya's entry into Palestine was a homecoming for her, but eventually she turns it into a tourist's journey. The United Nations High Commissioner for Refugees encourages repatriation in the face of threats in the home country. Despite these threats, a 'growing number of refugees [choose to return] home before conditions are safe for them to do so' (Ghosn et al. 2021: 982), which means that a lot of these journeys of repatriation or exile are about the 'human desire for traveling and homing' (Naficy 2001: 237). But the choice to come home is not available to everybody. Both *Salt of this Sea* and *Wajib* are films that centre around journeys: these journeys are complicated, multifarious, and in a state of flux where various identities or various intentions consistently transverge. More than being a movement towards some ultimate goal, the journeys in these films are an evaluation of multiple emergent possibilities. Overall, these are films of journeys, as they contain sites, means and meanings of journeys as well as journeying identities.

GENERATIONAL AND TRANSNATIONAL CONFLICTS IN *WAJIB*

Wajib employs a car journey to foreshadow the various journeys that the film uncovers. The car serves as a vehicle to gradually explore Nazareth as well as the grounds of familial and communal relationships. *Wajib* delves into politics more subtly because religio-politics affects Shadi and Abu Shadi in less explicit ways than the characters in Jacir's other films. Abu Shadi, who is a respected schoolteacher, sends Shadi to Italy because of the Israeli state's interference in his teaching, and an increasingly bitter Shadi has been living there since. In

Italy, Shadi renegotiates his identity into a complex of Palestinian and European influences, which is unpalatable to his father. Hence, the film portrays a conflict between parental expectations and migrant aspirations, and the resultant tension that the migrant youth must navigate.

Abu Shadi disapproves of Shadi's fashion choices as well as his career choices. He mocks Shadi's floral shirt, his pink trousers and his manbun. He also appears to have lied to his family and his friends about Shadi's profession and his country of residence, which creates a comedic confusion in the film. This misinformation symbolises the larger political and cultural differences between Abu Shadi and Shadi. Abu Shadi tells his friend Abbu Issa's family that Shadi is studying medicine in America. Contrary to their belief, Shadi is an architect in Italy. They believe Shadi to be single, though he lives with his girlfriend. Shadi disapproves of people's practical but aesthetically unpleasing architectural choices in Nazareth. He dislikes people's judgement of his mother for divorcing his father and remarrying. In its portrayal of the father–son relationship and extended family dynamic, the film is universally relatable, as it contains brief moments of comedy, warmth, sacrifice, tragedy and heartbreak. But it sets these transcultural human emotions and experiences in the specific Nazareth context at the intersection of an impending Christmas and Amal's wedding.

Figure 4.2 *Wajib*: Shadi and Abu Shadi accompany Amal to try on wedding dresses and to inform her that her mother won't be attending her wedding. Credit: Philistine Films

Shadi comes to Nazareth to perform his duty of distributing his sister Amal's wedding invitations. But on the pretext of this rather small act of duty, the film engages with the larger, collective conceptualisations of duty. What is a young migrant's duty to his family? To his city? To his compatriots? To his nation? To his religion? To his ancestral cultural traditions? To his national traditions? To the world at large? Jacir pushes the audience to examine these questions as she puts her characters' relationships with each other and with their communities under stress to show that human coexistence is possible because they are willing to perform their duties to each other despite borders. The film contains various incidents of familial, communal and national duties: Shadi and Abu Shadi witness men carrying a dead body to the graveyard, Abu Shadi intervenes in a street brawl and gets hurt, Shadi fixes the WiFi for an older family member when visiting her house. Shadi, despite living in Italy, still has emotional attachments, aesthetic visions and political aspirations for his homeland, but that is not enough for his father, who traces disloyalty even in Shadi's smallest choices such as sporting a manbun and wearing a floral shirt.

During Shadi and Abu Shadi's arguments, it becomes clear that Shadi has built a Palestinian community in Italy, but that Abu Shadi disapproves of this community. Despite Shadi's dutifulness, Abu Shadi perceives him as a traitor who has forgotten his roots – a tension that migrants consistently navigate. Abu Shadi taunts him about his girlfriend Nada's father: 'I don't want to go to Europe and wear fancy shirts and sit in the parlour with Nada and her daddy, talking about the liberation of Palestine. What's this Palestine you keep talking about? Where is it? I'm living it here.' But Shadi carries bitterness and anger towards the Israeli state for mistreating Abu Shadi in Nazareth. 'It's forbidden even to mention our own history. Forbidden to think. I grew up watching you beg them to recognize you, asking permission to exist, permission to breathe. You learned their language better than them, but you're invisible to them. Fuck this life.' Abu Shadi explains his reasons: 'I had a family to raise, you've no idea what I had to do to make sure you had a nice life. God damn you, boy.' While Arabic-speaking Muslim and Christian families and communities struggle to survive under political surveillance and financial strains, the migrants are viewed as disloyal to the homeland.

Abu Shadi considers both Nada's father and Shadi to be traitors, while Shadi views Palestinian residents as cowards; both believe that the other failed in performing their duties to their communities and to the country. Migrant and diaspora populations are never fully at home in their country of residence since the idea of home carries an irreplaceable sense of comfort for them. Despite their transnational locations, they carry idealised conceptions of the homeland. Abu Shadi is disillusioned with the Palestinian cause. Shadi, though politically sensitive and hostile to surveillance, is an idealist. Nada's father is a romantic nationalist who has preserved his memories of the homeland. He calls Shadi while he is driving in Nazareth with Abu Shadi, and asks to speak with his father:

> Nada's father: Nazareth, the homeland.
> Abu Shadi: Our homeland? It's beautiful . . . we hope to welcome you here. Nothing more beautiful than Palestine.

He asks Abu Shadi what he sees as they pull up in front of a Christmas shop:

> Abu Shadi: What do I see now? Orange trees and vineyards. Mountains. Mountain precipices. It's beautiful, very green this time of the year [as the camera shows a shabby house and a pile of rubbish in front of it], nothing more beautiful than the sea and fishing.

Nada's father, in this conversation, invokes stereotypical representations or referents such as oranges, vineyards and mountains – a view that mostly exists in the romantic imaginary. In this scene these referents are not visible, and Abu Shadi recalls them from memory just like Nada's father. These imaginary images also invoke sensory feelings that activate 'private memories and intensif[y] the feeling of displacement, a feeling that one may have suppressed in order to get on with life' (Naficy 2001: 28). The displaced subject, in response to their displacement, 'creates a utopian prelapsarian chronotope of the homeland that is uncontaminated by contemporary facts' and that includes open chronotopes of the homeland such as landscape and mountains and 'certain privileged renditions of house and home' (Naficy 2001: 152) – thus constituting a contradiction between the memorialised images and the lived images of the homeland.

This tragi-comic contradiction is clear both to the audience and to Shadi and Abu Shadi as they all stare at the urban garbage in front of them. This contradiction between the romantic images and lived realities of the homeland results from the perceptive ruptures caused by exile and the impossibility of a return to the lost past. Displacement, the displaced subject and the lost homeland carry different relationships according to the exilic, diasporic and postcolonial experiences and subjectivities of the experiencing subjects. They constantly reminisce about the homeland and carry the 'dream of a glorious homecoming' (Naficy 2001: 229). Shadi and Nada's father, as diasporic subjects, have 'horizontal and multisited' relationships that involve 'not only the homeland but also the compatriot communities elsewhere' (Naficy 2001: 229).[3] Abu Shadi and other residents in Nazareth struggle with financial pressures and freedom of expression, and mourn the loss of family members who leave the country, like Shadi's mother and Shadi. But the options for emigration are determined by material, political, legal, national and international factors more than the personal choices for both the residents and early exilic or diasporic subjects.

This desire to leave is markedly different across generations. Primarily young people harbour the desire to leave the homeland or visit other places: Emad in *Salt of this Sea* applies for a Canadian study visa four times; Fadya, who is a lawyer in Nazareth, dreams of visiting Italy; and Noura is utterly bored with her life in Nazareth. Noura's life is so dull that she risks her reputation and tries to hook up with Shadi. When she opens the door of her dark house and sees Shadi, her lips break into a smile. She invites Shadi into the dimly lit room with its closed curtains. She is alone at home and doesn't have much to share about her life other than how bored she is. She gradually inches closer to him as Shadi and the camera both unsteadily move away:

> Noura: Do you like living abroad? Nazareth is so boring.
> Shadi: What do you do?
> Noura: Who cares? It's boring.
> Shadi: Can't be that boring.
> Noura: Everything is boring.

Eventually, Noura pushes Shadi on to the couch and attempts to kiss him. He gets a rash on his lip from this interaction, though the audience never sees him leaving the apartment. By contrast, when Shadi and Amal meet Fadya, they are all jubilant and cheerful. They break into a dance to celebrate Amal's upcoming wedding. Shadi's interactions with Noura and Fadya show that Noura is bored with her life due to the lack of purpose, access and recreational activities, whereas Fadya is discontent with her location. Fadya and Amal receive cultural remittances that add transnational possibilities and perspectives to their lives.

Transnational migrants, people who simultaneously belong to two societies, often transfer social remittances to their homelands. These social remittances can be 'normative structures, system of practice, and social capital' (Levitt 2001: 59). These remittances are disseminated via 'identifiable pathways' when a migrant shares their experiences with a family member or speaks of a 'different kind of politics', and are then exchanged between people who share 'mutual social ties'. Their impact depends upon 'the gender, class, and life-cycle stage of the receiver' (Levitt 2001: 63–4). Fadya is part of the group that receives these transnational social remittances, as is clear from her conversation with Shadi. Her sister Dana also lives abroad and is 'never moving back [to Nazareth]. She has a good job, a good life, her family.' Neither Fadya nor Noura has any romantic companion in their lives. Abu Shadi laments Shadi's and Fadya's romantic lives. He comments that Fadya and her ex-boyfriend 'moved to Haifa together. They didn't marry. Everybody knew about it. She lived with him.

Then they broke up. That was it for her. That's how people think here'; he goes on to say that 'the guy got married, has three kids'. He subtly suggests that Shadi should marry her and laments that is it 'too bad cousins don't marry any more'. But marriage is not Fadya's concern as she never speaks of romance or marriage in her conversation with Shadi.

Though her life is informed by transnational practices as well as transnational possibilities, she expresses her disappointment with the limitations of life in Nazareth and dreams of visiting Europe:

Fadya: Families fighting over inheritance. Divorces. Parents kidnapping their own kids. The usual. How's Italy? Amazing, right?
Shadi: Amazing. You should visit.
Fadya: Really?
Shadi: It's an open museum.
Fadya: I want to see the Sistine chapel and the colosseum.
Shadi: . . . and the Pantheon, Piazza Navona. We'll go to the Spanish Steps and watch the world go by . . .
Fadya: . . . and make a wish in Trevi fountain . . .
Shadi: . . . dinner in Trastevere. Cacio o pepe . . .
Fadya: . . . red wine . . .
Shadi: . . . incredible wines. Cheaper than water.
Fadya: Oh my God.

As Fadya and Shadi finish each other's sentences in a song-like, dream-like rhythm, sharing the transnational dreams of their youthful hearts, Abu Shadi intervenes: 'Tell Shadi about your friends in the North who make wine', and reinstates the conversation in the local, national context.

These transnational aesthetic influences also recur in Shadi's comments on the urban infrastructure and exterior design choices of homes in Nazareth. He repeatedly expresses his disapproval of the plastic tarp that is used to cover roofs, walls and other spaces in Nazareth. Abu Shadi tells him that the tarp is 'practical', but Shadi comments, 'it is shit' as he walks out of the scene, a cinematic equivalent of angrily stomping out. Shadi expresses his exasperation: 'We live in one of the most ancient cities. Everybody puts tarp and plastic chairs everywhere. There's no taste? People have no sense of aesthetics.' Shadi, like Nada's father, also desires an image of Nazareth that does not exist. His aesthetic sensibilities perceive European architecture as the standard, which makes infrastructure architectural choices in Nazareth appear inferior to him. These contradictory idealised images of the homeland abound in the migrant imagination.

The film heightens this contradiction by positing dichotomies of closed versus open form, closed versus open spaces, wide roads versus narrow streets, sunlight versus dimly lit houses, old versus young people, romantic national idealism versus lived realism, and national versus transnational. These contradictions also highlight the diversity of lives in Nazareth, despite the limitations of mobility and the surveillance of the state. These desires and limitations are also determined by transnational politics and experiences. Nada cannot visit Palestine because she does not have a European passport yet, and she is not allowed entry on her Palestinian passport. Fadya, upon learning this, comments, 'We have to become European to visit our homeland.' This forced or opted rootedness of people in domestic or national locations poses a contrast to Shadi and Abu Shadi's mobile car and the progression of their conversation. This (im)possibility of transnational (im)mobility reflects the affective, communal and national violence that Nada and her father, Soraya's family, and Tarek and Ghayda embody in their rooted bodies which are not allowed to cross transnational borders.

DREAMS OF RETURN TO THE HOME/HOMELAND IN *WHEN I SAW YOU*

While *Salt of this Sea* and *Wajib* could be described as films of journeys, *When I Saw You* is a *bildungsroman* of locational rootedness of bodies that are otherwise determined and affected by transnational events, histories and cultures. This rootedness or immobility is reflected in the film's structure and narrative: it is slower paced, almost static since both the characters and audience remain in a perpetual state of anticipation for some life-altering event, which never take place – even the closing scene of the film leaves both the audience and the characters wondering about Ghayda and Tarek's location. A feeling of nostalgia is foregrounded in the characters, cinematography and dialogue; this nostalgia freezes characters' affective consciousness in the past when they left their homes and their loves ones. But simultaneously, they appear to have made peace with their refugee or exilic condition because, as one character points out, they have been living in that condition for decades. They have formed new friends and families both in the refugee camp and on the fedayeen training site in Jordan. They live between a stable house in the past and a hopefully temporary house in the present, thereby emotionally living on the border between hopefulness and hopelessness, on the border between a dynamic future and a frozen past. While the adults appear to have created a semblance of normalcy and routine, the traumatic shock of this eviction from home and the homeland manifests most visibly in younger characters, especially Tarek.

Salt of this Sea and *Wajib* focus on the homeland as a transnationally complex, affective site. Conversely, *When I Saw You* complicates both the home and the homeland as interdependent and interrelated – thereby capturing both the home and homeland as sites of affective, material, political, financial and cultural complexity and settler violence. Desire for a home, which coincides and/or alternates with the desire for a homeland and a return to it, remains the central motivation for the film's plot and characters. The adults and Tarek have distinct conceptions of the home and homeland, a pertinent distinction in the film. Tarek only remembers and desires a return to his home. On the contrary, Ghayda and the fedayeen desire to return to the homeland. This distinction obscures the affective perception of time in different age groups. When Tarek learns from an older woman in the group that she's been in the refugee camp for twenty years, he is incredulous. '1300 days?', he exclaims. 'Twenty years, these are 175,320 hours.' This realisation of the passage of time breaks the frozen moment in the past and he decides to cross the border into Palestine to find his home, instead of waiting for his father in the refugee camp in Jordan.

Tarek's attempt at border-crossing signals a cognitive and perceptive border-crossing. Despite his intelligence and mathematical competence, he had not registered the length of the refugees' stay in the camp since they are not connected to the outside world except for a radio, a tiny TV, and the incoming truck carrying more refugees and aid. Tarek's decisive moment arrives when his memories of his home, the world outside the refugee camp, start to slip away from him. Exasperated, he asks Ghayda, 'Where is our house? Which direction did we come from? . . . I don't know where our house is, I can't remember.' This loss of the memorialised route to the home is tantamount to the loss of the home itself as it solidifies the fear of no return. But Ghayda reminds him, and in the process reminds herself, of the location of their home: 'Remember that trip he took us on? Remember? Remember what he showed you? The stick. How the sun makes the shadow? Remember what he told you? The direction of the sun. That's where our home is.' Since the sun changes its direction and transcends borders and boundaries, Ghayda actually dislocates home and transposes it into a borderless temporal location.

But instead of portraying this as a perceptual rupture, the film converts it into a constructively determinative moment. Tarek leaves to go home in the direction of the sun but ends up at the fedayeen base, where his sense of self, companionship and family are all transformed – and resolved to an extent. The film replaces home with a sense of feeling at home: Tarek joins the fedayeen in their training, he dances with them, he becomes useful. His journey to his home in the homeland converts into a journey of self-discovery and adulthood. He confronts the various images of refugees in the host country during this journey of return to the home. An older woman recognises him as a child refugee and hands him a pomegranate to satiate his hunger. But then a group of stranded young people in Western clothes stops Tarek. Their car has broken down so they need help. Tarek first appears as a guide for the group since they need him to help them get out of there. But as soon as they learn he is a refugee, he is reduced to a vilified and useless entity to be signified upon. They comment, 'Look at how he speaks', 'Are you a refugee? He is a refugee', 'Do you want him to bring camp boys here?' and then they command him to leave: 'Please get out of here. Move it, what are you waiting for.' The only man in the group threatens the girl, 'I'll leave you with the camp boys tonight.' This vilification and criminalisation of a refugee child shapes both Tarek and the film's audience, since this antagonistic behaviour towards refugees remains prevalent transnationally. Tarek does not find his father, but he finds guides and models who teach him not only how to fight, but also how to live with his male body. In living with the fedayeen, he lives with both soft and difficult emotions. He sings, paints, dances and fights. Tarek, who previously constantly talked about his father, only mentions him when Ghayda, his mother, flirts with Layth, a fedayee. Despite his failure to cross transnational borders, he learns to navigate complex gendered and affective borders.

Though the film contains fewer explicitly transnational signifiers and elements, it is in some ways more transnational than *Salt of this Sea* and *Wajib*. The refugee experience bypasses the normative and privileged means of borders-crossing such as immigrant, study and visit visas. International communities and organisations help provide the necessities of life for refugees both in the camps and outside them. Despite this help, the refugee experience undermines human dignity, as refugees await aid, food and a chance at an agential life. Their future depends upon the international community and its support and intervention. The UN Relief and Works Agency reports that there are 5.8 million Palestinian refugees among the world's 26.6 million refugee population.[4] More than half of these refugees live in Jordan, with the rest in Syria, Lebanon, the West Bank, the Gaza strip and the rest of the world. While *Salt of this Sea* is charged with hostile confrontations or the possibility and anticipation of violence, *When I Saw You* rarely captures this visceral violence despite its constant anticipation. In the first half of the film, the audience and even the characters only witness the consequences of violence on different Palestinian generations. Both the audience and the characters anticipate the possible elimination of threats of violence and await the realisation of a peaceful return to the homeland, which is depicted through memorialised images and distant national scenery.

These natural elements are employed as 'powerfully cathected collective chronotopes that condense the entire idea of nation' (Naficy 2001: 160; Bakhtin 1981). The lack of access to what lies beyond the border is also made with visible in the long, panoramic, idyllic shots of the land, mountains, trees and valleys. Mountains, particularly when the 'nation's status is in dispute', signify not 'as a barrier but as a bridge that consolidates the national idea and heals the ruptures of exile' (Naficy 2001: 160). This film encapsulates the loss of the past, the stagnation of the present, and the uncertainty of the future in its focus on nature and natural reminders of the sovereignty and peace of the nation with which the characters associate themselves. This idyllic memory is also invoked in the songs that are sung in the fedayeen base:

> Long time ago, there was a house and a garden
> A garden full of colours, white jasmines and gardenias too
> Rid of poppies and pomegranate
> Green, pure of cactus and fig
> A paradise full of song
> Suddenly, I don't know how, wheat stalks, in their longing, bend
> Wait, O night, wait, don't go
> Once daylight comes, wounds will show
> A paradise full of songs
> Never once does the night last

Exilic or refugee subjects take emotional and physical refuge in this 'idyllic chronotope' (Bakhtin 1981: 225) and in the 'structural authority and certainty' that only nature can provide them in the refugee camp (Naficy 2001: 156). Nature serves not only as a reminder of the home lost in the homeland but also as a comforter in the present home in Jordan, since both the homeland and the host country share many signifiers. Simultaneously, the idyllic chronotope strengthens the possibility of return from the host country to the home country.

This nostalgia for the lost homeland and the return to it occurs in various affective, artistic, personal and collective forms, but the desire for the home emerges as the instigator to enliven the hope of a larger change: the hope for freedom not only from the settlers but also from transnational forms of oppression. The fight for the homeland and the fedayeen devotion to freedom is inspired by international political histories: the fedayeen and Abu Akram discuss class struggle, feudalism and freedom. They sing songs: 'From Acre's prison came the funerals of Mohammad Jamjoun and Fuad Hijazi, / And for the life of my people, avenge the High Commissioner and his accomplices', invoking global complicity in the atrocities committed against them. Fedayeen are romantic young revolutionaries: handsome, long-haired young men who are poets, singers, artists, musicians and readers. The power of resistance resides in their youth and their idealism. Abu Akram affirms this when talking to Tarek: 'the basic clay of our work is the youth'. They talk about home and the return, but ultimately the goal appears to be to keep the hope of the return, instead of the return itself, alive.

Stagnation and the romanticisation of the fedayeen life and cause is multilayered. Tarek and the fedayeen look at the homeland from afar. This visual connection makes it appear physically reachable, which is why Tarek, who is less familiar with the complexity of his refugee experience, attempts to reach

Figure 4.3 *When I Saw You*: The fedayeen commander, Abu Akram, trains fedayeen while Tarek assists him in keeping count of their sets of crunches. Credit: Philistine Films

home multiple times in the film. But for others, 'the desired return is postponed not out of anxiety about its possible disappointing outcome but because of timing, which may lead to a long-lasting deferral that further intensifies the desire for return' (Naficy 2001: 236). Sometimes for refugees or exiles, 'return is impossible, making a metaphoric, imaginative, or filmic staging of it a viable option' (Naficy 2001: 236). Fedayeen songs and their imaginative and narrative recollections of the past serve as this alternative staging, this alternative form of return to the homeland. The need for these alternative imaginaries arises from their nomadic lives and temporary homes, which exist at the fringes of both the homeland and the host country.

This necessary perception of their life as nomads helps safeguard them from the further trauma of sudden evictions or expulsions from the homes and families they have created in exile. The arbitrariness and fragility of their situation surfaces when Layth tells Ghayda and Tarek to pack their tent at midnight and erase all signs of their existence within minutes and restore the innocence of the land. After an inestimable time, the threat disappears and the fedayeen life is restored amid mountains and trees. Mountains, in this scene, emerge as the fatherly place of safety and trees as the motherly place of secrecy, completing the home in the host country.

While Jordan remains the main site of their physical location, they are informed upon and informed by various direct and indirect transnational structures. Their shoes are made in Belgium and China. Even though they can't access most of the blessings of neoliberal globalisation, their lives are deeply affected by it. The news that they receive in the refugee camp, the news that they hear on the radio during the peace talks between Israel and Palestine, the arms that the fedayeen use for their fight, and the training shoes that they wear – all are made in other countries. When Tarek and the fedayeen open a box of guns, one of them announces: 'Russia', identifying the guns as Russian. While these commodities can cross borders, human beings in the refugee camp cannot.

A white reporter takes photographs of two fedayeen. Their lean bodies, smooth skin, curly hair and poses make them look like figures that are shaped to be displayed on the pages of magazines, instead of in war. Abu Akram sarcastically comments, 'Hey, hero, think the enemy will be afraid of how pretty you look in the magazine?' But the fedayee responds, 'Let them know who we are', without any connotation of threat in his voice. Abu Akram comments, 'History is the judge.' These model fighters, when depicted in Western magazines, become the sole images of the Palestinian cause for most readers. Both comments by Abu Akram highlight the paradox of the way fedayeen images are read in the West and the larger cause that appears as a background for the film. Their uniform symbolically transforms them from humans in search of a home to fighters. When Ghayda wears uniform, she appears stronger, firmer and readier to fight than some male fedayeen.

The uniform, to the fedayeen, signals the only chance of return to the home or its reclamation. In the refugee camp, Ghayda is resigned to her status as a refugee in Jordan, despite the pitiable living conditions, but her resignation comes from her cognisance of her helplessness. This contrasts with the *Salt of this Sea*, a film marked by anxieties, fears and confrontations. Soraya possesses the characteristic American confidence about future possibilities. She leaves her safe life in Brooklyn to return to Palestine, whereas Ghayda cannot even provide an assurance of the possibility of a return to Tarek. While Ghayda was reticent about returning to the homeland from the refugee camp in Jordan, she is emboldened for a return to the homeland in the fedayeen camp. She joins the movement to bring the return closer. The fedayee uniform acts as a transformative tool that helps her embody that resistance. Both Ghayda and Tarek have an untainted view of Palestine and the possibility of return. Their return to the home is blocked, however, by multiple tightly secured borders that are enforced and informed by transnational politics. But Soraya's perception of the homeland and her desire to return are comparable to Tarek's.

While Emad and Marwan attempt to escape the homeland, Tarek and Soraya actively attempt to return to Palestine despite little knowledge of its challenges. The border is fenced and patrolled to block Tarek's entry, but it is structured to allow the entry of immigrants such as Soraya and Shadi. Soraya and Shadi have plural identities as residents of multiple locations and cultures, whereas Tarek's and Emad's identities are reduced to a singularity that increases the barriers to their locational, hierarchical and cultural mobility. Access to cultural and political multiplicities and identities enables Soraya to navigate and access further mobilities and identities. Transvergent transnationalism not only helps us understand transnational cinema and its constitutive transnational factors, such as identity, documents, capital, gender, age, language and accent, but also examines the multiplicities and fluidities that accommodate regular shifts in these constituents.

REFERENCES

Armes, Roy (2015), *New Voices in Arab Cinema*, Bloomington: Indiana University Press.
Bakhtin, Mikhail (1981), *The Dialogic Imagination: Four Essays*, ed. Michael Holquist, trans. Caryl Emerson and Michael Holquist, Austin: University of Texas Press.
Barlow, Helen (2013), '*Salvo*: Saleh Bakri Interview', *SBS Movies*, 2 October, https://www.sbs.com.au/movies/article/2013/10/02/salvo-saleh-bakri-interview (accessed 19 April 2023).
Bayraktar, Nilgün (2016), *Mobility and Migration in Film and Moving-image Art: Cinema Beyond Europe*, Abingdon: Routledge.
Bergfelder, Tim (2005), 'National, Transnational or Supranational Cinema? Rethinking European Film Studies', *Media, Culture & Society* 27.3: 315–31.
Bergfelder, Tim, Sue Harris and Sarah Street (2007), *Film Architecture and the Transnational Imagination: Set Design in 1930s European Cinema*, Amsterdam: Amsterdam University Press.
Buckwalter, Ian (2010), 'In "This Sea", Salt of Conflict is Strong on the Tongue', *NPR*, 12 August, https://www.npr.org/templates/story/story.php?storyId=129082782 (accessed 19 April 2023).
Crofts, Stephen (1998), 'Concepts of National Cinema', in *The Oxford Guide to Film Studies*, ed. John Hill and Pamela Church Gibson, Oxford: Oxford University Press, pp. 385–94.
Durovicová, Natasa, and Kathleen Newman (eds) (2010), *World Cinemas, Transnational Perspectives*, Abingdon: Routledge.
Enwezor, Okwui (2007), 'Coalition Building: Black Audio Film Collective and Transnational Post-colonialism', in *The Ghosts of Songs: The Film Art of the Black Audio Film Collective*, ed. Kodwo Eshun and Anjalika Sagar, Liverpool: Liverpool University Press, pp. 106–29.
Ezra, Elizabeth, and Terry Rowden (2006), 'General Introduction: What is Transnational Cinema', in *Transnational Cinema: The Film Reader*, ed. Elizabeth Ezra and Terry Rowden, Abingdon: Routledge, pp. 1–12.
Ezra, Elizabeth, and Terry Rowden (2009), 'Postcolonial Transplants: Cinema, Diaspora and the Body Politic', in *Comparing Postcolonial Diasporas*, ed. M. Keown, D. Murphy and J. Procter, Basingstoke: Palgrave Macmillan.
Farhat, Maymanah (2009), 'Finding a Sense of Home in "Salt of this Sea"', *The Electronic Intifada*, 15 April, https://electronicintifada.net/content/finding-sense-home-salt-sea/8184 (accessed 19 April 2023).
Ghosn, Faten, Tiffany S. Chu, Miranda Simon, Alex Braithwaite, Michael Frith and Joanna Jandali (2021), 'The Journey Home: Violence, Anchoring, and Refugee

Decisions to Return', *American Political Science Review* 115.3: 982–98, http://doi.org/10.1017/S0003055421000344.
Higbee, Will (2007), 'Beyond the (Trans)National: Towards a Cinema of Transvergence in Postcolonial and Diasporic Francophone Cinema(s)', *Studies in French Cinema* 7.2: 79–91, https://doi.org/10.1386/sfci.7.2.79_1.
Higbee, Will, and Song Hwee Lim (2010), 'Concepts of Transnational Cinema: Towards a Critical Transnationalism in Film Studies', *Transnational Cinemas* 1.1: 7–22, https://doi.org/10.1386/trac.1.1.7/1.
Higson, Andrew (2000), 'The Limiting Imagination of a National Cinema', in *Cinema and Nation*, ed. Mette Hjort and Scott Mackenzie, London: Routledge, pp. 57–68.
Hjort, Mette (2010), 'On the Plurality of Cinematic Transnationalism', in *World Cinemas, Transnational Perspectives*, ed. Kathleen Newman and Nataša Ďurovičová, Abingdon: Routledge, pp. 12–33.
Kinder, Marsha (1993), *Blood Cinema: The Reconstruction of National Identity in Spain*, Berkeley: University of California Press.
Levitt, Peggy (2001), *The Transnational Villagers*, Berkeley: University of California Press.
Lim, Song Hwee (2007), 'Is the Trans- in Transnational the Trans- in Transgender?', *New Cinemas: Journal of Contemporary Film* 5.1: 39–52.
Lim, Song Hwee (2019), 'Concepts of Transnational Cinema Revisited', *Transnational Screens* 10.1: 1–12, https://doi.org/10.1080/25785273.2019.1602334.
Lodderhose, Diana (2021), 'Filmmaker Annemarie Jacir on her Journey to Preserve Palestinian Cinema for Future Generations', *Deadline*, 8 July, https://deadline.com/2021/07/annemarie-jacir-filmmaker-palestine-cinema-cannes-magazine-disruptor-1234787507/ (accessed 19 April 2023)
Loska, Krzysztof (2016), 'Transnational Turn in Film Studies (Editorial)', *Transmissions: The Journal of Film and Media Studies* 1.2: 1–7.
Lu, Sheldon H. (1997), 'Historical Introduction: Chinese Cinemas (1986–1996) and Transnational Film Studies', in *Transnational Chinese Cinemas: Identity, Nationhood, Gender*, ed. Sheldon Hsiao-peng Lu, Honolulu: University of Hawai'i Press, pp. 1–31.
Lu, Sheldon H. (ed.) (1997), *Transnational Chinese Cinemas: Identity, Nationhood, Gender*. Honolulu: University of Hawai'i Press.
Marks, Laura (2000), *The Skin of the Film: Intercultural Cinema, Embodiment, and the Senses*, Durham, NC: Duke University Press.
Michel, Patrick, Adam Possamai and Bryan S. Turner (2017), *Religions, Nations, and Transnationalism in Multiple Modernities*, Basingstoke: Palgrave Macmillan.
Mundell, Ian (2008), '"Salt" to be Palestinian Oscar Entry', *Variety*, 22 September, https://variety.com/2008/film/awards/salt-to-be-palestinian-oscar-entry-1117992600/ (accessed 23 April 2023).
Naficy, Hamid (2001), *Accented Cinema: Exilic and Diasporic Filmmaking*, Princeton, NJ: Princeton University Press.
Novak, Marcos (2002), 'Speciation, Transvergence, Allogenesis: Notes on the Production of the Alien', *Architectural Design* 72.3: 64–71.

Nussbaum, Emily (2008), 'In Conversation: Gloria Steinem and Suheir Hammad', *New York Magazine*, 22 September, https://nymag.com/anniversary/40th/50664/ (accessed 19 April 2023).

Said, Edward (1990), 'Reflection on Exile', in *Out There: Marginalization and Contemporary Cultures*, ed. Russel Ferguson, Martha Gever, Trinh T. Minh-ha and Cornell West, Cambridge, MA: MIT Press, pp. 357–66.

Vertovec, Steven (2009), *Transnationalism*, Abingdon: Routledge.

Vertovec, Steven, and Robin Cohen (eds) (1999), *Migration, Diasporas and Transnationalism*, Cheltenham: Edward Elgar.

Woldt, Marco (2009), 'Palestinian Filmmakers Beat the Odds to Hit Silver Screen', *CNN*, 22 April, http://edition.cnn.com/2009/SHOWBIZ/Movies/04/22/palestinian.territories.cinema.challenges/index.html (accessed 19 April 2023).

NOTES

1. He particularly focuses on the cinemas of mainland China, Hong Kong and Taiwan.
2. Naficy also delineates the following features of accented cinema: it requires multiple 'spectatorial activities and competencies' in addition to 'watching, writing, listening, reading, translating'; its variegated forms, diverse cultures and sociopolitical impact make it a 'disparate and disperse' yet 'increasingly significant cinematic formation'; its accent mainly 'emanates' from filmmakers' 'displacement' and 'artisanal production mode', and partially from 'accented speech' and 'diegetic characters'; stylistic approaches that accentuate this cinema include 'fragmented, multilingual, epistolary, self-reflexive, and critically juxtaposed narrative structure; amphibolic, doubled, crossed, and lost characters; it is interstitial; it is simultaneously local and global; it resists and exploits existing cinematic production practices; it "signif[ies] and signif[ies] upon the exile and diaspora by expressing, allegorizing, commenting upon, and critiquing" the home, the host, and the deterritorialization of the filmmaker'; it 'signif[ies] and signif[ies] upon cinematic traditions via aesthetics and politics of smallness and imperfection and cross-generic narrative strategies'; it uses 'counterhegemonic' epistolarity through its 'multivocal, multiauthorial, calligraphic, and free indirect discourses'; it is invested in 'territoriality, rootedness, and geography' with some exceptions; its power 'derives not from purity and refusal but from impurity and *refusion*' (emphasis original); it is dialogically transnational; it is 'haunted' by indigenous culture, while attendant to its 'political agency' and 'political immediacy' which leads to its 'incorporative and resistive' strategies' (2001: 4–7).
3. Hence exilic and diasporic experiences differ because diasporic experience is characterised by 'plurality, multiplicity, and hybridity' whereas an exilic experience is built around 'binarism and duality' (Naficy 2001: 14).
4. Read more at https://www.unrwausa.org (accessed 19 April 2023).

CHAPTER 5

Characters at the Margins

Iqra Shagufta Cheema

The protagonists of Jacir's films remain the focus of both audience and scholarly attention, as has been the case throughout the previous chapters of this book. Despite constructing the many layers of the narrative world wherein the major characters operate, minor characters usually receive minimal, ephemeral attention. This is a paradoxical yet inevitable transgression that film creators must commit. This paradox becomes starker in films that are produced from the political periphery and that tell stories of people pushed to the spatial, political or cultural margins. One example is Palestinian narratives where the filmmaker cinematises the marginalised narrative but, in the process, creates characters who live at the margins of the narrative itself and whose stories remain either partially explored or untold.

Departing from the pattern of focusing only on major characters or on one central character, this chapter instead examines the ways in which minor characters contribute to the larger schema of narrative building and character development in Jacir's films. It explores and explicates the ways in which minor characters add to the multidimensionality of the main characters, the complexity of the plot, and the intricacies of a film's narrative. These minor characters are perceived not only through their limited appearance on screen 'but in the very manner in which they are "absorbed" or "expelled"' from the narrative (Woloch 2003: 69), or are 'overshadowed' (Woloch 2003: 112). If minor characters are not portrayed in all their complexity, their 'actualization' as 'human being[s] is denied' (Woloch 2003: 25). This interest in minor characters arises from the 'dissonance' between a character's presence on screen and their impact on the narrative itself (Woloch 2003: 37).

Alex Woloch invites the audience to perceive these characters in 'a distributed field of attention' (2003: 17) in which characters' roles and their presence on screen constantly shift either to draw attention or to be ignored, which results in a 'formed pattern of attention' (2003: 41). Thereby, minor characters become 'implied human being[s] who get constricted into a delimited role, but who ha[ve] enough resonance with a human being to make [them] aware of this constricted position as delimited' (2003: 40). These characters' reception depends upon their relatability with the audience or their ability to incite strong emotions. Depending upon their popularity, these characters are sometimes elaborated in subsequent series or narratives.

The elaboration of minor characters takes various forms in storytelling fields, such as literature and films. In literature, it has been termed 'minor-character elaboration' (Rosen 2016: viii) or 'minor-character investigation' (Reed 2019: 78). It is also defined as 'a genre constituted by the conversion of minor characters from canonical literary texts into the protagonists of new ones' (Rosen 2016: 1–2). Jeremy Rosen reads this genre in literature, citing works such as Christopher Moore's *Fool* (2009), Jean Rhys's *Wide Sargasso Sea* (1966), Christa Wolf's *Cassandra* (1983), Alice Randall's *The Wind Done Gone* (2001) and Margaret Atwood's *The Penelopiad* (2005), while Adam Reed offers Henry Williamson's *A Chronicle of Ancient Sunlight* (1951–69) as an exemplar of the genre of minor-character elaboration.[1]

While Jeremy Rosen writes about minor-character elaboration in literature and as an instance of 'recovery' or inclusion of minor characters into the literary canon, we shift and extend their framework to discuss characters who are not popular enough to receive their own separate narrative, but who, nevertheless, remain intriguing and invite the audience's affective attachments. In film, this trend or genre shows up as spin-offs: films or series that detail a particular aspect of a character's personality or elaborate a character who was only marginally explored originally. In Hollywood, some examples are series such as *Ocean's 8* (2018), *Annabelle* (2014) and *Maleficent* (2014).[2] We cite these examples as more familiar referents because these spin-offs or minor-character elaborations occur only in popular works that intrigue a large audience or that exhibit promising monetary potential – things that are impossible for a cinema that is already produced on the margins and struggles for funding.

In this chapter, we expand our discussion of minor characters such as Noura, Fadya, Marwan and Irit to offer a scholarly exploration and critical examination of minor characters so as to explore the many ways in which these characters form and inform Jacir's cinematic narratives and their efficacy. Herein, we show how these characters, despite forming only the narrative background, introduce perspectival complexity and diversity into the narrative. Even as minor characters, they introduce significant minoritised or rare perspectives which it is critical to address, as the succeeding discussion shows.

THE GOOD SETTLER AND THE BAD INVADERS IN *SALT OF THIS SEA*

Soraya and Emad have to hide their identities and their intentions in visiting Jaffa until they arrive at Soraya's grandfather's house. Once they arrive, disclosing their identities to the Israeli artist Irit (Iman Aoun) who lives there becomes a necessary risk. Unlike other locations in *Salt of this Sea* where Soraya and Emad have to fabricate lies about their identities and intentions, in this instance Soraya gets entry into the house because she shares her identity with the artist. This scene distributes the audience's attention almost equally to each character – between the major and minor characters – as the camera moves from Soraya who is walking around the house to Irit, Emad and Marwan who are sitting together, talking politics. Readers 'like to speculate about [the] motivations, desires, childhoods, and the consequences' of the actions of minor characters, 'even if these are nowhere mentioned' in the narrative (Rosen 2016: 154). The representation of the Israeli artist, as a minor character, assumes critical narrative significance as the backdrop to the increasing settler violence in the Palestinian territories.

The film never shows the artist's opposition to this violence beyond her interaction with Soraya in the house and some symbolic but hidden everyday commodities such as the coffee mugs in her kitchen cabinet. However, the audience intervenes and extends this viewpoint to the artist's larger life. The artist's rather simplistic and naive opposition to settler violence seems commendable, especially after the previous hostile encounters with Jewish Israelis. However, despite her expressions of sympathy for Soraya, there is an affective detachment. The artist never engages in a meaningful personal exchange with Soraya about her loss and the complicity of common citizens and their communities in this loss. She says, 'I think everyone wants peace except the leaders', showing her oblivious optimism. She also comments, 'It's so sad, I wish [those exiled during the Nakba] had stayed' – as if they chose to leave their homes and homeland to live as refugees in refugee camps, or as exiles in foreign lands. However, the artist does appear to be safe and open, because everyone else that Soraya and Emad meet acts like the police and attempts to trace their ancestral, residential and national origins. It makes one wonder if the artist would appear to be as opposed to the Israeli settlements and as supportive of Palestinians if her scenes were watched in isolation, removed from the larger picture, where most people they encounter in Israel are Zionists. And Jacir does indulge this question.

As the scene develops, Jacir not only highlights the multiple layers of Irit's political positioning on Israeli settlements in Palestinian territories and her responses to them, but also implicates her in the settlements. Irit is the only character who does not ask Soraya and Emad about the legality of their presence in Jaffa. She invites them in and lets Soraya explore her ancestral memories in the house where her grandparents lived until they were exiled in 1948. Despite her complicity as a citizen of the state of Israel and a resident in Soraya's ancestral house, she voices her opposition to Israeli settler violence in Soraya's presence. The artist's opposition to the Israeli settler violence is soon challenged and complicated when Soraya asserts her ancestral claim on the house and even offers to buy it from the artist.

Below is the dialogue between Soraya and the artist, with some mediative interruptions by Marwan:

> Soraya: This is my home. It was stolen from my family so it is for me to decide if you can stay. And you can't.
> The artist: Are you serious?
> Soraya: My father should have been raised in this house, not in a fucking camp.
> The artist: You wanna speak about the history, the past. Let's forget it.
> Soraya: Your past is my every day. My right now. This is not your home.
> The artist: It is now.
> Soraya: You can stay if you admit all of this is stolen.
> The artist: I can stay? This was your grandfather's home, they left.
> Soraya: They were forced to.
> Marwan: Take it easy, girl.
> Soraya: They didn't wanna leave. My grandfather laid this floor – what does that mean to you?
> The artist: She's crazy. I am extending the hand to you. I invited you to stay. I am being friendly.
> Soraya: Our doors. Our windows. Our fucking house. Admit it.
> The artist: Get out of my house.
> Soraya: Recognize it.

This exchange, which escalates quickly, highlights the irony of political solidarities: Irit not only refuses to acknowledge that her current house was stolen from Soraya's ancestors but readily mobilises the same violent Israeli state structures against Soraya, Emad and Marwan by threatening to call the police. Irit picks up the phone to call the police despite knowing that she could destroy the lives of Marwan and Emad – if not of American-born Soraya – by reporting their illegal presence in Israeli-occupied territories.

The artist, as a beneficiary of the Nakba and Israeli settlements, not only refuses to acknowledge and recognise the ways in which she has benefited from Israeli settler violence but also expresses her willingness to actively participate in state violence. She yells at Soraya, 'I invited you to stay. I am being friendly.' The scene becomes a replication of Soraya's ancestors' exile during the Nakba;

it's as if she is being expelled from her home once again. It appears that the artist invited them into the house less because she opposes the violence against them and more because she desires to be perceived as the good, kind, Jewish-Israeli who did them a favour by inviting them in when others would not even let them in the city.

If we assume the very real possibility of the artist being a bigoted nationalist like every other Jewish-Israeli character in the film, this would have brought the end of the film, when Emad goes to jail and Soraya is deported for her illegal presence in Jaffa, closer. The artist not only introduces a relatively uncommon Jewish political position on Israeli-Palestinian conflict but also facilitates Soraya's visit to her ancestral home, the memorialised home of her grandfather's life. Despite Soraya's ultimately failed visit to her ancestral homeland, she reaches closure as her visit to the house cements the irretrievability of her ancestors' material lives.

However, the artist is not the only person whose politics and ideological allegiance are put to the test. Marwan, Emad's friend, claims the most screen time among the minor characters in the film, but his character remains underexplored. This underexploration of Marwan's character incites more interest because he describes his profession as a filmmaker. Interestingly, we learn the most about Marwan's character when he visits Soraya's ancestral house with her – a place where he is an unpermitted body, with an illegal presence – but also the place where someone shows an interest in his life. Marwan appears to be besotted with the artist despite her hostility towards Soraya. Irit asks him questions about his life and interests while Soraya explores the house:

Marwan: I am a filmmaker – I wanna make films about love stories.
The artist: What kind of love stories?
Marwan: Crazy love stories.

During the hostile disagreement between Soraya and the artist, Marwan tells Soraya to 'take it easy' – despite being the bearer of the wounds of Nakba, despite losing the chance at a normal life, and despite not even being able to pursue his dream of making romantic films, he tells Soraya to take it easy so he can have a chance at love, validation from an Israeli artist. Eventually, Soraya and Emad leave but Marwan disappears, leaving the audience wondering if he stayed behind with the artist. The film, by posing these questions, investigates the affiliations and allegiances of both of these minor characters as well as of the audience. The audience must engage with the complexity of the characters and with their own feelings about them.

However, minor characters don't only complicate the narrative. At the start of the film, multiple minor characters also challenge the film's disillusioned desperation so as to suffuse it with vitality. Right after Soraya is allowed to enter

Palestine, she and the audience witness a dancing traffic constable in the road. After her dispiriting and humiliating experience with the airport security personnel, the traffic constable introduces the life of ordinary people in Palestine to Soraya and the audience, both of whom were left shocked by her earlier experiences at the airport. This first reminder of the tenacity of ordinary citizens in the face of increasing restrictions and violence provides a lesson in navigating her life in Palestine. She is soon seen applying this lesson in playfulness and joviality in her actions and interactions. Other characters in the film, like the child who Emad picks up from school and the group of women who Soraya meets, also serve as little human oases in the otherwise thorny events. The audience gets a nuanced and balanced portrayal of life as a result of the minor characters in the film.

The audience, then, engages in the meaning-making process in the film to expand it beyond what is said on screen. Audience awareness, engagement with and eventual rejection of the construction of minor characters as minor is termed 'doubleness' (Rosen 2016: 157). This 'doubleness' of the audience's engagement endows the minor characters with an 'autonomous existence that precedes the representation that constitutes' them and 'elucidates an array of cultural phenomenon' such as attachment to the characters and the desire to know more about their lives (Rosen 2016: 157). It also addresses the 'twofoldness' of characters: 'treating characters as if they had full lives', while simultaneously 'knowing that characters have a merely textual existence' (Rosen 2016: 157). Films, therefore, contain their own binary majoritised and minoritised worlds, and the audience does not get to choose which world they want to inhabit as engaged and invested subjects that assign a film its meaning or plurality of meanings.

COMMUNITIES AND REFUGEES IN *WHEN I SAW YOU*

While the minor characters in *Salt of this Sea* serve as interlocutors of complexity, the minor characters in *When I Saw You* serve more as mood sustainers and affect enhancers for the film, along with expanding the affective range of experiences. *Salt of this Sea* includes multiple politically homogeneous minor characters who are affected by the Nakba and the Israeli settlements in similar ways in terms of personal and familiar loss and access to education and professional opportunities, or else characters who predominantly hold similar Zionist ideologies or are complicit in the exercise of these ideologies even if they do not express them.

Minor characters in *When I Saw You*, however, are more diverse in terms of gender, age, emotions and ideology. This provides a perspectival diversity for the audience, who witness the intricacies of the impact of exile on children, women, men and older people, some of whom live with their families, some of whom only have epistolary contact with their families, some of whom have no contact with their families, and some of whom have been abandoned by their families. This diversity also leads to expansive affective expressions where characters seek familial attachments, form new families, long for their romantic partners, and ache to see the world as well as be seen by the world.

The film captures the first comparative conversation about the experience and effect of exile on refugee children in the conversation between Tarek and the young girl, where he shares how he misses his father, his house, his bed and his bathroom, and asks her if she misses her bathroom too. She says that she aspires to join the fedayeen once she grows up and that she plans on marrying a fedayee. However, this realisation is lost on Tarek who, until the very end of the film, remains hopeful of a return to his home and homeland. Despite the return serving as the main thread through the film, the characters remain suspended in a limbo – only training for the fight and never fighting. This limbo provides an affective space for a deeper investigation and expression of their emotions.

The training, then, becomes more a means for them to connect with each other and stay together. Their training together gives a reason for them to construct the space of the fedayeen base. Multiple scenes in the film capture them either hanging out together at night, singing together, talking about their families, or doing banal chores around the fedayeen base. In one scene, two fedayeen pose together with their guns for the white photographer. Complying with the popular portrayal of fedayeen in the Western media, they tell Abu Akram that they want the world to see who they are – by which they mean that they want the world to see them as capable of fighting and taking back their homes and homeland. But contrary to their statements, their body language and their bodies issue a completely different statement. They appear as harmless, lean young men who want to be seen and acknowledged by the world. They train to fight, but their songs are about beauty and peace. During their banter and arguments, they tease each other about their past lovers, lovers they had to leave behind in the homeland to pursue their lives as fedayeen, and the longing to find those lost lovers. They express their longing to touch their lovers again. These images counter the popular portrayal, and invite an empathetic perspective that views fedayeen as human beings with the desire for a life of dignity and love.

While many of these minor characters in the collective scenes remain unnamed, they constitute a communal space and community for Ghayda and Tarek when they move out of the refugee camp. The different encounters and interactions between the fedayeen in the camp encapsulate the complexity of the desire to return home when this is not an option immediately available to them. But the longing for home results in an emotional investment in the homes and families they have built in the fedayeen base. Without this centre, their community would be scattered. These minor characters construct and highlight intricate affective attachments between all the characters.

Essentially, it is only the minor characters that help build the collective character and mood of the film, while the major characters portray the more immediate and expansive impact of critical crises such as loss of the home, homeland, family, stability and security. However, minor characters remain instrumental in highlighting the kind of communities that emerge as a result of these losses and that serve as unofficial spaces of refuge and respite. Jacir spent considerable time preparing the characters who played the roles of fedayeen, only to learn later that many of them were the children of fedayeen. Particularly effective are the scenes in which the fedayeen sit around and chat and experience a version of normal lives.

Jacir had to start shooting the film before securing funding because of the fear that Mahmoud Asfa, who plays Tarek, might grow up if they didn't start on time.[3] Since *When I Saw You* can also be read as a coming-of-age film, we essentially learn about Tarek's personality and his growth via his interactions with other people. His interactions with the girl in the camp provide an insight into the psyche of two children growing up under the same circumstances but with different ambitions and expectations. His interactions with the travellers and the old woman on the road compare the various responses to refugees from urban and rural residents. His interactions with the fedayeen commander, Abu Akram, show us his leadership and learning potential. His interactions with the male fedayeen show the audience the kind of options he has in terms of role models and gender-conditioning. But overall, these interactions also show the audience that Tarek already has a strong enough personality that helps him to sustain his determination to return home despite everyone else's subtle resignation and acceptance of the reality of their lives.

These minor characters are not limited to the fedayeen base only. Two other scenes where we encounter minor characters occur when Tarek attempts to return to his house from the refugee camp. He meets an older woman who recognises him as a refugee and hands him a pomegranate. She prays for him and wishes for his enemies' destruction. Immediately after this, Tarek runs into a group of young tourists, who stand as if as if they are posing for an idyllic photoshoot. Upon seeing Tarek, they call to him:

Man: Can you help us? Our car broke down. I'm talking to you, boy. Do you know if there is a village nearby?
Tarek: No, I don't.
Woman 1: See how he speaks! Are you a refugee?
Man: He's a refugee.
Woman 1: You don't know if there's a village nearby?
Woman 2: And a camp?

Man: Do you want him to bring the camp boys here? Unbelievable.
(*He yells at Tarek*)
Please get out of here.
Yes, move it.
Yes, you. What are you waiting for?
Woman 2: Poor boy. You were mean to him.
Man: You like me mean, no?
Woman 2: No, I don't.
Man: Then I'll leave you here tonight with the camp boys, baby.

These contradictory experiences on his first excursion out of the refugee camp provide an outsider's perspective for both Tarek and the audience. These characters represent the variety of responses from the hosts to the refugees.

Observing Tarek's interactions with the old woman and the young people comparatively highlights two categories of responses towards refugees – both implicated in class. The old woman is wearing a traditional headcovering. She looks wise and appears to understand the political history of the Palestinian crisis and its impact on different refugees. She is sympathetic to Tarek's desperation and desire to return home – but is also realistically aware of the impossibility of this desire despite wishing him well. By contrast, the group of young tourists are wearing Western clothing and fanning their faces. They are inconvenienced by the heat. They talk to Tarek contemptuously. This comparison highlights that negative responses towards Palestinians are class-based, where people who are socio-economically underprivileged incline to be more understanding of the struggles of those who lose their homes and possessions, and as a result, their economic stability and sense of safety. These minor characters make visible the difficulties of refugees in terms of sociocultural communal mobility. Additionally, this highlights that the task of becoming a functional human being in society becomes harder for refugees, because most educational and economic opportunities are navigated through sociocultural connections between communities. These instances go on to highlight the critical significance of the community that Tarek and Ghayda find for themselves in the fedayeen base. These are also the only points in the film when the audience witnesses outsiders' perspectives and interactions with the refugees.

Beyond these interactions with people, the rest of the film focuses on the interaction with Palestinian exiles and refugees or outsiders' perspectives on the situation only via radio broadcasts and reportage. While the characters in the refugee camp and the fedayeen base also present complex affective positionalities, it is really the minor characters in *When I Saw You* that represent the wide range of sociopolitical and affective complexities of Palestinian subjects both in the context of indigenous and transnational politics.

MINOR IN ABSENCE: MINOR CHARACTERS IN *WAJIB*

Unlike *Salt of this Sea* and *When I Saw You*, where characters form friendships and choose families at will after being separated from their genetic families, Jacir's third film, *Wajib*, mostly contains characters who have been family members or close friends for decades. The audience gets to observe the minor characters only ephemerally in *Wajib*. Most of the characters in *Wajib* are minor characters who highlight some aspect of Shadi and Abu Shadi's relationship, introduce their past familial history, explain the conflict between them, or portray the impact of local politics on the residents. The various family members and friends who they visit provide an insight into the lifestyles, preferences, fears and anxieties of those living in Nazareth and those who have left. Hence, the place and the city also emerge as characters in *Wajib* – characters that form and inform human lives. While some of these characters appear on screen, many remain absent, and the audience only hears about them but never sees them.

Nada, Nada's father, Ronnie, Shadi's mother and Shadi's mother's husband are a few of the minor characters who inform the most critical decisions in the film but who remain invisible. These characters incite the strongest reactions from Shadi or Abu Shadi, but their life stories remain only partially explored. Their names serve as sites of contention and elaboration for Shadi and his father. The relationship between Shadi and Abu Shadi is deeply haunted by the memories and shadows of his broken marriage. More than the estrangement of his son, Abu Shadi carries the residual anger and frustration about his wife's decision to leave him and marry another man. His children, however, have made peace with the decision. His children are set to start their own families, which marks the initiation of a new period of loneliness for Abu Shadi, but he does not have the tools to navigate this new stage of his life. Alongside these deep familial connections, Ronnie and Nada's father also posit imaginative oppositions regarding the contentious history between Shadi and Abu Shadi.

Fadya, Noura and Shadi's sister are characters who intrigue the audience and who also make an appearance on screen. Minor characters who also make an appearance on screen include older couples in their semi-lit homes, the older woman who has a crush on Abu Shadi, the neighbour who talks to Shadi about how much Abu Shadi loves him, the people carrying the dead body in the street, the young guys in the street brawl – all reflect the diversity of lived experiences in Nazareth, some of which Shadi misses but most of which he complains about. The film presents an opposition to the other two films where the central characters are displaced, exiled or diasporic, but all desire a return to the homeland. The characters in *Wajib* have more socioculturally stable lives but they are also more affectively chaotic.

While Shadi does appear to love his life in Italy, this is primarily because he has found a family with Nada and Nada's father. However, Abu Shadi considers Nada's father responsible for Shadi's decision to stay in Italy as well as his laxity regarding his traditions. Conversely, this same perspective applies to Shadi's opinion of Ronnie. Shadi believes that Ronnie was responsible for forcing Abu Shadi to send Shadi away at a young age to keep him safe. Abu Shadi believes this to have been an intentional decision on his part. While the audience witnesses some phone calls between Ronnie and Abu Shadi and Nada's father and Abu Shadi, their characters remain elusive and unexplored, while also the most critical for Shadi and Abu Shadi's relationship. In a way, Shadi and Abu Shadi consistently live in the shadows of these characters.

One of the most striking things about *Wajib* is its portrayal of the diversity of life in Nazareth. The audience travels through the streets of Nazareth, a city with large Christian and Muslim populations, with a father and son who find a way to perform a generations-old tradition of delivering wedding invitations despite their own personal differences. In a way, *Wajib* also becomes the story of how numerous people who are no longer an active part of Shadi and Abu Shadi's lives serve as an archive of their personal familial history, but also of the history of the city itself. While these characters highlight the smaller details of Shadi and Abu Shadi's relationship, they also portray the frustrations of ordinary citizens about the banality of their lives. *Wajib* is different from *Salt of this Sea* and *When I Saw You* because the minor characters highlight not political and cultural chaos and turmoil, but the everyday lives and frustrations of different people who all form parts of a family and a community.

These minor characters in Jacir's films become foundational in adding layers of complexity to the major characters. However, all three films provide a widely different range of affective, familial, political, cultural and locational challenges. Reading these minor characters comparatively provides the audience with a diverse understanding of the Palestinian experience. These minor characters might not get to tell their own individual stories, but the larger stories would remain incomplete without them, and that is where their strength lies.

REFERENCES

Galef, David (1993), *The Supporting Cast: A Study of Flat and Minor Characters*, University Park, PA: Pennsylvania State University Press.

Johnson, Joyce (1983), *Minor Characters*, New York: Houghton Mifflin.

McDonald Werronen, Sheryl (2017), 'Women Helping Women, and Other Minor Characters', in Sheryl McDonald Werronen, *Popular Romance in Iceland*, Amsterdam: Amsterdam University Press, pp. 171–94.

McNally, John (2013), 'Minor Characters', in John McNally, *Vivid and Continuous: Essays and Exercises for Writing Fiction*, Iowa City: University of Iowa Press, pp. 53–62.
Reed, Adam (2019), 'Reading Minor Characters: An English Literary Society and its Culture of Investigation', *PMLA* 134.1: 66–80, doi:10.1632/pmla.2019.134.1.66.
Rosen, Jeremy (2013), 'Minor Characters Have Their Day: The Imaginary and Actual Politics of a Contemporary Genre', *Contemporary Literature* 54.1: 139–74, doi:10.1353/cli.2013.0003.
Rosen, Jeremy (2015), 'An Insatiable Market for Minor Characters: Genre in the Contemporary Literary Marketplace', *New Literary History: A Journal of Theory and Interpretation* 46.1: 143–63, doi:10.1353/nlh.2015.0001.
Rosen, Jeremy (2016), *Minor Characters Have Their Day: Genre and the Contemporary Literary Marketplace*, New York: Columbia University Press.
Willis, P. W. (1999), 'Approaching a Major Novel through its Minor Characters', in *Approaches to Teaching Stendhal's The Red and the Black*, ed. D. de la Motte and S. Haig, New York: Modern Language Association of America, pp. 104–11.
Woloch, Alex (2003), *The One vs. the Many: Minor Characters and the Space of the Protagonist in the Novel*, Princeton, NJ: Princeton University Press.

NOTES

1. *Fool* 'retells Shakespeare's King Lear from the perspective of Lear's jester'; *Wide Sargasso Sea* focuses on the now famous 'madwoman in the attic'; *Cassandra* 'revisits the Trojan War and the story of Agamemnon's homecoming from the perspective of the eponymous Trojan prophetess'; *The Wind Done Gone* 'imagines a slave half-sister for *Gone with the Wind*'s Scarlett O'Hara'; and *The Penelopiad* 'converts Penelope and a chorus of the twelve maids hanged by Odysseus into dueling narrators' (Rosen 2016: 1–2).
2. *Ocean's 8* focuses on the character of Debbie Ocean, Danny Ocean's sister, who wasn't featured in the original films; *Annabelle* features the doll from the first *The Conjuring*; and *Maleficent* turns the antagonist of *Sleeping Beauty* into the main character.
3. https://www.kpbs.org/news/arts-culture/2014/06/13/interview-annemarie-jacir-director-when-i-saw-you (accessed 19 April 2023).

CHAPTER 6

Curatorial Politics and Practices

Stefanie Van de Peer

In 2003 Annemarie Jacir was an MFA student in New York. She worked with Columbia University professor Hamid Dabashi on the Dreams of a Nation project, a film festival that took place in both New York and Palestine, in which they showcased Palestinian films from across the decades since the Nakba. Some of the earliest films they screened dated from the 1960s and 1970s, including revolutionary films by the PLO-funded Palestine Film Unit (PFU). Dabashi edited the first scholarly book on Palestinian cinema as a result of the film screenings, and Columbia University now hosts one of the largest Palestinian film archives in the world. Jacir was the main curator of the festival, as she had established a network with many (Palestinian) filmmakers and custodians of the older films, scattered throughout the world. The impulse behind this project was Edward Said's passion for the preservation of archives and cultural products created in and about Palestine, as well as Dabashi's realisation that if he wanted to teach Palestinian cinema at Columbia, he needed access to the films for his students, and gaining access to them was a struggle.

In this chapter, we discuss the significance of film festivals for Palestine's cultural identity and for its filmmaking trends, focusing on Jacir's curatorial practices for Dreams of a Nation and other projects she has led. Chief among Jacir's projects is Philistine Films, founded in 1997, an independent film production company located in Palestine and Jordan which produced, among other projects, Dreams of a Nation. Later on, the Jacir family repurposed their ancestral home in Bethlehem as a cultural centre for the arts and research, Dar Jacir. As a cultural centre within Palestine, the significance of this house cannot be overstated, but its successes as well as its failures are directly linked to its materiality and its location in Bethlehem. The fact that Annemarie Jacir was exiled from Palestine in 2007 plays a role in the house's significance. The differences between her curatorial practice for Philistine Films, Dreams of a Nation and Dar Jacir shape the thread of this chapter.

PHILISTINE FILMS

Philistine Films is a production company 'created to support new voices and to offer a platform for the emerging independent Arab film scene' (Philistine Films website), with a focus on supporting filmmakers working outside of the mainstream. The vision of the company came from the understanding that filmmaking is a collaborative process, and like a true collective, they work together and support and mentor one another with the films they make. They have (co-)produced *Huda's Salon* (Hany Abu-Assad, 2021), *The Translator* (Rana Kazkaz, Anas Khalaf, 2020), *3000 Nights* (Mai Masri, 2015) and many others, including Jacir's own films. These are all exceptional films by auteurs whose work has garnered awards around the world at the most significant film festivals, such as Berlinale, Cannes and Toronto. They are also films by filmmakers who have a well-established reputation for highly political and challenging work that does not shy away from controversial or taboo subjects. As such, Philistine Films celebrates truly independent and political films.

Apart from producing fiction and documentary films by the well-established names of contemporary Palestinian cinema, Philistine Films also invests in the training and education of young, new talent from the Arab film world, with development and screenwriting workshops, director and crew training. In an interview with *Deadline*, Jacir commented:

> When I first started in the business I had so many questions and I didn't know who to go to or how to start [. . .] But there is so much talent out there, and there are so many stories and so many creative people, so when I started doing a lot of workshops in Palestine, I just felt like I had to share whatever knowledge I had and spread it to the younger generation. (Lodderhose 2021)

With its work, Philistine Films develops local Arab film crews. It also emphasises its efforts to produce films that are entirely funded by, produced in and using staff from the Arab region, without the intervention of Western (co-)producers. It has made it its mission to be not only truly independent from the colonial past and the occupied present, but also to disrupt the film industry's tendency to continue the hierarchical appreciation of international co-productions. Jacir clearly thrives on collaboration, working as an editor, screenwriter and producer on young filmmakers' films. She has also taught and mentored screenwriters through Philistine

Films at workshops for organisations across the globe, such as Birzeit University and the Doha Film Institute.

The importance of creative writing for Jacir must be highlighted. She is perhaps less known as a novelist and poet, but poetry has a central role in her life and creative practice. In poems such as 'Azraq', 'Landscape', 'In Arms', 'Untitled Exile Poem', 'End of Autumn' and 'To Juan Pablo Nasser – Lost in Barranquilla',[1] the main motifs are memory, longing and a rooting of love in the material qualities of human beings and the land they live in. Food, drink, sounds and textures take centre stage amid the many people inhabiting Jacir's poems. The same is true in her films – they showcase sensuous human beings on journeys both in emotional and in material terms. These narratives offer space for complex Palestinian realities that speak to the humanity of an international audience. The travel journeys in her films emphasise a narrative arc that is familiar to Jacir herself, unable to settle in Palestine. She says: 'I want to tell stories that I feel are real stories that are interesting to me, that are complicated and aren't just black and white. I want to ask and leave questions' (Lodderhose 2021).

She has won numerous awards as a screenwriter for her own films, including her first feature *Salt of this Sea*, for which she was awarded the Muhr Arab Award for Best Screenplay. She credits her education in literature, her interest in poetry and her first job in the LA film industry as a reader of scripts with giving her the inspiration and growing confidence to start to write and format the scripts of her own films.

Philistine Films also organises cine-clubs and film screenings. While production of Palestinian films is increasingly recognised globally, Palestinians themselves very rarely see these films – Palestinian films are most often seen abroad, in a global arthouse cinema network. Livia Alexander (2005) argues that Palestinian film is in essence a transnational cinema, but that in thematic terms, issues of the national dominate. In our understanding of and approach to Palestinian cinema, we prefer to qualify the word transnationalism with the adjective transvergent, as explained in Chapter 5. What Alexander does explain well is how Palestinian films often feel as though they are produced for the international film festival circuit, through external funding for production, distribution and exhibition, and as such are well-incorporated into a Euro-American system, which is, of course, what dominates the transnational markets for cinema. Philistine Films experienced this first-hand, and through its preoccupation with developing the independent Arab film scene it started to screen its films to Palestinian audiences in historic Palestine, the Occupied Territories and in Palestinian refugee camps around the Arab world. It has made considerable contributions to the local and regional film infrastructure, including developing a local audience interested in their own stories. In fact, it was this sense of estrangement between Palestinian audiences and their films that inspired Dreams of a Nation to hold a parallel festival in Palestine. Jacir said that 'one of the aims of the Dreams of a Nation project was to provide access to Palestinian films after the organizers had heard many stories of people who could not view these works' (Oumlil 2016).

FESTIVALS OF PALESTINIAN FILM

Before we explore the complex reality of the Dreams of a Nation festival and archive, we want to engage more with the ideas and theories surrounding the role of festivals and films in and of Palestine. Around the world, Palestine has become a 'cause', and, as Nick Denes (2014) and other festival scholars interested in Palestinian film have shown, a plethora of festivals around the world are dedicated to Palestine and its cinema. Most of these have been established since the 2000s, in response to the Second Intifada, which infused Palestinian politics with an awareness of and interest in the capacity of cultural products to build identity and solidarity. As Edward Said showed in his work in the 1980s and 1990s,[2] international interest in the Arab world – and in the Palestinian cause – comes in waves and is usually rooted in political events with huge repercussions on the international community. However, this interest in Palestine is often one-sided and temporal. This is also the case for films dealing with Palestine.

As (co-)production funding comes so often from European nations, the outlook of Palestinian films is decidedly international in scope and the significance of these films at film festivals internationally (for example through winning awards) illustrates how the particular production circumstances of Palestinian films translate into significant and expansive distribution and exhibition opportunities. The quick succession of significant historical moments and the changes brought about in emotional and material terms for the nascent film culture in the 1980s and 1990s resulted in a multiplicity of realities for Palestinians – their cinema is national in content and transnational in ambition. The international audience requires international productions, which comes with its own possibilities (funding) and limitations (specificity of the stories). Alexander shows how Palestinian film festivals are in fact often global events at which global audiences see Palestinian films more readily than do people living in Palestine. She claims: 'Palestinians might read about Palestinian films, but they had few chances to view them' (2005: 156). The diaspora is extensive, and the storytelling powers formidable.

Explaining the circumstances in Palestine as determining the infrastructure of festivals, Alexander illustrates how film culture changed with the First Intifada in the late 1980s, which saw 'investment in the infrastructure for the development of a national cinema inside Palestine' (2005: 155). However, the material culture of cinema makes it vulnerable in the Occupied Territories. Israeli forces closed down cinemas in major Palestinian cities one by one, and the clashes of the First Intifada struck the final blow to any remaining theatres. An absence of local venues in historic Palestine and the Occupied Territories impacts the potential domestic market. In historic Palestine there is also the growing conservative influence of the Islamist movement, and competition from television and home video. Attempts to develop local venues during the post-Oslo era came to a halt with the Second Intifada. Israeli forces destroyed many of these institutions and organisations, which turned producers towards an international market for film and resulted in 'the creation of films addressing the broadest common denominator, and global viewers' (Alexander 2005: 156), thus turning away (however involuntarily) from a Palestinian audience.

The lack of a nation-state and the dominance of the global market for Palestinian films reflects the pendular movement of obsession with space on the one hand (the land, its borders and travel across them) and time on the other (the histories of the Nakba and 1948, the Naksa and 1967, the First and Second Intifadas, and so on). The conflict with the oppressive Israeli occupier is played out through the denial of exactly these concepts of time and space for Palestinians in Palestine. Indeed, Viviane Saglier calls Palestinian film culture a 'not-yet' industry precisely because of these factors. She shows how this 'not-yet' industry consists of individual initiatives that are part of a non-centralised, non-institutionalised and fragmented community (2020: 131). She points out that the late 2000s, post-Second Intifada, saw the creation of several film production companies, collectives, festivals, courses and diplomas, and also the increased visibility of Palestinian films internationally. The film festivals that take place within Palestine are, according to Saglier, mostly multi-site festivals in the largest cities and refugee areas, where they are impacted by constant instability: cancellations, postponements and changes of location are commonplace. These inconsistencies destabilise programmes and threaten events with discontinuance, illustrating the structural precariousness of Palestinian life under settler colonialism, with checkpoints, curfews, confiscations and denial of entry.

These interruptions also affected Dreams of a Nation in New York, where screenings were interrupted because of the poor quality of the subtitles or projection. This parallel between New York and Palestinian-based screenings of Palestinian films broadens the meaning of how '[i]n Palestine, fully engaging with visual pleasure means, purely materially, not being interrupted, not being captured, and keeping control over the viewing space [and time]' (Saglier 2020: 137). These are things that a New York audience would take for granted, but are exceptional in a Palestinian context. As such, Palestinian film economies do not conform to European ideals of stable film festivals.

Likewise, the usual discourse around nationhood and identity does not yet go quite far enough for our understanding of the ultra-importance of festivals of Palestinian film such as Dreams of a Nation taking place on Palestinian soil. In fact, as Annemarie Jacir herself writes, if films can be used 'for cultural purposes' only, then in the Palestinian case – where national identity is constantly contested and threatened – culture is what keeps identity stubbornly alive. Cultural identity is what cinema in the Arab world is rooted in and contributes to, as Viola Shafik so thoroughly illustrates (2016: 6). Joseph Massad asserts that 'people survive as people only if their culture survives' (2006: 32). It is true that in the absence of a Palestinian state, cinema suffers limited production and a lack of even a starting point for spatial and temporal continuity. But still, the productivity and quality of Palestinian films is exceptional and its contribution to cultural identity, however imagined, is significant. As such, the limits of nationalist discourse do not translate directly to film culture and display the limited usefulness of the national in the discussion of film cultures.

So, with the fragmentation of space and in the absence of a material, public space, where communities and identities can be formed on and off screen, the question remains whether film festivals can create an imagined space, or a dream of a nation. As I have argued elsewhere (2022), Benedict Anderson's imagined communities might be more usefully replaced with Appadurai's 'imagined worlds', theorised through various 'landscapes' (Appadurai 1990: 295–310). In this thinking, films are coherent creations *despite* deconstructed time and space, and festivals are 'mediascapes': metaphors by which people live, which subvert centre–periphery models and instead blur the lines between nations and cultures. Films can shape time and be spaces that enable a shared crossing of borders through the cinematic imagination. As such, domestic audiences can function in the context of world cinema, with highly sophisticated Palestinian films being screened around the world before they come to Palestine. At that point, then, the films have already done their jobs of showing global audiences that Palestine is not in fact just an idea or a dream, but a material place with a harsh reality and a past that consists of continuous disruptions. The aestheticisation of brutal politics effectively creates global solidarity through film festivals. Tawil-Souri's statement that creating culture *is* political resistance (2011: 146), and Dabashi's assurance that films can show the 'aesthetic presence of a political absence' (2006: 11), make the films even stronger and the festivals in Palestine even more important. The more recent tendency of filmmakers to deal with the absurdity of being Palestinian equally shows that the Palestinian issue is as much a cultural as a material struggle (Rastegar 2002: 276).

DREAMS OF A NATION

What sets the Dreams of a Nation film festival apart among the many film festivals dedicated to Palestinian film around the world was its parallel curation of a programme of films screened in New York and in Palestinian cities. These screenings ensured a Palestinian as well as a New York audience for the films. The festival in New York took place over the course of four days at venues across Columbia University, in lecture halls and event rooms. It was described by a festival critic as 'organizationally and technically more than a little messy, and naturally hit and miss (as most festivals are) [. . .] nevertheless, by its very existence, an exciting and important achievement' (Rapfogel 2003). As an example of its 'messy' nature, this reviewer explains that *Fertile Memory* by Michel Khleifi (1980) was shown, but that the print was of such poor quality that they had to interrupt the screening and replace it with another film. The word choice in the review of the festival is interesting, and occurs in much academic and journalistic writing about Palestine: 'important' is a relatively vague term, but implies the urgency with which the world should acknowledge and address the awful truth about the protracted Palestine–Israeli conflict. Similarly, emphasising the 'naturally hit and miss' nature of festivals is something critics do not usually do when reviewing festivals. The reviewer praised the political impetus of the festival, drawing a distinction between smoothly run professional festivals and more urgent, idealistic curation: 'not simply a celebration of a national culture, but a far more political assertion of a national identity' (Rapfogel 2003).

The urgency with which this festival and its film screenings were imbued was evident both in immediate audience reactions and the way in which the press reported on it. The 'urgency' also perhaps highlights the materiality of film and the speed with which we are losing film history due to its deterioration. In the opening addresses to the festival, both Hamid Dabashi and Edward Said pointed out its uniqueness in terms of its taking place both in New York and in the Palestinian territories, as well as the significance of the archive of Palestinian films and documents that was to come out of the festival and the book publication, which was at the time the first of its kind to focus entirely on Palestinian cinema. The festival showcased the films, then preserved them in the newly established archive which, alongside the documentation garnered through the festival and its adjacent research, became a world-leading resource on Palestinian cinema and cultural identity. The current Palestine Studies Centre at Columbia University grew out of this archive in 2010.

The archival role of the festival was significant in the context of the Palestinian cultural identity, in that it brought films from a scattered exiled people together in a trusted context at a respected centre of learning. In many ways, this gave legitimacy to the identity of the filmmakers whose work was collected, digitised and made accessible. Its increased visibility and accessibility stand in stark contrast to the legendary 'missing' Palestinian film archive. As scholars have explained (Marks 2015: 111–14), and as filmmakers have explored (see Azza El Hassan's documentary *Kings and Extras: Digging for a Palestinian Image*, 2004), the archive of the PLO Film Unit contained the revolutionary films of the early days of the

PFU administered by the PLO, which present a self-determined Palestinian identity. In 1982, during the Israeli siege of Beirut, this archive was moved, stolen or destroyed – its fate remains uncertain.[3] Over the decades, content from the archive has slowly resurfaced in both likely and unlikely places, which has contributed to its mythologisation. But even an archive that is presumed lost remains a living thing, and so Azza El Hassan's work in restoring and making these films newly available with The Void project[4] belies the static nature of the myth and unfolds the history of the films' content and their very existence.

As Helga Tawil-Souri (2011: 152) writes, the constant destruction and theft of (moving) images by Israeli forces is a large part of the Israeli project to erase Palestinian history and silence their culture. Through aesthetic erasure, in deleting the past, they erase the legitimacy of claims to the ownership of Palestinian land and as such continually enforce the establishment of the Israeli state on Palestinian land. As Tawil-Souri and El Hassan both show, in their cultural praxis, Palestinians preserve the(ir) past and reproduce its images and its discourse, and simultaneously represent and recreate the present, whether in exile, in refugee camps, in ghettos or open-air prisons. The way the myth of the archive is deconstructed in Azza El Hassan's film and work, and the way in which Columbia University has gradually constructed the biggest archive of Palestinian cinema, accessible to all and available online, indeed contradicts the national loss of Palestinian land and power with its cultural gain of stories and identity.

Like El Hassan's project, Dreams of a Nation continues to contribute to the preservation of Palestinian film history, initiated through the personal and professional network of a young woman filmmaker, Annemarie Jacir, who accessed her own networks in the film world in order to open up a cinematic past that belies the absolute loss of this work. The power of these archival images is acknowledged in the way in which they return in fragmentary form in many Palestinian fiction and documentary films, among others Jacir's own *When I Saw You*, which re-enacts and refers directly to some of the iconic images of Palestinian freedom fighters or fedayeen. It is in this context of the reuse of these iconic images, and the creative response to the images in their films, that Anna Ball explains the self-reflexivity of Palestinian filmmakers. She shows how self-scrutiny seems inherent to many of the filmmakers who reference and use the archival footage. She connects this directly to the 'political as well as cultural significance of projects such as "Dreams of a Nation" [. . .] which aims to create an archive of Palestinian cinema and connected resources to replace that which was lost or destroyed' (2012: 2). Indeed, Dreams of a Nation moves beyond the obsession with the past of the Palestinian revolutionary film archive and connects the past directly to the present through the pairing of historical work with contemporary films. As such, Dreams of a Nation illustrates that the role of a festival is indeed also to think of posterity, and those moving images that will become part of a Palestinian archive in the future. As such, its title 'dreams' refers to the ambitions of the project, in terms of where an initiative can lead when the right avenues of discovery are tapped.

Including films from the 1970s, 1980s and 1990s, as well as films from the early 2000s, the festival showcased the long history of Palestine's moving image legacy, especially in foregrounding some of the very early films made in the Occupied Palestinian Territories. Michel Khleifi's *Fertile Memory* was accompanied by a screening of *Palestine: A People's Record* by Kais al-Zobaidi, also from the early 1980s. The festival opened with Khleifi's *Tale of Three Jewels* (1995) and dedicated a significant part of the programme to the mid-1990s: Omar Al-Qattan's *Going Home* (1996), Elia Suleiman's *Chronicle of a Disappearance* (1996), Rashid Mashharawi's *Haifa* (1996) and Ali Nassar's *The Milky Way* (1997). These films were made during or immediately after the First Intifada, and appropriately deal with the dream of returning to the homeland, observing the absurdities of everyday life under occupation and the quest for a cultural identity that is consistently undermined by the occupier and by the internal difficulties of the Palestinian political parties and traditions.

Most of the films on the 2003 programme in New York, however, dated from the early 2000s, the first years of the Second Intifada: Hazim Bitar's *Jerusalem's High Cost of Living* (2001); Akram Safadi's *Song on a Narrow Path: Stories from Jerusalem* (2001); *Divine Intervention* (2002) by Elia Suleiman; Hany Abu-Assad's *Ford Transit* (2002) and *Rana's Wedding* (2002); *Mahali (Local)* (2002) by a team of first-time filmmakers; *A Number Zero* (2002), a short documentary by Saed Andoni, now known mainly for his animated documentary *The Wanted 18* (2014); *Crossing Kalandia* (2002), by Sobhi al-Zobaidi; and Leila Sansour's *Jeremy Hardy vs. The Israeli Army* (2003). Of her curatorial choices, Jacir stated that her main aim was to introduce Palestinian cinema to US audiences in all its qualities, diversity and power. She had been disappointed by the cultural discourse on Palestine in the West, and approached her role as principal curator as one in which she had to introduce nuanced and compelling work from Palestinian filmmakers around the world in contrast to a static vision of Palestine as a territory of terrorism. In a total of 34 films, she was able to include work from the early days of Palestinian filmmaking, which contained 'images invested with dangerous or emancipatory powers' (Jacir 2006: 23).

Due to the stereotypes of the Palestine–Israeli conflict in the US political sphere and the power of anti-Palestinian lobbyists in the US, the run-up to the festival was fraught with problems both in Palestine – where the films came from – and the US – where they were screened first. In Palestine, occupation and the destruction of local infrastructure during the Second Intifada meant that film transport was hugely complex. Again, the films' materiality contributed to the complexity of curation. Jacir testifies:

Curating the film festival from New York hinged on having someone in Palestine who could physically gather the tapes – since Palestinians in various parts of the West Bank and Gaza are under different levels of military curfew and are often not allowed to leave their homes, let alone to venture to a post office to mail videotapes. This made even the mundane details of receiving copies of films for the festival a major difficulty, often requiring sophisticated planning and execution by parties both inside and outside of Palestine. (Jacir 2006: 27)

It is interesting, then, to think about how objects can travel and people cannot. The films, due to their material existence, were able to travel, 'for cultural purposes only', to America, even if Palestinian people less privileged than Jacir cannot. As curator, she additionally experienced emotional and concrete setbacks through pressure and bullying from anti-Palestinian extremists, via hate mail, personal attacks and even death threats. Due to this coordinated campaign, Columbia University was 'forced to release a public statement defending the rights of academic and artistic freedoms where the film festival was concerned' (2006: 30). Jacir's testimony of how difficult it was for her personally, and for the faculty she was affiliated with, speaks to the censorship that Palestinian filmmakers continually face, even outside Palestine. She is simultaneously pragmatic about it, as 'that's the case for all Palestinian filmmakers I think – and all we can do is keep making films, art, and believing in what we do' (Oumlil 2016).

In Palestine, Dreams of a Nation became the largest travelling film festival ever to have taken place, including archival and contemporary films screening for the first time on Palestinian soil. Jacir says: 'I knew it was both appropriate and essential to try to open the festival with these films in the heart of Palestine – Jerusalem – to honor the work of these brave filmmakers' (A. Jacir 2007). The difficulties of organising the festival in Palestine were even greater than those in the US, in material terms. Jacir describes how cultural institutions are constantly targeted by the occupiers as part of a campaign to destroy and dismantle Palestinian cultural infrastructure and civil life. Through aesthetic erasure, by destroying cultural centres, cinemas and cinematheques, images of the Palestinian past are prevented from being shared in a communal space and thus become erased from memory, which translates into the erasure of the historical, cultural and national identity of the Palestinian audience. It is part of an Israeli tactic of separation as a method of control, through which social cohesion erodes.

For Jacir, and many other filmmakers and curators, resisting the disappearance of the visual past is 'a matter of survival, of resisting our culture's disappearance' (2006: 27). As such, the locations of the screenings throughout Palestine were crucial for their symbolic meaning of resistance to the occupiers' ideas about the disintegration of a Palestinian cultural identity and social cohesion, but also in their concrete, material resistance to the destruction of infrastructure: screenings took place in significant spaces such as the Yabous Cultural Organisation in Jerusalem, the Cinematheque in Nazareth, the Popular Arts Centre and Sakakini Cultural Centre in Ramallah, and the Cultural Centre Cinema in Gaza. They also managed to hold a lecture by Chilean-Palestinian filmmaker Miguel Littin at the al-Qattan Foundation in Ramallah, and in Jerusalem they hosted a panel discussion with Mustafa Abu Ali, Daoud Barakat, Nisar Hassan, George Khleifi, Najwa Najjar and Ula Tabari, bringing together for the first time a very significant number of filmmakers, thus contributing to the strengthening of their identities as filmmakers and to new alliances and collaborations.

Especially momentous was the successful screening of *They Do Not Exist* and the presence of the filmmaker Mustafa Abu Ali. *They Do Not Exist* is a 25-minute docu-fiction about Nabatia refugee camp, made in collaboration with other PFU filmmakers, Sulafa Jadallah and Hani Jawhariya, and made specifically to undermine the speech by Prime Minister Golda Meir in which she claimed that the Palestinians do not exist. Jacir explains that Abu Ali – who, as Azza El Hassan shows in *Kings and Extras*, was a temporary custodian of the legendary PFU film archive until 1982 – was exiled from Palestine and forbidden to enter Jerusalem, his home town. For the purpose of the screening of the film, Dreams of a Nation applied for a permit to allow Abu Ali into Jerusalem, which was denied multiple times. And yet the festival smuggled him into Jerusalem anyway. As Jacir explains, this short journey was perilous for the old man, but they persisted and he arrived at the 'screening [of] his film in a theater we had built ourselves at the YMCA, as the Israeli authorities forced Palestinian movie theaters to shut during the First Intifada in the 1980s' (A. Jacir 2007). She testifies to the stress they both experienced throughout the journey and his contribution to the festival, but she also highlights the importance of screening the film in Jerusalem and in the presence of the filmmaker. She writes: 'More than thirty years after their production, we managed to publicly screen two of the most important films of the Palestinian resistance cinema for the first time in Palestine' (A. Jacir 2007). The filmmaker made concrete the Palestinian dream of return, illegally but in a symbolically significant way, so as to enable the festival and the audience to experience the film in his presence. There is a tragic parallel for Jacir herself, who was later also banned from entering the Palestinian territories,

> and has not been able to go back after screening *Salt of This Sea* there; she has been living in Jordan since then. She spoke about how she could see the land right in front of her (from Jordan), but yet has not been able to get to it. This simultaneous closeness and inaccessibility inspired the theme of her new film, *When I Saw You* (2012). (Oumlil 2016)

This illustrates the power of film and filmmakers, and their importance for the cultural identity of Palestinian history.

The afterlife of Dreams of a Nation is both material and intellectual: the festival lives on in several screenings and other film-related initiatives, some of which are undertaken by Annemarie Jacir and her sister Emily, both in Palestine and in the diaspora. In February 2007, for example, Emily Jacir curated a programme of revolutionary Palestinian cinema in New York, with a focus on the period between 1968 and 1982, at the New York Arab and South Asian Film Festival. At this showcase they screened Mustafa Abu Ali's work from when he was a part of the Palestinian Film Unit working with a collective of other filmmakers such as Khadija Habashneh (formerly Abu Ali), Sulafa Jadallah and Hani Jawharia. Screenings included *They Do Not Exist* (Mustafa Abu Ali, 1973) as well as *Return to Haifa* (Kassem Hawal, 1981) and *Away from Home* (1969) and *The Visit* (1970) by Kais al-Zubaidi. Films about and from the Palestinian revolutionary period were accompanied by talks and presentations, and Emily credits her meeting of Mustafa Abu Ali and her interviews with his ex-wife Khadija Habashneh with a growing shared knowledge of the films from this period, and the role of the PFU archive which was disappeared in 1982 (E. Jacir 2007).

In 2011 the Dreams of a Nation festival at Columbia University screened Annemarie Jacir's own debut feature film *Salt of this Sea* (2008) along with *Pomegranates and Myrrh* (Najwa Najjar, 2008) and *The Time that Remains* (Elia Suleiman, 2009) and many other films. It was also the occasion on which the Dreams of a Nation film archive was inaugurated. Housed at the Centre for Palestinian Studies at Columbia University, this archive serves as a source for cinephiles and scholars, and is accessible online.[5] The sheer existence of this archive in New York serves as a counter-narrative to the discourse of a forgotten past and melancholy around the history of Palestinian cinema, and in particular its revolutionary work of the 1960s and 1970s, its obsession with the materiality of the land in the 1980s and 1990s, and the more stubborn representations of trauma and political subversion in the 2000s. Coincidentally, this (simplified) categorisation of Palestinian film history is reflected in Gertz and Khleifi's book *Palestinian Cinema: Landscape, Trauma and Memory* (2008). Alongside academic publications, such as *Dreams of a Nation* (Dabashi 2006) and the Gertz and Khleifi book, this archive is material proof of the existence of Palestinian film culture embedded in its memorialisation of the past. It contributes significantly to the historiography of Palestine, where elsewhere this history is neglected or ignored. Oumlil (2016) goes so far as to theorise that 'creating a physical archive relates to [. . .] a feminist archaeological method, which involves digging for and bringing to light "lost" stories (or films in this case)'. This digitisation and renewed accessibility of the Palestinian film archives – both the Dreams of a Nation archive and Azza El Hassan's restoration work of the PFU archive – act, according to Oumlil (2016), against the 'male chauvinism as perceived as inherent to the Palestinian identity and against the lack of feature-length fiction films by women and about women'. Certainly, an emancipatory and expansive effort goes into the guardianship of the cinematic past, and it seems to be the case that a lot of women are indeed working on this (Khadija Habashneh (Abu Ali), Annemarie Jacir, Azza El Hassan). But the term 'feminism' is not always welcomed by Arab or Palestinian filmmakers or custodians of culture. Jacir herself is hesitant in embracing the label, and does 'not believe in women's cinema' (Nussair). Being a representative sits uneasily with her, for any category, and she recognises her privilege and her uniqueness. This is reflected in a later project, Dar Jacir, about which more follows below.

At the inauguration of the archive, Dabashi stated: 'Today, our festival is one of many national and international tributes to the collective identity of Palestinians, in their unity and their fragmentation' (Mullenaux 2011). As such, Dreams of a Nation may have been the first and most elaborate Palestinian film festival to be held in parallel in the US and Palestine, but it has also spurred the founding and subsequent success of a plethora of Palestinian film festivals around the world. It confirms the sizeable importance of Palestine's film culture and the important role Palestinian film plays in the cultural resistance against occupation and the erasure of history and memory. While the Palestinian nation may remain a dream for now, cultural production and the bold curation of culture contribute significantly to an 'imagined world' of internationally located Palestinian artists that keeps the memory of the Palestinian nation alive.

DAR JACIR IN BETHLEHEM

By way of conclusion, We want to focus on the paradox between Palestinian film culture around the globe and Palestinian film in Palestine. It was not only with Dreams of a Nation and the networks created through the festival that Annemarie and Emily Jacir worked together in terms of the curation of Palestinian films. As we explained above, Emily Jacir's curation of films of revolution and both sisters' interest in the role of the Palestinian film archive through their acquaintance with Khadija Habashneh and Mustafa Abu Ali came out of the first Dreams of a Nation screening of *They Do Not Exist* in Jerusalem in 2003, in the presence of Mustafa Abu Ali.

Emily Jacir is a conceptual and (moving) image artist. Like Annemarie, Emily's artistic practice and her curatorial interest equally focus on the significance of keeping the past of Palestine alive in collective memory. She is an important voice on the international art scene and – like Annemarie – often problematises in her work her own privilege as a Palestinian with an American passport. The sisters' curatorial strengths lie in a shared preoccupation with a highly political yet nuanced engagement with Palestinian memory and amnesia, bringing history into the contemporary age. They also often bring their own material realities into the images they create by documenting and using in their works the situations they encounter while filming or creating other images. Concepts that they are preoccupied with are mobility and journeying across borders, and the impact of generational differences on storytelling and the incongruous memories of people on the material reality of Palestine.

This shared understanding of the value of material archives resulted in their inauguration of Dar Yusuf Nasri Jacir for Art and Research in Bethlehem. After having worked closely with many diverse cultural and arts centres throughout the Palestinian territories, they decided to open up their ancestral home for the curation and development of arts and artists interested in and hailing from different areas of Palestine. Their dedication to younger generations of people, whether these are Western students or young Arab artists, comes from an acute awareness of their own privilege as transnational artists descended from a well-to-do family. Together, they search for platforms where they can educate, train and tutor younger generations. The website of the organisation states that

> Dar Yusuf Nasri Jacir for Art and Research is a grass-roots independent artist-run initiative founded in 2014 and is located in our 19th century family home in Bethlehem. Originally built in the late 1880s by al Mukhtar Yusuf Jacir, the site serves as a place in which the history and contemporary conditions of Bethlehem meet, enabling the exchange and production of new art works and visions towards the future.

The use of the plural pronoun 'our' showcases the shared ambitions for the house as a place for learning, experiencing and creating, which – significantly – includes agricultural learning in their grounds. They describe it as 'an experimental learning hub for the Bethlehem community and beyond – a place to ask questions, exchange ideas, to dream and to grapple with our contemporary situation' (Dar Jacir website). Annemarie runs one of the residency programmes, Bled Residency, where she has hosted filmmaker Mahdi Fleifel and writer Rashed A. This once again shows Annemarie's interest in developing writing for film and creative writing, and both residents of Dar Jacir have gone on to win important prizes for their work.

The history of the house itself is a fascinating story, reflecting not only the reality of power and occupation in Palestine since the late nineteenth century, but also the changing functions of the house that are reflected in its directors' mission statements. The house was built by Yusuf and later his son Suleiman Jacir, who was mayor of Bethlehem for a while. However, it was lost by the family as a result of bankruptcy in 1929, after which it functioned as a prison, a school (for boys for a long time but also for girls at one point), a residence and a boarding house. After the Nakba, one of the original owner's grandsons became a teacher at the school located in the house, and in the 1980s Nasri and Marguerite Jacir managed to buy the house back. They lived there until, in 2014, Annemarie and Emily's father, Yusuf Nasri Jacir, became the sole owner of the house and co-founded, with his daughters, the arts and research centre it has become. Together, they are completely dedicated to providing an 'alternative' space of knowledge production, away from the grand narratives of Israeli and Palestinian historiography, in the spirit of Philistine Films' shared ambitions for a truly independent art scene.

Exiled from Palestine, Annemarie curates from a distance. While it is devastating on a personal level, her immateriality at the house makes space and creates opportunities for her family, friends and colleagues to embody its full potential. Her absence also results in her missing out on destruction. In 2021 the house was attacked and ransacked by Israeli forces. There was a fire in the urban farm that damaged the house. Books, films and equipment were stolen. The management of the house posted photos of bullet casings found on the site, and of the damage to the house and the adjacent charred fields on its social media pages. Their statement included expressions of devastation and anger about the loss of equipment, concern for the resident artists who had to find alternative accommodation and whose belongings and artworks were stolen or damaged, but in the same breath also expressed a stubborn resistance to the culprits, not shying away from loaded language. This blatant attempt at aesthetic erasure was countered with defiance, the will to continue to create cultural memories and a refutation of material loss and damage. The statement asserted that they would continue to 'protect cultural life and heritage for thousands of artists, students and community members' (Ditmars 2021). This resilience perhaps best illustrates the frustration and absurdity of being an artist and curator of Palestinian cultural production, as a universal event. As we saw earlier in this chapter, it is not only in Bethlehem that the blatant bullying had material consequences; in New York Annemarie Jacir equally suffered loss and destruction. The continued aesthetic erasure of Palestinian cultural production is perpetrated globally, whether the artistic expressions serve 'cultural purposes only' or not. The production of films by Philistine Films and Dar Jacir, and the curation and exhibition of them at Dar Jacir and Dreams of a Nation, give shape to the material *and* immaterial richness of Palestinian culture at events across the world.

REFERENCES

Alexander, Livia (2005), 'Is There a Palestinian Cinema? The National and Transnational in Palestinian Film Production', in *Palestine, Israel, and the Politics of Popular Culture*, ed. R. L. Stein and T. Swedenburg, Durham, NC: Duke University Press, pp. 150–72.

Appadurai, Arjun (1990), 'Disjuncture and Difference in the Global Cultural Economy', *Theory, Culture and Society* 7: 295–310.
Ball, Anna (2012), *Palestinian Literature and Film in Postcolonial Feminist Perspective*, New York: Routledge.
Dabashi, Hamid (ed.) (2006), *Dreams of a Nation: On Palestinian Cinema*, London: Verso.
Dar Jacir webpage (n.d.), https://darjacir.com/Home-Page (accessed 19 April 2023).
Denes, Nick (2014), 'An Overburdened "Brand"? Reflections on a Decade with the London Palestine Film Festival', in *Film Festival Yearbook 6: Film Festivals and the Middle East*, ed. Dina Iordanova and Stefanie Van de Peer, St Andrews: St Andrews Film Studies, pp. 251–64.
Ditmars, Hadani (2021), 'Artist-run Dar Jacir Center in Bethlehem Damaged', *The Art Newspaper*, 19 May, https://www.theartnewspaper.com/2021/05/19/artist-run-dar-jacir-center-in-bethlehem-damaged (accessed 19 April 2023).
Gertz, Nurith, and George Khleifi (2008), *Palestinian Cinema: Landscape, Trauma and Memory*, Edinburgh: Edinburgh University Press.
Iordanova, Dina, and Ruby Cheung (eds) (2010), *Film Festival Yearbook 2: Film Festivals and Imagined Communities*, St Andrews: St Andrews Film Studies.
Iordanova, Dina, and Stefanie Van de Peer (eds) (2014), *Film Festival Yearbook 6: Film Festivals and the Middle East*, St Andrews: St Andrews Film Studies.
Jacir, Annemarie (2006), '"For Cultural Purposes Only": Curating a Palestinian Film Festival', in *Dreams of a Nation: On Palestinian Cinema*, ed. Hamid Dabashi, London: Verso, pp. 23–31.
Jacir, Annemarie (2007), 'Coming Home: Palestinian Cinema', *The Electronic Intifada*, 27 February, https://electronicintifada.net/content/coming-home-palestinian-cinema/6780 (accessed 19 April 2023).
Jacir, Annemarie (2021), 'Poems', in *Mostra Mulheres Arabes: Cinema & Poesia*, ed. Anna Claudia Martins, WIFT Brasil, Krassiva Produções, https://issuu.com/wiftbrasil2/docs/macp_catalogo_en-final (accessed 19 April 2023).
Jacir, Emily (2007), 'Palestinian Revolution Cinema Comes to NYC', *The Electronic Intifada* 16 February, https://electronicintifada.net/content/palestinian-revolution-cinema-comes-nyc/6759 (accessed 19 April 2023).
Lodderhose, Diane (2021), 'Filmmaker Annemarie Jacir on her Journey to Preserve Palestinian Cinema for Future Generations', *Deadline*, 8 July, https://deadline.com/2021/07/annemarie-jacir-filmmaker-palestine-cinema-cannes-magazine-disruptor-1234787507/ (accessed 19 April 2023).
Marks, Laura U. (2015), *Hanan al-Cinema: Affections for the Moving Image*, Cambridge, MA: MIT Press.
Massad, J. (2006), 'The Weapon of Culture: Cinema in the Palestinian Liberation Struggle', in *Dreams of a Nation: On Palestinian Cinema*, ed. Hamid Dabashi, London: Verso, pp. 32–9.
Mullenaux, Lisa (2011), '"Dreams of a Nation" Celebrates Palestinian Cinema', *Washington Report on Middle East Affairs*, April, pp. 56–7, https://www.wrmea.org/011-april/music-arts-dreams-of-a-nation-celebrates-palestinian-cinema.html (accessed 19 April 2023).

Nusair, Isis (2018), 'Refusing the Separation: An Interview with Palestinian Filmmaker Annemarie Jacir', *Jadaliyya*, 6 September, https://www.jadaliyya.com/Details/37878 (accessed 19 April 2023).

Oumlil, Kenza (2016), 'Re-writing History on Screen: Annemarie Jacir's *Salt of this Sea*', *Arab Studies Quarterly* 38.3: 586–600.

Rapfogel, Jared (2003), 'A Report of Dreams of a Nation – A Palestinian Film Festival', *Senses of Cinema* 25 (March), https://www.sensesofcinema.com/2003/festival-reports/dreams_of_a_nation/ (accessed 19 April 2023).

Rastegar, Kamran (2002), 'Conference Report: Dreams of a Nation: A Palestinian Film Festival', *Edebiyât* 13.2: 273–6.

Saglier, Viviane (2020), '"Not-Yet" an Industry: The Temporalities of Contemporary Palestinian Cinema', in *Cinema of the Arab World: Contemporary Directions in Theory and Practice*, ed. T. Ginsberg and C. Lippard, London: Palgrave Macmillan, pp. 125–46.

Said, Edward (1981), *Covering Islam: How the Media and the Experts Determine How We See the Rest of the World*, London: Routledge & Kegan Paul.

Shafik, Viola (2016), *Arab Cinema: History and Cultural Identity*, Cairo: The American University in Cairo Press.

Tawil-Souri, Helga (2011), 'The Necessary Politics of Palestinian Cultural Studies', in *Arab Cultural Studies: Mapping the Field*, ed. T. Sabry, London: I.B. Tauris, pp. 137–61.

Van de Peer, Stefanie (2022), 'Arab Documentary Landscapes. Transnational Flow of Solidarity at Festivals', in *Documentary Filmmaking in the Middle East and North Africa*, ed. Viola Shafik, Cairo: The American University in Cairo Press, pp. 153–76.

Wadi, Shahd (2016), 'A Palestinian Film We Call Home: Women's Cinematic Bodies Out of Place', in *Mediations of Disruption in Post-Conflict Cinema*, ed. A. Martins, A. Lopes and M. Dias, Basingstoke: Palgrave Macmillan, pp. 187–93.

NOTES

1. The poems are available online at https://issuu.com/wiftbrasil2/docs/macp_catalogo_en-final (accessed 19 April 2023).
2. For example, *Covering Islam* (1981).
3. Recently (we are writing in July 2022), people active in the cultural sector in Palestine have revealed on social media that the IDF has released some of the works that were part of this archive, suggesting that at least some of it was, indeed, stolen.
4. https://www.thevoidproject.org/palestinianrestoredfilms (accessed 19 April 2023).
5. http://palestine.mei.columbia.edu/dreams-of-a-nation (accessed 19 April 2023).

CONCLUSION

An Interview with Annemarie Jacir

For this interview, we emailed our questions to Annemarie Jacir. Jacir was working on her next project and wrote her responses to the questions during breaks from work.

I & S: What inspired you to use camera as a means of creative expression or as a means of telling a story? What do you like the most about this medium?
AJ: Cinema brings everything I love together – photography, poetry, music, storytelling, writing, editing, working with people. It's a wide universe and it feels like an endless place to create and explore.

I & S: Who are the international and Palestinian filmmakers that have inspired you?
AJ: Claire Denis, John Cassavetes, Abbas Kiarostami, Spike Lee, Tsai Ming-liang, Jim Jarmusch, Jane Campion, Steve McQueen, Abdelrahman Sissako, Agnes Varda, Federico Fellini, Godard and Truffaut, Scorsese, Sidney Lumet. As for Palestinian filmmakers, Elia Suleiman and Hany Abu Assad – for different reasons.

I & S: Your films are exceptionally diverse. Each is markedly distinct from the other. What inspires these characters, stories and settings?
AJ: Each film is a time for me to explore something new and to learn something. The research period for each film is critical and I also enjoy it very much. Perhaps this is one of the things I like best about filmmaking – one is constantly exploring a new interest and delving deeply into it. It's a way to continuously challenge myself and push myself out of any comfort zone I have built up. Opening up to a new character or story is that.

I & S: Your characters have complex and emotionally charged relationships with Palestine. This complexity also seeps into their familial relationships. How do you envision or imagine this relationship between family and a nation or a country?

AJ: This is not something intentional for me but probably more organic and natural. I believe everyone has emotionally charged relationships with their home (homelands, home towns, homes) and with their family. These are both the most mundane and the most passionate relationships we have I would imagine.

I & S: Which character do you personally identify with or like the most in your films?

AJ: This is an impossible question to answer because they are all me. They are all in me. I identify with Tarek in *When I Saw You* but also with Ghayda and Emad. In *Salt of this Sea*, of course Soraya, and I also see myself in Abu Shadi and in Shadi in *Wajib* . . . there is a part of me in all of them. Of course, So I identify with them, I do – I wrote them.

I & S: Space assumes an active role in your films. Much of the emotional strength of your films lies in the way you narrate and capture space. We are especially interested in the poetic portrayal of space in *Wajib*. At some points, the story almost becomes more about the space than the characters themselves. What is your process/vision in presenting Palestinian space?

AJ: Absolutely. Space or location is always a character. In *Wajib*, a big part of the story is how these two men navigate not only their relationship to each other but also their individual relationships to their space. The ending of the film is absolutely about reaching an understanding of that space. The fact is also that they both love that space and exhibit it in very different ways.

I & S: Another approach we see appear in your oeuvre is the tragi-comic. Even in the most difficult situations, the characters can experience joyful moments, where it becomes just about ordinary humans experiencing something emotionally intense in the most banal situations. Is that something you intentionally attempt to do in your films?

AJ: I don't think it's something I intentionally set out to do. I think films very much resemble the filmmaker behind them. There is so much pain in this world, and it is why we need these moments of relief, of laughter. It is absolutely ordinary, and it is what I'm most interested in. I find that emotion comes at us in all kinds of ways and is impossible to define. Our hearts break and we experience death, and we laugh or dance madly as a reaction. Or as a way to keep on going. I know I need that. Especially in the bleakest moments.

I & S: You treat time very differently in each film. *Salt of this Sea* spans a few weeks, *When I Saw You* spans fewer weeks, and *Wajib* takes place in one day. Does the compression of time reflect a particularly Palestinian experience for you, or is it a narrative challenge, or something entirely different?

AJ: It is more about the particular story itself and how it needs to be told or rather asks to be told. The compression of time, or sometimes it's the expansion of time, is entirely dependent on the particular narrative of that specific film.

I & S: To what extent does your identity as a Palestinian filmmaker, or as a woman filmmaker, affect your work or its international distribution?

AJ: I would not say it affects my work — I have many identities, but this is not something that is directly tied to how I tell stories necessarily. In terms of international distribution, I think it's more the core of the film that determines what kind of distribution it gets. A film about Palestine may be unpopular or popular, may get mainstream distribution or not – but what determines that, aside from the artistic side, is not necessarily whether it's about Palestine or not but rather is it at its core radical or not. Making a film that is anti-occupation is expected and even celebrated in some places. Of course, that's not radical at all – even some right-wing Israelis are anti-occupation. But making a film about the right of return for example, you will find yourself blocked out of much mainstream distribution.

I & S: What is your preferred form of filmmaking, feature films or documentary?
AJ: Fiction filmmaking without a doubt. I prefer the freedom it offers.

I & S: Your films have complex titles, they contain historicity. How do you arrive at the titles?
AJ: I love titles. Some of them come quickly – even before I finish the script. Some of them arrive after I've shot, even after I've edited the film. I am very attracted to titles.

I & S: In terms of production, what have been the most challenging circumstances in your career?
AJ: It's boring to say but it's true – financing. Getting the funds to make each film. The funding landscape constantly shifts, it has changed so much over the last twenty years, and it feels a bit like surfing in a huge ocean. You look for that wave, you fall a million times, you feel you might drown, and you feel exhilaration when you finally can move.

I & S: Do you have a particular vision of how your films are distributed?
AJ: I feel very strongly that our films should first and foremost be seen by our own audience. That is the reason that one of our main goals when we began

Philistine Films was to locally distribute, find grassroots ways, unconventional ways to make sure the films we made were being seen by the local audience. When *Salt of this Sea* was accepted to Cannes, it was critical to me to premiere the film first in Palestine before heading to Cannes.

I & S: To what extent have your personal experiences affected your filmmaking approach, or the distribution of your work?
AJ: Everything is personal. Everything is political.

I & S: How has filmmaking changed for you throughout your career?
AJ: It changes all the time. I wouldn't be interested in it if it didn't. I only hope that I continue to learn, to challenge myself, and to improve my craft. I always want to do something new for me.

I & S: Do you think you want to/could move away from representing Palestinian stories and people?
AJ: Does anyone ever really move away from who they are?

I & S: Some say that audience members with Palestinian roots often cannot or do not want to watch the 'difficult' contemporary independent films by Palestinian filmmakers. How does that sit with you? Who is your preferred audience?
AJ: I don't think it's true that Palestinians do not want to watch contemporary independent films by Palestinians. In fact, I think it's quite the opposite. People want to watch stories on the screen that reflect their own lives, that challenge their own societies and worlds. People want to hear their own accents and see people they recognise. When you are part of a marginalised and villainised community, this is even more meaningful.

My main audience is the Palestinian audience, and I am aware that my films are not truly understood by a non-Palestinian audience. The Palestinian audience understands all the small nuances, references, and critiques. However, as an artist I know that we do not choose our audience. A film will speak to each person differently and I've discovered through the years a wider audience than I imagined and also that people will connect to a film for very personal reasons. I am constantly amazed by the audience.

I & S: The archive of Palestinian cinema plays a significant, even 'mythical' role. You have explained that access to the past of Palestinian cinema was subject to its materiality (Dabashi 2006). With the rediscovery of Palestinian archival work, and the restorations of these films, do you feel the plethora of Palestinian film festivals around the world benefit from the digital developments in distribution and exhibition? How, in your opinion, does the digital offer new possibilities for a future of Palestinian cinema's past?

AJ: Digital has certainly changed things for all of us. It has made filmmaking cheaper and more affordable, and more democratic. The Palestinian archives have become something of a fashionable trend in the last ten years but it's a good trend. Digitising the works from our past, so many people working on the archives, finding places to screen these films – all means that our history has not been erased, as hard as some people tried to make that happen.

I & S: How do you see Palestinian cinema's future?
AJ: So bright! There are so many amazing Palestinian filmmakers right now, it's truly inspiring.

There remain issues of funding and distribution and we have to be sure we remain a film community where those who don't have access to funding or who don't have the money to get their films distributed are still put in the front. Unlike many countries, Palestine's cinema has always been quite diverse and not only for a certain class. My biggest concern is that we turn into a situation where only the rich are able to make films.

I & S: Which project are you currently working on?
AJ: In terms of the company, Philistine Films has just wrapped shooting on our fourth feature film this year. Like everywhere, COVID hit hard and halted many projects. But this year we were able to get moving again. On a personal level, yesterday I premiered a short experimental film at the Locarno Film Festival, called *From Palestine With Love*, which is part of a collection of films by international filmmakers, a 'Postcard from the Future'. I am also in development on my next feature and hoping to close financing in the next few months so we can go ahead. And this year I directed my first TV episode – Season 3 of *Ramy*.

Index

3000 Nights, 124

A Chronicle of Ancient Sunlight, 113
A Few Crumbs for the Birds, 3, 24, 31, 33
A Number Zero, 131
A Post-Oslo History, 27, 36, 127
A Revolutionary Tale, 27
A World Apart in 15 Minutes, 24, 33
Abourahme, Dahna, 4
Abu Ali, Mustafa, 133, 134, 135
Abu Assab, Tarek, 8
Abu Assad, Hany, 7, 124, 140
Abu Moch, Ashraf, 8
Abu Sbaih, Reem, 8
Abu Wael, Tawfiq, 7
Abu-Assad, Hany, 131
Academy Award, 9, 11, 14
accented cinema, 87
aesthetics, 24, 32, 101, 110
affinitive transnationalism, 90
affinitive, 88, 90
agricultural idyll, 75, 76, 77
al Funun, Darat, 4
Al Malhi, Um Hussein, 9
Alayan, Muayad, 7
Alexander and Bonin, 4
Algaralleh, Anas, 12, 46
al-Qattan Foundation, 133

al-Qattan, Omar, 131
al-Zobaidi, Sobhi, 131
al-Zubaidi, Kais, 134
Amari refugee camp, 10
Americanness, 55, 92
Amnesty International, 89
An Explanation (and then burn the ashes), 3, 24, 29, 30, 31
Andoni, Saed, 131
Annabelle, 112
Appadurai, Arjun, 42
Arab cinema, 6, 8, 18
Arab–Israel War, 45
archival spirit, 10
Asfa, Mahmoud, 11, 12, 13, 118
Asmahan, M.I.A., 10
Atwood, Margaret, 112
Augustus Films, 9
auteur, 2, 18, 88, 124
Away from Home, 134

Bakhtin, Mikhail, 74, 75, 81, 104, 105
Bakri, Mohammad, 7, 14, 15
Bakri, Saleh, 9, 10, 12, 14, 75, 89
Barakat, Daoud, 133
Barakat, Yahya, 9
Bawardi, Ossama, 3, 4, 14, 16, 18
Beckettian imagination, 72

Beirut Art Center, 4
Berlinale Co-Production & Talent Project, 10
Best Foreign Language Film, 4, 9, 11, 14
Bethlehem, 2, 4, 7, 11, 27, 72, 123, 135, 136, 137
Bhabha, Homi K., 42
Birzeit University, 4, 125
Bitar, Hazim, 131
Blal, Ruba, 11, 12
Bonnie and Clyde, 10
border, 11, 12, 24, 25, 31–3, 36, 58, 72, 76, 79, 92, 94, 95, 96, 102–4, 107
border-crossing, 92, 94, 95, 96, 103
Bristol Palestine Film Festival, 3, 7, 18
Brooklyn, 9, 40, 53, 55, 58, 86, 91, 94, 95, 107

Canadian, 40, 54, 100
Cannes Film Festival, 3, 4, 8, 10, 27, 90, 92, 124, 143
carnivalesque, 81, 82
Cassandra, 112
Cassavetes, John, 10, 140
Chavez, Hugo, 35
checkpoint, 3, 8, 16, 24–9, 34, 36, 54, 58, 67, 69, 89, 92, 94, 127
Chinese transnational cinema, 87
Chronicle of a Disappearance, 112, 131
chronotope, 74, 75, 99, 104, 105
cinema of transvergence, 88
Cinematheque in Nazareth, the, 133
Clarity World Films, 9
closed-form, 87
cognitive memories, 73
Columbia University, 3, 4, 27, 29, 30, 123, 129, 130, 132, 134
coming-of-age story, 6, 9, 118
commemorative sites, 68
conceived space, 41
conceptual abstraction, 44
construction, 17, 36, 39, 40, 49, 52–5, 58, 59, 66, 67, 88, 92, 116
continuities, 64, 65, 67, 128

cosmopolitan, 88
counterhegemony, 87, 110
counter-sites, 42
Crossing Kalandia, 131
cultural remittance, 100

Dabashi, Hamid, 26, 27, 30, 123, 128, 129, 134, 135, 143
Dabbag, Ismael, 8
Dar Yusuf Nasri Jacir for Art and Research, 4, 136
Darwish, Mahmoud, 7, 10
Dawayima, 54, 55, 57, 92, 95
deterritorialisation, 64, 66, 110
diaspora, 17, 43, 86–9, 99, 100, 110, 120
Dickinson, Kay, 24, 25, 26, 28, 34
diegetic characters, 110
discursive space, 48, 49
disjunctive frames, 42
displaced subject, 99
displacement, 1, 12, 16, 65, 77, 99, 110
distributed field of attention, 111
Divine Intervention, 131
documentary, 10, 14, 24, 26, 31, 65, 66, 85, 90, 124, 129–31, 142
Dog Day Afternoon, 10
Doha Film Institute, 125
Dreams of a Nation (book), 134
Dreams of a Nation (film festival), 4, 30, 123, 124, 126–8, 130, 132, 134, 135, 137
Drigov, Dana, 9
Dubai Film Festival, 11
Duraie, Zain, 4
duty, 6, 15, 52, 80, 98

Elayan, Ali, 12, 45
El-Hassan, Azza, 36, 47, 129, 130, 133, 134, 135
empirical border place, 92
epiphany, 88
estrangement, 94, 120, 125
eulogised space, 55

INDEX

Europe, 6, 7, 10, 14, 16, 18, 51, 52, 55, 63, 87, 97, 98, 101, 102, 126, 127
exilic, 1, 17, 33, 70, 82, 86, 87, 88, 89, 92, 100
expatriate, 64, 80, 87
experimental transnationalism, 88
extraordinary simultaneities, 43

facilitative tool, 93
fantasy, 12
feature film, 4, 9, 17, 23, 25, 39, 62, 64, 89, 142
fedayee, 11, 13, 14, 43–8, 52, 59, 61, 64, 71, 72, 74–9, 82, 86, 102–7, 117–19, 130
Fertile Memory, 129, 131
financiers, 7, 45
Firstspace perspective, 41, 43
Firstspace, 41, 43
Fool, 112
Ford Transit, 131
formed pattern of attention, 112
Foucault, Michel, 39, 40, 42, 49

Gaza strip, 11, 85, 104
gender-conditioning, 118
generational trauma, 9
Ghayda, 11, 43–8, 59, 64, 73, 74, 76–9, 86, 102, 103, 106, 107, 117, 119, 141
globalising, 88
Going Home, 131
Guggenheim Museum, 4
Gun Crazy, 10

Habashneh, Khadija, 134, 135
Habibi, Emile, 7
Haifa, 131
Haifa, 5, 9, 16, 65, 92, 100, 131, 134
Hammad, Suheir, 9, 10, 89
Harir refugee camp, 11, 76
Hassan, Nisar, 133
Hawal, Kassem, 134
heterochronies, 42
heterogeneous space, 42

heterogeneous, 42, 86
heterotopia of crisis, 45, 47
heterotopia of deviation, 45
heterotopia, 17, 39–43, 48, 49, 51, 53, 55, 57, 59, 60
heterotopology, 42, 49
Holiday, Billie, 10
Hollywood, 3, 18, 88, 112
home, 86–108, 115, 117–19, 123, 127, 131, 133, 134, 136, 141
homecoming, 96, 99
homeland, 2, 5, 9, 12, 16, 17, 23, 43–9, 52–8, 62–83, 86–108, 113, 115, 117, 118, 120, 131
hostile space, 55
Huda's Salon, 124
hybridity, 42, 110

Ideis, Riyad, 9
identity markers, 39, 68
idyll, 47, 71, 74–7, 104, 105, 118
idyllic symbols, 75
imagination, 106, 120
independent cinema, 1, 4
international cinema, 2
internationalism, 86
interstitial, 42, 87, 110
Intifada, 4, 8, 23, 25–8, 35, 37, 126, 127, 131, 133
invitation, 14, 15, 39, 49, 80, 98, 121
Irish Museum of Modern Art, 4
Israel, 5, 7, 10, 11, 12, 15, 16, 30, 39, 45, 85, 91, 93, 106, 113, 114, 137
Israeli Defense Forces (IDF), 45, 139

Jacir, Emily, 2, 4, 5, 134, 135, 137
Jadallah, Sulafa, 133, 134
Jaffa, 9, 10, 55, 56, 58, 59, 62, 68, 91, 93, 94, 113, 114, 115
Jawhariya, Hani, 133
JBA Production, 9
Jeremy Hardy vs. The Israeli Army, 131
Jerusalem, 3, 5, 8, 16, 27, 28, 33, 34, 36, 57, 65, 85, 90, 95, 131–3, 135

Jerusalem's High Cost of Living, 131
Jewish-Israeli, 113, 115
Jordan, 3, 4, 11–13, 31, 35, 36, 45, 64, 73, 85, 86, 89, 102–7, 123, 133
Jordanian army, 12
journeys of repatriation, 96

Kanopy, 9
Kazkaz, Rana, 124
Khalaf, Anas, 124
Khalidi, Walid, 10
Khateeb, Raja'i, 8
Khleifi, Michel, 129, 130, 134
King, Martin Luther, 35
Kings and Extras: Digging for a Palestinian Image, 129, 133

Lebanon, 4, 85, 86, 91, 104
Lefebvre, Henri, 39, 40, 41, 44
life histories, 56
Like Twenty Impossibles, 3, 8, 24, 27, 29
Littin, Miguel, 133
lived space, 40
Los Angeles, 2
Louverture Films, 9

magazine, 1, 18, 107
Mahali (Local), 131
Maleficent, 112
Masharawi, Rashid, 7
Mashharawi, Rashid, 131
Masri, Mai, 4, 124
material culture, 68, 126
meaning-making, 116
Mediapro, 9
Meir, Golda, 133
memory, 5, 16, 17, 23, 49, 52, 53, 55, 62–83, 87, 99, 105, 125, 129, 131, 132, 134–6
metaphor, 106
milieu-building, 88
Milky Way, The, 131
minor character, 17, 111–13, 115–18, 120, 121

mobility, 25, 64, 79, 87–91, 94, 95, 102, 107, 119, 136
modern revolutionaries, 45
modernising, 88
Muhr Arab Award, 125
Mussalem, Rami, 8

Naficy, Hamid, 1, 75, 87, 88, 92, 96, 99, 104–6, 110
Najjar, Najwa, 7, 133, 134
Naksa, 11, 13, 63, 127
Nassar, Ali, 131
national liberation, 45
national sovereignty, 87
nature, 14, 24, 26, 31, 32, 34, 35, 45, 79, 96, 104, 105, 129, 130
neoliberal globalisation, 106
News Time, 36, 47
non-state, 45
nostalgia, 31, 32, 102, 105

Ocean's 8, 112
open-form, 87, 101
opportunity, 88
oral storytelling, 67
Oscar, 3, 4, 9, 90
Oslo Accords, 27, 36, 127
Owen, David, 7

Palestine Film Unit, 123, 130, 133, 135
Palestine is Waiting, 27
Palestine: A People's Record, 131
Palestine: Summer 2006 (I), 3, 33
Palestine: Summer 2006 (II), 34
Palestinian cinema, 1, 6, 7, 8, 17, 18, 23, 37, 39, 63, 75, 89, 123–5, 129–31, 134, 143, 144
Palestinian filmmaking, 1, 131
Palestinian Liberation Organization (PLO), 14
Palestinian refugees, 11, 72, 73, 104
Palestinian woman filmmaker, 1, 3
Palestinian-American, 2, 9, 64, 86

Paris Cinema Project, 9–10
Paul Robeson Foundation, 9
Penelopiad, The, 112
perceived space, 41
peripeteia, 70
Philistine Films, 4, 9, 27, 123–5, 137, 142, 144
points of reference, 68
Popular Arts Centre, 133
postcolonial, 87, 99
postmodern, 40
Pre-Nakba Palestine, 71
production of space, 39, 59

Ramallah, 9, 15, 33, 34, 53, 59, 67, 90, 91, 92
Rana's Wedding, 131
Randall, Alice, 112
Rastegar, Kamran, 4, 23, 29, 128
refugee child, 64, 104
refugee, 2, 4, 5, 9–13, 16, 17, 43–8, 52, 58, 59, 63, 64–6, 71–9, 81, 82, 86, 89, 96, 102–7, 113, 116–19, 125, 127, 130, 133, 134, 141–3
regulatory force, 87
relations of 'propinquity', 42
religious liberation, 45
reterritorialized, 92
Return to Haifa, 134
revolution, 5, 135
revolutionary, 12, 13, 23, 25, 27, 81, 123, 129, 130, 134
Rhys, Jean, 112
Rice, Condoleezza, 35
Right to Return, 27, 58
Rios, Catherine, 4
rites of entrance, 45
rootedness, 87, 89, 102, 110
Rotana Film Production, 9

Safadi, Akram, 131
Said, Edward, 30, 63, 126, 129
Sakakini Cultural Centre, 133
Salamy, Suzy, 4

Sallam, Darin J., 6
Salt of this Sea, 3, 4, 8–12, 37, 39, 40, 41, 52, 53, 56, 58, 62–5, 69, 71, 72, 79, 82, 86, 89, 90, 96, 100, 102, 104, 107, 113, 116, 120, 121, 125, 133, 134, 141–3
Sansour, Leila, 131
Satellite Shooters, The, 3, 27
second order memory, 68
secondspace perspective, 41, 43
secondspace, 41, 43, 50
self-regulating state, 45
Sembène, Ousmane, 36
Shadows, 10, 75, 120, 121
Shamshoum, Ruba, 12, 13
signification, 49, 71, 78
signifier, 49, 70, 94, 104, 105
situatedness, 43
social remittance, 100
Soja, Edward, 39–42, 44, 46, 50, 52, 66
solidarities, 28, 114, 126, 128
Song on a Narrow Path, Stories from Jerusalem, 131
Sound of the Streets, 24, 34, 36, 47
space of multiplicity, 42
Spateen, Taqi, 7
spatial experience, 39
spatiality, 41, 42, 43, 48, 60
spatiality-historicality-sociality, 41, 43
spatio-political territories, 45
Spivak, Gayatri Chakravorty, 36
Srour, Ahmad, 12
state, 17, 23, 30, 35, 43–5, 50, 51, 56, 57, 70, 71, 73, 76, 93, 95, 96, 98, 102, 114, 127, 128, 130, 131
Steinem, Gloria, 89
subjecthood, 55, 66, 87
Suleiman, Elia, 7, 27, 131, 133–6, 140
Sundance Screenwriters Lab, 9
symbolic weight, 70
Syria, 12, 31, 85, 104

Tabari, Ula, 133
Tale of Three Jewels, 131
tank, 79
Tarek, 9, 11–13, 40, 41, 44–6, 48, 56, 59, 63, 64, 72–9, 82, 86, 102–7, 117–19, 141
Taybeh, Firas W., 12, 45
The Time that Remains, 134
The Translator, 124
Thelma Film AG, 9
They Do Not Exist, 133, 134, 135
They Drive by Night, 112
third space, 42
thirdspace, 39–44, 46, 48, 49, 50, 52, 58, 59
topology, 65
traffic constable, 116
transcultural, 94, 95, 97
translingual, 88, 94
transnational cinema, 87
transreligious, 94
transvergent transnationalism, 17, 23, 86–9, 91, 93, 96, 97, 99, 101, 103, 105, 107
trauma, 9, 11, 16, 23, 26, 27, 29, 58, 63, 72, 73, 75, 78, 82, 106, 134
traumatologist, 82
TSR, 9
twofold, 116
typology, 88

United Nations Relief and Works Agency for Palestine Refugees (UNRWA), 2, 85

utopian thought, 41
utopias, 41, 42, 99
utterance, 42, 72

Visit, The, 134
vudu, 12

Wajib, 4, 14, 15, 39, 41, 43, 49, 50–2, 56, 62, 64, 79–81, 86, 96, 97, 102, 104, 120, 121, 141, 142
Wanted 18, The, 131
West Bank, 3, 8, 10, 11, 16, 85, 89, 92, 93, 104, 132
When I Saw You, 4, 6, 11, 12, 14, 39, 41, 43, 45, 49, 52, 56, 59, 64, 71–4, 78, 79, 82, 87, 102, 104, 106, 116, 118–22, 130, 133, 141, 142
Whitechapel Gallery, 4
Wind Done Gone, The, 112
Wide Sargasso Sea, 112
Williams, Saul, 10
Williamson, Henry, 112
Wolf, Christa, 112
woman filmmaker, 1, 3, 130, 142

Yabous Cultural Organisation, 133
Yacub, Nadia, 24, 25, 29
Yasin, Rami, 4
Young Artist Award, 12

Zayyad, Tawfiq, 7, 29
Zidane, Zinedine, 35
Žižek, Slavoj, 95
Zumorrod, Shadi, 8

EU representative:
Easy Access System Europe
Mustamäe tee 50, 10621 Tallinn, Estonia
Gpsr.requests@easproject.com

www.ingramcontent.com/pod-product-compliance
Lightning Source LLC
Chambersburg PA
CBHW051129160426
43195CB00014B/2407